HISTORY AND HISTORICAL WRITING IN ANCIENT ISRAEL

STUDIES IN THE HISTORY AND CULTURE OF THE ANCIENT NEAR EAST

EDITED BY

B. HALPERN AND M.H.E. WEIPPERT

VOLUME XVI

HISTORY AND HISTORICAL WRITING IN ANCIENT ISRAEL

Studies in Biblical Historiography

BY

TOMOO ISHIDA

BRILL
LEIDEN · BOSTON · KÖLN
1999

This book is printed on acid-free paper.

Library of Congress Cataloging-in-Publication Data

Ishida, Tomoo, 1931–
History and historical writing in ancient Irsrael : Studies in biblical historiography / by Tomoo Ishida.
p. cm.— (Studies in the history and culture of the ancient Near East, ISSN 0169-9024 ; v. 16)
Includes bibliographical references and index.
ISBN 9004114440 (cloth : alk. paper)
1. Jews—History—To 586 B.C. 2. Jews—History—To 586 B.C.–
–Historiography. 3. Bible. O.T. Former Prophets—Criticism, interpretation, etc. 4. Bible. O.T. Samuel, 2nd, IX-XX–
–Historiography. 5. Bible. O.T. Kings, 1st, I-II—Historiography.
I. Title. II. Series.
DS121.3.I75 1999
933—dc21 99-13402
CIP

Die Deutsche Bibliothek – CIP-Einheitsaufnahme

Ishida, Tomoo:
History and historical writing in ancient Israel : studies in biblical historiography / by Tomoo Ishida. - Leiden ; Boston ; Köln : Brill, 1999
(Studies in the history and culture of the ancient Near East ; Vol. 16)
ISBN 90-04-11444-0

ISSN 0169-9024
ISBN 90 04 11444 0

PRINTED IN THE NETHERLANDS

To Kazuko
My wife, friend, and colleague

CONTENTS

ACKNOWLEDGEMENTS

I wish to acknowledge my gratitude to the following institutions and publishers for permission to reprint the following 14 essays in revised versions. They are as follows:

1. “The Leaders of the Tribal Leagues <Israel> in the Pre-Monarchic Period”, *RB* 80 (1973), pp. 514–530.
2. “‘The People of the Land’ and the Political Crises in Judah”, *AJBI* 1 (1975), pp. 23–38.
3. “‘The House of Ahab’”, *IEJ* 25 (1975), pp. 135–137.
4. “נגיד: A Term for the Legitimization of the Kingship”, *AJBI* 3 (1977), pp. 35–51.
5. “The Structure and Historical Implications of the Lists of Pre-Israelite Nations”, *Bib* 60 (1979), pp. 461–490.
6. “Solomon’s Succession to the Throne of David—A Political Analysis”, in T. Ishida (ed.), *Studies in the Period of David and Solomon and Other Essays*, Tokyo/Winona Lake, 1982, pp. 175–187.
7. “‘Solomon who is greater than David’: Solomon’s succession in 1 Kings i–ii in the light of the inscription of Kilamuwa, king of *y’dy*-Śam’al”, in J.A. Emerton (ed.), *Congress Volume*, Salamanca 1983 (VTSup 36), Leiden, 1985, pp. 145–153.
8. “Solomon’s Succession to the Royal Throne—Problems about History and Historiography”, *Biblical Studies* 19 (1985), pp. 5–43 (Japanese).
9. “Adonijah the Son of Haggith and His Supporters: An Inquiry into Problems about History and Historiography,” in R.E. Friedman and H.G.M. Williamson (eds.), *The Future of Biblical Studies. The Hebrew Scriptures*, Atlanta, 1987, pp. 165–187.
10. “Royal succession in the kingdoms of Israel and Judah with special reference to the people under arms as a determining factor in the struggles for the throne”, in J.A. Emerton (ed.), *Congress Volume*, Jerusalem 1986 (VTSup 40), Leiden, 1988, pp. 96–106.
11. “Nathan’s Prophecy—A Historiographical Interpretation”, in S. Arai et al. (eds.), *The Message of the Bible—Ways of its Communication. Essays in Honour of Professor Masao Sekine on the Occasion of His Seventy-Seventh Birthday* (Biblical Studies 23), Tokyo, 1989, pp. 147–160 (Japanese).

12. "The Role of Nathan the Prophet in the Episode of Solomon's Birth", in M. Mori, H. Ogawa, and M. Yoshikawa (eds.), *Near Eastern Studies. Dedicated to H.I.H. Prince Takahito Mikasa on the Occasion of His Seventy-Fifth Birthday* (Bulletin of the Middle Eastern Culture Center in Japan 5), Wiesbaden, 1991, pp. 133–138.
13. "The Succession Narrative and Esarhaddon's Apology: A Comparison", in M. Cogan and I. Eph'al (eds.), *Ah, Assyria . . . Studies in Assyrian History and Ancient Near Eastern Historiography. Presented to Hayim Tadmor* (Scripta Hierosolymitana 33), Jerusalem, 1991, pp. 166–173.
14. "The Story of Abner's Murder: A Problem Posed by the Solomonic Apologist", in S. Aḥituv and B.A. Levine (eds.), *Avraham Malamat Volume* (Eretz-Israel. Archaeological, Historical and Geographical Studies 24), Jerusalem, 1993, pp. 109*–113*.

I wish also to acknowledge my sincere gratitude to Professor Baruch Halpern for his steadfast friendly encouragement to complete this book. Without his persevering support I could have never finished the work. I owe thanks to Professor M.H.E. Weippert for accepting this book in the series: *Studies in the History of the Ancient Near East.* I wish also to thank Mr. Masamichi Yamada for his help in preparing the manuscript and Ms. Patricia Radder, desk editor of Ancient Near East and Asian Studies of E.J. Brill, for her patient waiting for the completion of my manuscript.

Tomoo Ishida
Bach Grove, Tsukuba, Japan
January, 1999

ABBREVIATIONS

AASOR	*The Annual of the American Schools of Oriental Research*, New Haven, Cambridge, Mass.
AB	The Anchor Bible, Garden City, N.Y.
ABD	*The Anchor Bible Dictionary*, New York, 1992.
AfO Beih.	Archif für Orientforschung Beiheft, Graz.
AHw	W. von Soden (ed.), *Akkadisches Handwörterbuch*, Wiesbaden, 1965–81.
AJBI	*Annual of the Japanese Biblical Institute*, Tokyo.
AnBib	Analecta Biblica, Rome.
ANET	J.B. Pritchard (ed.), *Ancient Near Eastern Texts Relating to the Old Testament*, Princeton, 1969^3.
AnOr	Analecta Orientalia, Rome.
AO	Der Alte Orient, Leipzig.
AOAT	Alter Orient und Altes Testament, Neukirchen-Vluyn.
AOS	American Oriental Series, New Haven.
ARM	Archiv Royales de Mari, Paris, 1950–.
ArOr	*Archiv Orientální*, Prague.
ATD	Das Alte Testament Deutsch, Göttingen.
BA	*The Biblical Archaeologist*, New Haven, Cambridge, Mass.
BASOR	*Bulletin of the American Schools of Oriental Research*, New Haven, Cambridge, Mass.
BBB	Bonner Biblische Beiträge.
BDB	F. Brown, S.R. Driver, and C.A. Briggs, *A Hebrew and English Lexicon of the Old Testament*, Oxford, 1906.
BHK	R. Kittel (ed.), *Biblia Hebraica* (3. ed.), Stuttgart, 1937, 1961^{12}.
BHS	K. Elliger and W. Rudolph (eds.), *Biblia Hebraica Stuttgartensia*, Stuttgart, 1967–77.
Bib	*Biblica*, Rome.
BibOr	Biblica et Orientalia, Rome.
BKAT	Biblischer Kommentar: Altes Testament, Neukirchen-Vluyn.
BN	*Biblische Notizen*, Bamberg.
BWANT	Beiträge zur Wissenschaft vom Alten und Neuen Testament.

BZ	*Biblische Zeitschrift*, Paderborn.
BZAW	Beiheft zur Zeitschrift für die Alttestamentliche Wissenschaft, Berlin/New York.
CAD	*The Assyrian Dictionary of the Oriental Institute of the University of Chicago*, 1956–.
CAH	*The Cambridge Ancient History*, revised edition, I–II, Cambridge, 1961–.
CBOTS	Coniectanea Biblica: Old Testament Series, Lund.
CBQ	*Catholic Biblical Quarterly*, Washington, DC.
CRB	Cahiers de la Revue Biblique, Paris.
DBSup	*Dictionnaire de la Bible. Supplément*, Paris, 1928–.
DDD	*Dictionary of Deities and Demons in the Bible*, Leiden/New York/Köln, 1995.
DISO	C.-F. Jean and J. Hoftijzer, *Dictionnaire des Inscriptions Sémitiques de l'Ouest*, Leiden, 1960–65.
DNWSI	J. Hoftijzer and K. Jongeling, *Dictionary of the North-West Semitic Inscriptions* I–II, Leiden/New York/Köln, 1995.
EHAT	Exegetisches Handbuch zum Alten Testament, Münster i. Westf.
ETL	*Ephemerides Theologicae Lovanienses*, Gembloux.
FRLANT	Forschungen zur Religion und Literatur des Alten und Neuen Testaments, Göttingen.
HALOT	L. Koehler, W. Baumgartner, and J.J. Stamm, (tr. and ed., M.E.J. Richardson), *The Hebrew and Aramaic Lexicon of the Old Testament*, Leiden/New York/Köln, 1994–.
HAT	Handbuch zum Alten Testament, Tübingen.
HdO	Handbuch der Orientalistik, Leiden/New York/Köln.
HSM	Harvard Semitic Monographs.
HSS	Harvard Semitic Studies.
HUCA	*Hebrew Union College Annual*, Cincinnati.
ICC	The International Critical Commentary, Edinburgh.
IDB	*The Interpreter's Dictionary of the Bible*, Nashville/New York, 1962.
IDBSup	*The Interpreter's Dictionary of the Bible. Supplementary Volume*, Nashville, 1976.
IEJ	*Israel Exploration Journal*, Jerusalem.
Int	*Interpretation*, Ritchmond, VA.
JANES	*Journal of the Ancient Near Eastern Society of Columbia University*, New York.
JAOS	*Journal of the American Oriental Society*, New Haven.

JBL	*Journal of Biblical Literature*, Atlanta.
JBS	Jerusalem Biblical Studies.
JNES	*Journal of Near Eastern Studies*, Chicago.
JQR	*Jewish Quarterly Review*, Philadelphia.
JSOT	*Journal for the Study of the Old Testament*, Sheffield.
JSOTSup	Journal for the Study of the Old Testament Supplement Series, Sheffield.
JSS	*Journal of Semitic Studies*, Manchester.
JTS	*Journal of Theological Studies*, Oxford.
JWH	*Journal of World History*, Neuchatel.
KAI	H. Donner and W. Röllig, *Kanaanäische und aramäische Inschriften* I, Wiesbaden, 1971[3]; II, 1973[3]; III, 1969[2].
KB	L. Koehler and W. Baumgartner, *Lexicon in Veteris Testmenti Libros*, Leiden, 1953.
MVÄG	Mitteilungen der Vorderasiatisch-Ägyptischen Gesellschaft, Leipzig.
NCB	New Century Bible Commentary, London.
Or	*Orientalia*, Rome.
OTL	Old Testament Library.
OTS	*Oudtestamentische Studiën*, Leiden.
OTWSA	Die Oudtestamentiese Werkgemeeskap in Suid-Afrika, Pretoria.
PEQ	*Palestine Exploration Quarterly*, London.
POTT	D.J. Wiseman (ed.), *Peoples of Old Testament Times*, Oxford, 1973.
RA	*Revue d'Assyriologie et d'Archéologie Orientale*, Paris.
RB	*Revue Biblique*, Paris.
RHA	*Revue Hittite et Asianique*, Paris.
RIMA	The Royal Inscriptions of Mesopotamia: Assyrian Periods, Toronto/Buffalo/London, 1987–.
RLA	*Reallexikon der Assyriologie*, Berlin/Leipzig, 1932–.
SBLM	Society of Biblical Literature Monograph Series.
SBM	Stuttgarter Biblische Monographien.
SBS	Stuttgarter Bibelstudien.
SBT	Studies in Biblical Theology, London.
SBTS	Studies in Biblical Theology, Second Series, London.
SEÅ	*Svensk Exegetisk Årsbok*, Uppsala.
SHANE	Studies in the History of the Ancient Near East, Leiden.
SPDS	T. Ishida (ed.), *Studies in the Period of David and Solomon and Other Essays*, Tokyo/Winona Lake, 1982.

TGUOS	*Transactions of the Glasgow University Oriental Society.*
TH	Texte der Hethiter, Heidelberg.
TLZ	*Theologische Literaturzeitung*, Leipzig, Berlin.
TS	Theologische Studien, Zürich.
TWAT	*Theologisches Wörterbuch zum Alten Testament*, Stuttgart/Berlin/Köln, 1970–.
TZ	*Theologische Zeitschrift*, Basel.
UT	C.H. Gordon, *Ugaritic Textbook* (AnOr 38), Rome, 1965.
VAB	Vorderasiatische Bibliothek, Leipzig.
VT	*Vetus Testamentum*, Leiden.
VTSup	Supplements to Vetus Testamentum, Leiden.
WHJP	E.A. Speiser (ed.), *World History of the Jewish People* I/I: *At the Dawn of Civilization*, Tel-Aviv, 1964; B. Mazar (ed.), *World History of the Jewish People* I/III: *Judges*, Tel-Aviv, 1971.
WMANT	Wissenschaftliche Monographien zum Alten und Neuen Testament, Neukirchen-Vluyn.
WO	*Die Welt des Orients*, Göttingen.
WZ	*Wissenschaftliche Zeitschrift* (der Universitäten der DDR).
ZA	*Zeitschrift für Assyriologie und Vorderasiatische Archäologie*, Berlin.
ZAW	*Zeitschrift für die Alttestamentliche Wissenschaft*, Berlin.
ZDPV	*Zeitschrift des Deutschen Palästina-Vereins*, Leipzig/Wiesbaden.
ZTK	*Zeitschrift für Thelogie und Kirche*, Tübingen.

INTRODUCTION

This book is a collection of essays which I published in periodicals, collections of studies, and *Festschriften* in 1973–93. All the essays in this book are previously published articles revised with reference to recent studies. But it was impossible for me to discuss anew in this book various issues raised there. Therefore, by posing some fundamental questions which have arisen in my mind while I was studying recent discussions about historical studies of the Hebrew Bible, I will here express my view on biblical history and historiography in accordance with which I have pursued my studies.

To begin with, what I felt to be problematic is the title of the very source material of our study: the Hebrew Bible, generally called the Old Testament according to the Christian tradition.[1] It is clear that the title Old Testament demonstrates the Christian theological view that the Hebrew Bible is to be understood as the first volume of the Holy Scriptures of which the concluding second volume is the New Testament. However, the canonization of the Hebrew Bible had been completed by Jews who had nothing to do with the Christian theology before the New Testament was authorized in the Christian church.[2]

Therefore, from the purely historical point of view, it is hardly legitimate to consider the title Old Testament appropriate to historical studies. Moreover, *Biblia Hebraica* is not the original text of *Vetus Testamentum* in the strict sense of the term. They are traditionally different from each other in the order of the books as well as the division of chapters and verses. Therefore, the great majority of scholars in practice employ the Masoretic texts in *BHK* and/or *BHS* for the original source. Under these conditions it seems illogical that

[1] For an illuminating discussion about the issue see J.D. Levenson, "The Hebrew Bible, the Old Testament, and Historical Criticism", in R.E. Friedman and H.G.M. Williamson (eds.), *The Future of Biblical Studies. The Hebrew Scriptures*, Atlanta, 1987, pp. 19–60.

[2] For the history of the canonization of the Hebrew Bible see J.A. Sanders, "Hebrew Bible" in "Canon", in *ABD* I, New York, 1992, pp. 837–852; for the New Testament see H.Y. Gamble, "New Testament" in ibid., pp. 852–861.

they still stick to the title *Vetus Testamentum* in critical studies in which they develop radical theses independent of Christian theology. For it has become the consensus of the scholarly opinion that the disciplines of historical research belong to a different sphere from theological interpretation. Undoubtedly scholars have been aware of the inconsistency, but there seem to be other considerations than the historical that hinder them from adopting the title Hebrew Bible instead of the Old Testament. Without making a research into the problem, it seems that a firm continuity of religious traditions in Western society is one of the most fundamental causes of the conservative use of the title *Vetus Testamentum.*

If the religious tradition still has such a great influence on modern society, we may safely suppose that traditions exercised still stronger power in the ancient world. In fact, extensive research has established that they acted as a force binding together the society in the ancient Near East. It is possible to find a typical example of the continuity of traditions, among others, in the large number of literatures that were transmitted through millennia.[3] In view of the circumstances, it is only too natural that it has long been supposed that the Hebrew Bible, a collection of documents from the ancient Near East, also contains traditions transmitted from the remote past. Moreover, it is a distinctive feature that its main part consists of a large collection of traditions in the order which corresponds to the chronological sequence of the events described. In other words, the first nine (or eleven) books of the Hebrew Bible, i.e., from Genesis to Kings in the Pentateuch and the Former Prophets, tell consecutive stories of the Israelite/Jewish people from the creation of the world to the Babylonian exile.

Needless to say, scholars hesitate to call this large complex of traditions history. But we may find in it a certain historical development with relations of cause and effect running through the *tôlᵉḏôṯ*,[4] i.e., the successive generations, of ancient Israel. Therefore, one can hardly dismiss the impression that the first nine (or eleven) books of the Hebrew Bible were compiled as a sort of historiographical work,

[3] A.L. Oppenheim calls this sort of literature "the stream of the tradition", see *Ancient Mesopotamia. Portrait of a Dead Civilization,* Chicago, 1964, p. 13; about the continuity of the language and literary genres in ancient Egypt see J.A. Wilson, *The Culture of Ancient Egypt,* Chicago, 1951, pp. 76 f.

[4] About *tôlᵉḏôṯ* see J. Schreiner, "תולדות", in *TWAT* VIII, Stuttgart, 1994–95, cols. 571–577.

though they contain many other genres than historical narratives, such as myths, legends, laws, cultic sayings, songs and poems, and so on.[5] In fact, a majority of scholars today seem to accept the thesis that this large complex of traditions consists of two large historiographical corpora compiled by the Deuteronomistic historian(s) and the Priestly writers,[6] though there are still wide differences of opinion about its analysis.[7] And there is also a variant historiography in 1 and 2 Chronicles.

I have no intention at present to enter the discussions on the analytico-redactional problems of the Pentateuch and the Former Prophets. I agree with modern studies, in principle, that this great complex of traditions in the Hebrew Bible was eventually formed through the complicated process of redactional works over a long period of many centuries. What I feel questionable is the scholarly methodology for the reconstruction of the redactional process in the course of history of ancient Israel. When handling biblical traditions, it seems, much scholarship today sets out to be rather more skeptical of the validity of historical information there than to assume its reliability.[8] The skepticism stems from the criterion of judgement based on compatibility with modern thinking.[9]

However, it is an invariable principle in historical research that any document for source materials demands interpretation according to the historical milieu in which the document in question was produced. In studies on ancient Near Eastern texts, tradition as a force binding of society is to be counted as one of the most important elements of which the historical milieu consists. As to the large

[5] Cf. J.A. Soggin, *Introduction to the Old Testament. From its origins to the closing of the Alexandrian canon*, London, 1980², pp. 37 ff.

[6] For the classical study on this thesis see M. Noth, *Überlieferungsgeschichtliche Studien. Die sammelnden und bearbeitenden Geschichtswerke im Alten Testament*, Tübingen, 1943, 1957²; idem, *Überlieferungsgeschichte des Pentateuch*, Stuttgart, 1948.

[7] About various opinions and discussions see Soggin, *Introduction to the Old Testament*, pp. 138 ff., 161 ff.

[8] E.g. J. van Seters, *In Search of History. Historiography in the Ancient World and the Origins of Biblical History*, New Haven/London, 1983; N.P. Lemche, *Early Israel. Anthropological and Historical Studies on the Israelite Society Before the Monarchy* (VTSup 37), Leiden, 1985; T.L. Thompson, *Early History of the Israelite People. From the Written and Archaeological Sources* (SHANE 4), Leiden, 1994.

[9] A.R. Millard argues against the modern historian's interpretation of the biblical historiography, "Story, History, and Theology", in A.R. Millard, J.K. Hoffmeier, and D.W. Baker (eds.), *Faith, Tradition, and History. Old Testament Historiography in Its Near Eastern Context*, Winona Lake, 1994, pp. 37–64.

historiographical complex in the Hebrew Bible, consequently, it is legitimate to suppose that traditions played a decisive role to provide its compilation with not only the source materials but also the scheme of the framework. Thus I am of the opinion that the historiographical nature of the complex did not come from the last redactors such as the Deuteronomistic historian(s) and the Priestly writers but originated in ancient traditions.[10]

My approach is sometimes criticized as conservative. But I base my judgements just on the conservatism inherent in the very nature of tradition. Needless to say, however, I do not think that information in historical traditions in the Hebrew Bible as it is conveys history in the modern sense of the term. I agree with the view that few traditions are free from tendency, bias, or distortion. Even more, no historiography is composed without a certain historical view and a definite object. Moreover, history is a dynamic process of human activity through which traditions undergo metamorphosis in greater or lesser degree.

Based on the above understanding, I propose the following handling of the biblical texts as a working principle for study:

a) First of all, before resorting to braking a text into sources or layers to rationalize so-called discrepancies and repititions in it, we must try to give an explanation for each historical tradition *in toto* to elucidate its contents and intention.

b) The distinctive phraseologies or vocabularies of the Deuteronomists or the Priestly source indicate who were responsible for the last compilation of the texts but do not always show with whom the tradition in the texts originated. There always remains a possibility that the tradition stemmed from earlier generations.[11]

c) It is very likely that political and religious motivation played the leading role in the composition of the biblical historiography. Consequently, there must have been a decisive moment for it. It is

---

[10] For critical surveys of skeptical views on the historicity of biblical traditions and positive arguments for the reconstruction of history of ancinet Israel see, e.g., B. Halpern, *The First Historians. The Hebrew Bible and History*, San Francisco, 1988; E. Yamauchi, "The Current State of Old Testament Historiography", in *Faith, Tradition, and History*, 1994, pp. 1–36.

[11] About the Deuteronomistic historian's "sources" integrated in his history see N. Na'aman, "The 'Conquest of Canaan' in the Book of Joshua and in History", in I. Finkelstein and N. Na'aman (eds.), *From Nomadism to Monarchy. Archaeological and Historical Aspects of Early Israel*, Jerusalem, 1994, pp. 227–230.

difficult to assume that any historiography in the Hebrew Bible was composed as a purely literary work.[12]

d) Undoubtedly, extrabiblical sources and archaeological findings are useful for interpreting biblical texts. They often provide evidence indispensable to understanding the situation correctly. Nevertheless, they are auxiliary sources. They must be carefully treated especially when a conclusion is drawn from the absence of evidence.[13]

In the essays which follow I present research into various phases of historical traditions in the Hebrew Bible. In the first part I will deal with certain appellations, terminologies, or formulae which underwent changes in meaning in the course of history of the Israelite/Jewish people in the biblical period. In the second part I will shed light upon the historiographical problems of the Succession Narrative.

---

[12] According to S. Yamada, "The Editorial History of the Assyrian King List", *ZA* 84 (1994), pp. 36 f., three motives are found in compilations of the Assyrian King List, i.e., genuine interest in royal history-chronology, royal legitimation, and the ancestor cult. It seems to me, however, that the first motive requires further study.

[13] N. Na'aman, in *From Nomadism to Monarchy*, pp. 218 ff., is of the opinion that the "most important evidence for dating the rise of historiography" in the kingdoms of Israel and Judah comes from archaeological research which attests the sudden diffusion of alphabetic writing in the seventh century B.C. Based on the absence of tablets or inscriptions in Israel and Judah before the mid-eighth century B.C., he refutes the view of the beginning of historical writing in Israel in the period of David and Solomon. It is difficult for me, however, to regard this as decisive evidence. There remain many other problems to solve to search into the matter. E.g., Na'aman argues that "the development of historiography is necessarily connected with the emergence of a wide circle of readers" (p. 221) but, supposing public readings were given, historiographies could be appreciated not only by professional scribes in the royal courts but also by the general public who were illiterate.

PART ONE

DYNAMISM IN HISTORY AND HISTORIOGRAPHY

CHAPTER ONE

THE LISTS OF PRE-ISRAELITE NATIONS*

1. *From 2 to 12 Nations in 27 Lists*

Seven nations are enumerated in the Book of Deuteronomy 7:1 as the original inhabitants of the Promised Land, who were doomed to be dispossessed by the Israelites. These seven nations, or part of them, are mentioned mostly in list form, sometimes together with others. We can find altogether twenty-seven such passages in the Hebrew Bible. They seem stereotyped, but both the number and the order of the nations show great variation, as the following diagram indicates. (In this study, the following six nations are referred to by their initials: the Canaanites, the Amorites, the Hittites, the Perizzites, the Jebusites, and the Girgashites, and the letter V stands for the Hivites).

Table I

No.	Nations in order as found	No. of nations	Biblical passages
1	Canaan, Sidon, Heth, J A G V, Arkites, Sinites, Arvadites, Zemarites, Hamathites	12	Gen 10:15–18a
2	C P	2	Gen 13:7
3	Kenites, Kenizites, Kadmonites, H P, Rephites, A C G J	10	Gen 15:19–21
4	C P	2	Gen 34:30
5	C H A P V J	6	Exod 3:8
6	C H A P V J	6	Exod 3:17
7	C H A V J	5	Exod 13:5
8	A H P C V J	6	Exod 23:23
9	V C H	3	Exod 23:28
10	C A H P V J	6	Exod 33:2
11	A C H P V J	6	Exod 34:11
12	Amalek, H J A C	5	Num 13:29
13	H G A C P V J	7	Deut 7:1

* This essay is a revised version of the study which appeared in *Bib* 60 (1979), pp. 461–490.

Table I (*cont.*)

No.	Nations in order as found	No. of nations	Biblical passages
14	H A C P V J	6	Deut 20:17
15	C H V P G A J	7	Josh 3:10
16	A C	2	Josh 5:1
17	H A C P V J	6	Josh 9:1
18	C A H P J V	6	Josh 11:3
19	H A C P V J	6	Josh 12:8
20	A P C H G V J	7	Josh 24:11
21	C P	2	Judg 1:4–5
22	C H A P V J	6	Judg 3:5
23	A H P V J	5	1 Kgs 9:20
24	C H P J, Ammonites, Moabites, Egyptians, A	8	Ezra 9:1
25	C H A P J G	6	Neh 9:8
26	Canaan, Sidon, Heth, J A G V, Arkites, Sinites, Arvadites, Zemarites, Hamathites	12	1 Chr 1:13–16
27	H A P V J	5	2 Chr 8:7

Although it is explicitly stated in Deut 7:1 that they were "seven nations", the number in the various lists actually ranges from two to twelve. Moreover, the order of entries in one list is so different from that in another that it looks as though the listings of the nations were made incidentally. In fact, so far none of the attempts to find a principle in accordance with which these lists were composed has been very successful.[1] It is difficult to imagine, however, that so many lists, altogether twenty-seven, could have been compiled without following any rule.

[1] E.g., in his excursus about the "lists of the nations", W. Richter, *Die Bearbeitungen des "Retterbuches" in der deuteronomischen Epoche* (BBB 21), Bonn, 1964, p. 41, admits that "So wird man hinter dem Wechsel der Reihenfolge kaum eine Absicht vermuten können". On the other hand, G.E. Mendenhall, *The Tenth Generation. The Origins of the Biblical Tradition*, Baltimore/London, 1973, p. 144, n. 5, declares: "There is no evidence for a 'canonical list'". For previous studies regarding the lists of the pre-Israelite nations, *inter alia*, see S.R. Driver, *A Critical and Exegetical Commentary on Deuteronomy* (ICC), Edinburgh, 1902[3], pp. 97 f.; F.M.T. de Liagre Böhl, *Kanaanäer und Hebräer. Untersuchungen zur Vorgeschichte des Volkstums und der Religion Israels auf dem Boden Kanaans* (Beiträge zur Wissenschaft vom Alten Testament 9), Leipzig, 1911, pp. 63 f.; E.A. Speiser, "Man, Ethnic Divisions of", in *IDB* III, Nashville/New York, 1962, p. 237; N. Lohfink, *Das Hauptgebot. Eine Untersuchung literarischer Einleitungsfragen zu Dtn 5–11* (AnBib 20), Roma, 1963, p. 123; idem, *Die Landverheissung als Eid. Eine Studie zu Gn 15* (SBS 28), Stuttgart, 1967, pp. 65 f., 98 f.; Richter, *Bearbeitungen*, pp. 41–43; M. du Buit, "Populations de l'ancienne Palestine", in *DBSup* VIII, Paris,

It is true that we cannot find one single principle of compilation for all the lists. In such a case, we must suppose that there was originally more than one method of classification governing the grouping of the lists. According to our analysis, these twenty-seven lists can be classified under the following five categories: a) six-name lists with variations, b) lists of representative nations, c) geographical lists, d) the list in the Table of Nations, and e) lists in later sources.

2. *Six-Name Lists with Variations*

The six-name lists, which consist of the same six nations, though lined up in various orders, are predominant among our lists. They account for eleven instances (I:5, 6, 8, 10, 11, 14, 17–19, 22, 25)[2] out of the twenty-seven, while there are four five-name lists (I:7, 12, 23, 27), four two-name lists (I:2, 4, 16, 21), three seven-name lists (I:13, 15, 20), two twelve-name lists (I:1, 26), a ten-name list (I:3), an eight-name list (I:24) and a three-name list (I:9). This fact justifies us in regarding the six-name lists as an independent category.[3] However, not all of these eleven instances belong to the same category, since, according to our classification, the list in Josh 11:3 (I:18) is to be counted as one of the "geographical lists" and that in Neh 9:8 (I:25) should be included in the "lists in later sources". On the other hand, we may classify all the seven-name lists (I:13, 15, 20) as well as two of the five-name lists (I:7, 23) under the heading of variations of the six-name lists. The seven-name lists are made up of the same six nations as are found in the six-name lists, with the additional entry of the Girgashites. It is likely that these seven-name lists were composed as expanded forms of the six-name lists, with the

1972, cols. 112–114; J.G. Plöger, *Literarkritische, formgeschichtliche und stilkritische Untersuchungen zum Deuteronomium* (BBB 26), Bonn, 1967, pp. 73 f.; M. Caloz, "Exode, XIII, 3–16 et son rapport au Deutéronome", *RB* 75 (1968), 33 f.; F. Langlamet, "Israël et 'l'habitant du pays', vocabulaire et formules d'Ex., XXXIV, 11–16", *RB* 76 (1969), p. 332; idem, *Gilgal et les récits de la traversée du Jourdain* (Jos iii–iv) (CRB 11), Paris, 1969, pp. 109 f.; J. van Seters, "The Terms 'Amorite' and 'Hittite' in the Old Testament", *VT* 22 (1972), pp. 67–72; Mendenhall, *The Tenth Generation*, pp. 144 f.; R. North, "The Hivites", *Bib* 54 (1973), pp. 43–46.

[2] The numbers refer to "Table I no. 5, no. 6, no. 8, etc.".

[3] The nature of the six-name lists as the basic formula has been observed in one way or another, e.g., Speiser, in *IDB* III, p. 237; Richter, *Die Bearbeitungen*, p. 41; North, *Bib* 54 (1973), p. 45.

intention of making the number of nations up to seven by means of the inclusion of the Girgashites.[4] We will deal with the problem of the omission of the Perizzites and the Canaanites from the lists in Exod 13:5 (I:7) and 1 Kgs 9:20 (I:23), respectively, later.

Thus we have altogether fourteen lists in the category "six-name lists with variations". Can we find a principle in accordance with which these fourteen lists have been composed? Once again, we can resort to statistics, according to which we shall find that twelve lists out of the fourteen include the Canaanites, the Amorites and the Hittites in the first half, though in various orders (II:1, 3–8, 10–14), and ten of the lists have the Perizzites, the Hivites and the Jebusites in this fixed order in the latter half (II:1–3, 5–7, 11–14). These statistics make it clear that our first task is to find how to order the irregularities in the first half.

Before taking up this task, it is to be noted that there is a striking contrast between these two groupings. The three nations in the first half, the Canaanites, the Amorites and the Hittites, are well known peoples in both biblical and extra-biblical sources. On the other hand, not only are the nations of the latter half, the Perizzites, the Hivites, and the Jebusites, scarcely attested in extra-biblical sources,[5] but the information in the Hebrew Bible itself is scanty and vague about them. Undoubtedly, the six-name lists have a structure made up of two parts: the first consisting of three major nations, and the second of three minor.

The almost completely fixed order of the minor nations in the second half of the six-name lists suggests that the order decided upon among the three became fossilized after the original formula for compiling the six-name lists had been made up. This fossilization reflects a situation in which not only had the existence of these nations already come to an end in reality but also memory of them was no

---

[4] In the LXX seven of the six-name lists (I:5, 6, 8, 10 [codex Alexandrinus], 11, 14, 17) and in the Samaritan Pentateuch six of the six-name lists (I:5, 6, 8, 10, 11, 14) have been expanded to seven-name lists by adding the Girgashites, and two of the five-name lists (I:7, 23) have also been made "complete" by adding the Perizzites and the Girgashites or the Canaanites and the Girgashites.

[5] Attempts have been made to find their names in extra-biblical sources, but none of the suggestions has been unanimously accepted; cf. D.J. Wiseman, "Introduction: Peoples and Nations", in D.J. Wiseman (ed.), *POTT*, Oxford, 1973, pp. xv f.; N. Na'aman, "The Conquest of Canaan' in the Book of Joshua and in History", in I. Finkelstein and N. Na'aman (eds.), *From Nomadism to Monarchy. Archaeological and Historical Aspects of Early Israel*, Jerusalem, 1994, pp. 239–243.

longer alive in Israelite traditions. On the other hand, the great diversity in the order of the major nations in the first half shows that the connotations of these names continued to change after the original formulation of the lists. This accords with the fluidity and multiplicity of the implications of these three appellations in biblical as well as extra-biblical sources. Indeed, recent studies have made it clear that the terms Canaanites, Amorites, and Hittites each underwent a long historical development in the ancient Near East. Without entering into an intricate discussion of this subject, we may review the conclusions reached about the development of the connotations of these terms as follows:

a) Canaanites[6]—The discoveries in Ebla and Mari have demonstrated that the terms "Canaan" and "Canaanites" were used as early as in the third millennium B.C.[7] But the exact application of the term in these early documents has not yet been fully clarified. It is from the middle of the fifteenth century B.C. onward that the term "Canaan" was clearly used as a geographical name referring to western Palestine, including the Phoenician coast, and hence it became the administrative designation of an Egyptian province.[8] Therefore the term "Canaanites" was primarily applied to the whole population of the above region or province; however, where further distinction is required, biblical sources place the "Canaanites" in the coastal regions and the Jordan valley, and in later times the term implied "merchants" or "traders", especially "Phoenician traders". Naturally,

---

[6] See B. Maisler (Mazar), *Untersuchungen zur alten Geschichte und Ethnographie Syriens und Palästinas* I, Gießen, 1930, pp. 54–74; idem, "Canaan and Canaanites", *BASOR* 102 (1946), pp. 7–12; A. van Selms, "The Canaanites in the Book of Genesis", *OTS* 12 (1958), pp. 182–213; W.F. Albright, "The Role of the Canaanites in the History of Civilization", in G.E. Wright (ed.), *The Bible and the Ancient Near East. Essays in Honor of William Foxwell Albright*, London, 1961, pp. 328–362; J.C.L. Gibson, "Observations on Some Important Ethnic Terms in the Pentateuch", *JNES* 20 (1961), pp. 217–220; E.A. Speiser, "Amorites and Canaanites", in E.A. Speiser (ed.), *WHJP* I/I: *At the Dawn of Civilization—A Background of Biblical History*, Tel-Aviv, 1964, pp. 162–169, 364 f.; Y. Aharoni, *The Land of the Bible. A Historical Geography*, London, 1966, pp. 61–70; R. de Vaux, "Le pays de Canaan", *JAOS* 88 (1968), pp. 23–30; idem, *Histoire ancienne d'Israël. Des origines à l'installation en Canaan*, Paris, 1971, pp. 123–129; A.R. Millard, "The Canaanites", in D.J. Wiseman (ed.), *POTT*, Oxford, 1973, pp. 29–52; P.C. Schmitz, "Canaan (Place)", in *ABD* I, New York, 1992, pp. 828–831.

[7] For Ebla see G. Pettinato, "The Royal Archives of Tell Mardikh-Ebla", *BA* 39 (1976), p. 48; for Mari see G. Dossin, "Une mention de Canaanéens dans une lettre de Mari", *Syria* 50 (1973), pp. 277–282.

[8] See W. Helck, *Die Beziehungen Ägyptens zu Vorderasien im 3. und 2. Jahrtausend v. Chr.* (Ägyptologische Abhandlungen 5), Wiesbaden, 1962, pp. 279 f.

the use of the terms "Canaan" and "Canaanites" for western Palestine and the whole population of the region, respectively, became obsolete after the Israelites had changed the Land of Canaan (Gen 13:12; 17:8, etc.) into the Land of Israel (1 Sam 13:19; 1 Chr 22:2, etc.).[9]

b) Amorites[10]—Recently, scholars have become more and more skeptical about establishing any direct relationship between the term "Amorites" in the Hebrew Bible and the ethnic designation Amurru (MAR.TU), i.e., Western Semites who were active in Mesopotamia and Syria from the Old Akkadian and Ur III periods down to the middle of the second millennium B.C. Neither are they certain that they can find a distinction between the Amurru (MAR.TU) people and the Canaanites. They only agree that "Amorites" in some biblical passages refer to the geographical term Amurru, which appears mainly in Mari texts and the Amarna letters as the designation for a specific region or a state in Syria but that the biblical references to the Amorites as one of the pre-Israelite populations should be regarded as unhistorical, or remain, at best, vague.

However, it is not easy to believe that the biblical references to the Amorites in the mountains of western Palestine and the Transjordan have no historical value.[11] The distinction between the Canaanites living along the coast and the Amorites living in the mountainous regions must have stemmed from the experiences of Israelites entering the Promised Land. However, the term "Amorites" did lose its

[9] For the relationship between the Land of Canaan and the Land of Israel see Z. Kallai, "Tribes, Territories of", in *IDBSup*, Nashville, 1976, pp. 920–923; idem, "The Patriarchal Boundaries, Canaan and the Land of Israel: Patterns and Application in Biblical Historiography", *IEJ* 47 (1997), pp. 69–82; M. Ottosson, "ארץ", in *TWAT* I, Stuttgart, 1970–73, cols. 431 f.; cf. BDB, p. 76; *HALOT* I, p. 90.

[10] See Maisler (Mazar), *Untersuchungen* I, pp. 1–53; M. Noth, "Beiträge zur Geschichte des Ostjordanlandes I. Das Land Gilead als Siedlungsgebiet israelitischer Sippen" (1941), in *Aufsätze zur biblischen Landes- und Altertumskunde* I, Neukirchen-Vluyn, 1971, pp. 94–101; Gibson, *JNES* 20 (1961), pp. 220–224; Speiser, in *WHJP* I/I, pp. 162–169; K.M. Kenyon, *Amorites and Canaanites*, London, 1966; H. Klengel, *Geschichte Syriens im 2. Jahrtausend vor unserer Zeitrechnung* II: *Mittel- und Südsyrien*, Berlin, 1969, pp. 178–263; A. Haldar, *Who were the Amorites?*, Leiden, 1971; de Vaux, *Histoire ancienne d'Israël*, pp. 129–131; van Seters, *VT* 22 (1972), pp. 64–67, 72–78; idem, *Abraham in History and Tradition*, New Haven/London, 1975, pp. 43–45; M. Liverani, "The Amorites", in D.J. Wiseman (ed.), *POTT*, Oxford, 1973, pp. 100–133; W.G. Dever, "Prolegomenon to a reconsideration of archaeology and patriarchal backgrounds", in J.H. Hayes and J.M. Miller (eds.), *Israelite and Judaean History* (OTL), London, 1977, pp. 102–111; G.E. Mendenhall, "Amorites", in *ABD* I, New York, 1992, pp. 199–202.

[11] E.g., de Vaux, *Histoire ancienne d'Israël*, p. 130, maintains that "'Amorite' n'a, dans la Bible, aucune signification historique ni ethnique"; cf. also van Seters, *VT* 22 (1972), p. 78.

specific meaning later in the Hebrew Bible, when it was used replacing the term "Canaanites" as the designation of the whole population of pre-Israelite Palestine. But this use of the term seems to have originated in later times under the influence of the term "Amurru" as found in Neo-Assyrian inscriptions from the ninth century B.C. on, which signified the entire Syro-Palestinian region and its populations.[12]

c) Hittites[13]—Of the names of the three major nations, the appellation "Hittites" changed its signification most drastically during the more than two millennia in question, and a fourfold distinction in the use of the term has become well established, with these values given to it: (i) The name of the original inhabitants of Anatolia who are otherwise called "Hattians" to distinguish them from the second group; (ii) The designation of the Indo-Aryan immigrants who conquered the Hattians about 2000 B.C. and established their "Old kingdom" in the eighteenth century B.C., and thereafter the Empire which dominated not only Anatolia but also Syria as far south as the northern border of Palestine in the fourteenth and thirteenth centuries B.C.; (iii) A generic name for the small kingdoms in Syria which sprang up as successors to the great Hittite Empire after its dissolution around 1200 B.C.—these are often called "Neo-Hittites" to distinguish them from the second group; (iv) A general term for the whole of the inhabitants of Syria-Palestine, which first appeared in Neo-Assyrian inscriptions in the ninth century B.C. as a synonym for the term "Amurru" as used in the same sense, but which had

---

[12] Noth, in *Aufsätze* I, pp. 98 f., holds that the general use of the name Amorites in the Bible came not from the Neo-Assyrian but from the Old Babylonian use of the term; but see Liverani, in *POTT*, p. 123. The term Amurru as the general designation for Syria was first attested in the inscriptions of Aššurnaṣirpal II (883–859 B.C.), see Liverani, in *POTT*, pp. 119 f.

[13] See Maisler (Mazar), *Untersuchungen* I, pp. 76–80; B. Mazar, "החתים במקרא", in *Encyclopaedia Biblica* III, Jerusalem, 1958, cols. 355–357 (Hebrew); L. Delaporte, "Les Hittites sont-ils nommés dans la Bible?", *RHA* 4 (1938), pp. 289–296; idem, "Hittites", in *DBSup* IV, Paris, 1949, cols. 103–109; O.R. Gurney, *The Hittites*, Harmondsworth, 1961², pp. 59–62; Gibson, *JNES* 20 (1961), pp. 224–227; I.J. Gelb, "Hittites", in *IDB* II, Nashville/New York, 1962, pp. 612–615; A. Kammenhuber, "Hethitisch, Palaisch, Luwisch und Hieroglyphenluwisch", in *Altkleinasiatische Sprachen* (HdO I/II 1–2/2), Leiden/Köln, 1969, pp. 119–127; H.A. Hoffner, "Some Contributions of Hittitology to Old Testament Study", *Tyndale Bulletin* 20 (1969), pp. 27–37; idem, "The Hittites and Hurrians", in D.J. Wiseman (ed.), *POTT*, Oxford, 1973, pp. 197–221, 226–228; de Vaux, *Histoire ancienne d'Israël*, pp. 131–133; van Seters, *VT* 22 (1972), pp. 64–67, 78–81; J.D. Hawkins, "Ḫatti: the Ist millennium B.C.", in *RLA* IV, Berlin/New York, 1972–75, pp. 152–159; G. McMahon, "Hittites in the OT", in *ABD* III, New York, 1992, pp. 231–233; Na'aman, in *From Nomadism to Monarchy*, pp. 239 f.

supplanted the latter by the middle of the first millennium B.C.[14]

Although the above four distinctions in the use of the term "Hittites" are unanimously accepted, the question of how the Hittites in the Hebrew Bible fit into this picture is still a thorny one on which opinions vary. It is not so difficult to identify some biblical references to the Hittites with either the territory of the Hittite Empire in Syria or the Neo-Hittite kingdoms.[15] However, although the Hebrew Bible often mentions the Hittites among the original inhabitants of the Promised Land, we have had so far no definite evidence of a Hittite presence in Palestine in the second millennium B.C. Therefore recent studies are reluctant to regard biblical references to the Hittites in Palestine as historical.[16]

Nevertheless, there is enough evidence in the Hebrew Bible to justify the belief that the Israelites who settled the Promised Land did find a group of inhabitants in southern Palestine[17] who regarded themselves as descendants or relatives of the Hittites of Anatolia and Syria. We do not know exactly how this community came into being.[18] It must have been a small community formed by descendants

[14] On the progressive shift of the designation Amurru to an archaic term and the use of Ḫatti for the entire region of Syria-Palestine, see Liverani, in *POTT*, pp. 119–123.

[15] The term Hittite(s) in 1 Kgs 10:29 (= 2 Chr 1:17); 1 Kgs 11:1; 2 Kgs 7:6, certainly refers to the Neo-Hittites. Maisler (Mazar), *BASOR* 102 (1946), p. 11, n. 25; idem, in *Encyclopaedia Biblica* III, col. 356, thinks that "all the land of the Hittites" in Josh 1:4, also designates the Syrian regions, which were once under the rule of the Hittite Empire, as opposed to "Canaan", but opinions are divided on this interpretation.

[16] E.g., de Vaux, *Histoire ancienne d'Israël*, p. 132; van Seters, *VT* 22 (1972), p. 81.

[17] It is remarkable that every reference to the Hittites as indigenous to Palestine places them in southern Palestine: Ephron the Hittite who sold the field in Machphelah to Abraham was a citizen of Kiriath-arba (= Hebron) (Gen 23), while the Hittite wives of Esau came, it seems, from the region of Beer-sheba (Gen 26:33–34). A reference to the Hittites in the hill country (Num 13:29) also implies a Hittite settlement in the Judaean hills, cf. Gelb, in *IDB* II, p. 613. Note also that, in these texts, the Hittites in Hebron are called "the people of the land" (Gen 23:7, etc.), and Esau's Hittite wives are referred to as "daughters of the land" (Gen 27:46) or "daughters of Canaan" (36:2). From this, van Seters, *VT* 22 (1972), p. 79, has concluded that "'Canaanite' and 'Hittite' are largely synonymous terms". However, it seems more probable that the Hittites are regarded here as *one* of the populations in the Land of Canaan, called either "the land" or "Canaan".

[18] Several theories have been advanced to prove Hittite penetration into Palestine in the second millennium B.C. E.O. Forrer, "The Hittites in Palestine", *PEQ* 68 (1936), pp. 190–203; 69 (1937), pp. 100–115, spoke of a certain Kurustamma-people from Anatolia coming into Egyptian territory as fugitives in the fourteenth century B.C., to become the "Hittites" in the hill country of Judah. C.H. Gordon, "Abraham and the Merchants of Ura", *JNES* 17 (1958), pp. 28–31, suggested that the Hittites whom Abraham met in Hebron were merchants from the Hittite Empire.

of immigrants or fugitives, which had been totally assimilated to its Semitic surroundings but still retained the memory of its relation to the Hittites in Anatolia and Syria.[19] As a good parallel example we may refer to the Philistines, who migrated from the Aegean basin to the coast regions of Palestine in the twelfth century B.C. Both biblical and extra-biblical sources together with archaeological discoveries show that they were rapidly and fully assimilated to the surrounding Semitic world in material as well as spiritual aspects, but they retained a sense of independence claiming descent from the Philistines migrated from the Aegean islands throughout the first millennium B.C. (cf. Amos 9:7).[20]

In the light of the foregoing assessment, we may sum up the shift in the signification of the three major appellations in biblical sources as follows:

a) The term "Canaanites", besides being the name for the ethnic group dwelling by the sea coast and in the Jordan valley, signified the entire population of Palestine, but lost its significance after the establishment of the Israelite monarchy.

b) The designation "Amorites" was at first employed for the original inhabitants of the mountains of western Palestine and the Transjordan, but later took the place of "Canaanites" as a generic name for the whole population of pre-Israelite Palestine, when the term Canaan had become obsolete as the name of the country.

K.A. Kitchen, *Ancient Orient and Old Testament*, Chicago, 1966, p. 52, n. 91, has tried to collect evidence for Anatolians in Palestine in the Patriarchal period. None of these suggestions has met general approval, see Hoffner, *Tyndale Bulletin* 20 (1969), pp. 28–32.

[19] Hoffner, *Tyndale Bulletin* 20 (1969), pp. 32–37; idem, in *POTT*, pp. 199 f., does not find any Hittite characteristics either in the personal names of the "Hittites" in the Bible or in the customs pertaining to the real-estate transaction between Abraham and Ephron the Hittite in Gen 23. However, taking the biblical evidence of a native population called "Hittite" as historical, he suggests that these "Hittites" were native Semites who had nothing in common with the Hattians and Indo-European Hittites in Anatolia or the Neo-Hittites in Syria. A similar suggestion had already been made by G.B. Gray, *A Critical and Exegetical Commentary on Numbers* (ICC), Edinburgh, 1903, p. 148; Cf. also E. and H. Klengel, *Die Hethiter. Geschichte und Umwelt*, Wien/München, 1970, pp. 50 f. Hoffner's argument seems convincing but for the last suggestion. It is difficult to assume that the phonetic similarity between the Hebrew terms *ḥittî* and *ḥet* and the Akkadian term *ḫatti* is "due to chance conflation" (*POTT*, p. 214) with regard to the Hebrew vocalization of the name, see H.G. Güterbock, "Hethiter, Hethitisch", in *RLA* IV, Berlin/New York, 1972–75, p. 372.

[20] See K.A. Kitchen, "The Philistines", in D.J. Wiseman (ed.), *POTT*, Oxford, 1973, pp. 67–70.

c) The appellation "Hittites" designated, at first, a small community of Hittite origin in southern Palestine, but later took on an expanded meaning when the Israelites came into touch with the Neo-Hittites, and finally came to be used to represent the original nations inhabiting the land prior to the Israelite settlement.

We are now in a position to rearrange the irregular sequences of the three major nations in the first half of the six-name lists according to certain rules. This arrangement will enable us to chart the fourteen six-name lists as a diagram showing their historical development. The following are the rules in accordance with which the diagram may be read, and the signs employed to indicate deviation from the norm:

a) The order of the lists is determined by the promotion of the Hittites from the third position to the second and then the first, and the demotion of the Canaanites from the first to the third. The lists in which the Amorites occupy the first position are to be subordinated to the scheme determined by the order of the Hittites and the Canaanites.

b) After the expected positions of the six components have been fixed for each list in accordance with the above rule, those components deviating from the regular fixed positions have been inserted between the regularly placed components. Since the Girgashites cannot be regarded as a regular entry, they are always charted in between the regular components.

c) When a component deviates from its regular position, this vacant position is marked by the sign *, which is connected with the deviating component by a line.

d) The lack of a component is indicated by the sign –.

The chart shows a clear coordination between the promotion of the Hittites and the demotion of the Canaanites, as well as the secondary role played by the Amorites in this system. It also makes it clear that there is irregularity in the order of the entries only in three lists (II:4, 9, 10), in which either the Amorites occupy the first position or the Girgashites have been added. Although II:3 and 11 form an exception to this rule, it is possible to regard the lists in which either the Amorites take the first position instead of the Canaanites or the Girgashites have been inserted in the six-name system as secondary developments.

In order to find out the historical development of the formulae for compiling the six-name lists, special attention should be paid to

Table II

No.	Nations in order as found										No. of nations	Biblical passages
1	C		A		H	P		V		J	6	Exod 33:2
2	–		A		H	P		V		J	5	1 Kgs 9:20
3	A		C		H	P		V		J	6	Exod 34:11
4	A	P	C		H	*	G	V		J	7	Josh 24:11
5	C		H		A	P		V		J	6	Exod 3:8
6	C		H		A	P		V		J	6	Exod 3:17
7	C		H		A	P		V		J	6	Judg 3:5
8	C		H		A	–		V		J	5	Exod 13:5
9	C		H	V	*	P	G	*	A	J	7	Josh 3:10
10	A		H	P	C	*		V		J	6	Exod 23:23
11	H	G	A		C	P		V		J	7	Deut 7:1
12	H		A		C	P		V		J	6	Deut 20:17
13	H		A		C	P		V		J	6	Josh 9:1
14	H		A		C	P		V		J	6	Josh 12:8

the three-stage promotion of the Hittites in the lists. All the four lists in which the Hittites occupy the first position (II:11–14) are found in the Book of Deuteronomy and in Deuteronomistic passages in the Book of Joshua,[21] and the order of the three major nations in these lists, the Hittites, the Amorites, and the Canaanites, corresponds exactly to the situation in Neo-Assyrian inscriptions of the seventh century B.C., where the expression "Ḫatti land" denotes the whole region of Syria-Palestine, but the term "Amurru" mostly implies the West in a general archaic manner,[22] while the designation "Kinaḫḫu",

[21] Langlamet, *Gilgal et les récits*, p. 110, recognizes that these four lists belong to the "Deuteronomistic type", and the formula "C H A P V J" to the "Yahwist type". According to the analysis of M. Noth, *Das Buch Josua* (HAT 7), Tübingen, 1953², pp. 57, 71, Josh 9:1 is post-Deuteronomistic and Josh 12:8b is an addition to ch. 12, whose composition is Deuteronomistic.

[22] It is true that when Esarhaddon calls himself "King of Subartu, Amurru, Gutium, the great land of Ḫatti . . ." (R. Borger, *Die Inschriften Asarhaddons Königs von Assyrien* [AfO Beih. 9], Graz, 1956, p. 80, lines 27–28), the two terms Amurru and Ḫatti are devoid of any specific geographical sense, but in other inscriptions, the term Ḫatti is employed as a concrete designation for Syria-Palestine; see Borger, *Inschriften Asarhaddons*, p. 48, line 80; p. 60, line 72. Note also that, in ḪAR-gud E_3, rev. 6–8, 10–11, "Subartu", "Amurru", and "Gutium" are found in the second column, while "Ḫatti" appears in the third. This seems to show that the first three terms were already archaic by the late Neo-Assyrian period, the probable time of writing of the third column, and that the designation Ḫatti was used as an equivalent geographical term, see E. Reiner and M. Civil, *Materialien zum sumerischen Lexikon* XI, Rome, 1974, p. 35. I owe the last note to Prof. K. Deller.

i.e., "Canaan", is completely absent. We cannot but conclude, therefore, that the formula "H A C P V J" was composed under the influence of the common use of the terms Ḫatti and Amurru in the Near East in the seventh century B.C.

If our thesis is correct, we may further assume that the placing of the Hittites in the second and the third positions in the six-name lists also reflects two sets of historical situations, in which the Israelites recognized certain people called Hittites: the Hittites in the second position denote the Neo-Hittites, whose contact with the Israelites is mentioned in the Hebrew Bible from the time of David (2 Sam 8:9–10, etc.) and Solomon (1 Kgs 11:1, etc.) down to the days of the prophet Elisha (2 Kgs 7:6),[23] while the Hittites in the third position must imply one of the genuine native populations in Palestine in the pre-Davidic period. From the foregoing analysis, we may conclude that the formula "C A H P V J", which is preserved in a complete form only in Exod 33:2 (II:1), was the original of the six-name lists, and that the other formulae developed from it later.

There remains one question to be answered, however. Why were the Hittites as one of the pre-Israelite populations in Palestine priviledged to be included among the three major nations, although they actually formed only a tiny little community in the southern part of Palestine in fact smaller than even the Hivites?[24] But before proceeding to discuss this problem, we must examine the historical background against which the original formula of the six-name lists was compiled, since the answer is bound up with it.

---

[23] It is documented in biblical sources that Hamath, the southernmost Neo-Hittite kingdom, continuously maintained contact with Israel until its destruction by Sargon in 720 B.C. However, the kingdom of Hamath was no longer "Hittite" after Zakkur, an Aramaean, assumed its control in the first half of the eighth century B.C., see J.D. Hawkins, "Hamath", in *RLA* IV, Berlin/New York, 1972–75, p. 68; W.T. Pitard, *Ancient Damascus. A Historical Study of the Syrian City-State from Earliest Times until its Fall to the Assyrians in 732 B.C.E.*, Winona Lake, 1987, pp. 170 f.

[24] The dwelling places of the Palestinian Hittites were, as has been mentioned, confined to the regions around Hebron and Beer-sheba, while Hivite settlements were located in Mount Lebanon (Judg 3:3), at the foot of Hermon (Josh 11:3), in Shechem (Gen 34:2) and Gibeon (Josh 9:7; 11:19), that is, they were scattered between Sidon and Beer-sheba (2 Sam 24:6–7). E.A. Speiser has advanced a theory that the term Hivite is the result of a textual confusion of Horite and Hittite, "Ethnic Movements in the Near East in the Second Millennium B.C.: the Hurrians and their Connection with the Ḫabiru and Hyksos", *AASOR* 13 (1933), pp. 29–31; idem, "Hivite", in *IDB* II, Nashville/New York, 1962, p. 615; for critical views of this theory see S.E. Loewenstamm, "חוי", in *Encyclopaedia Biblica* III, Jerusalem, 1958, col. 45 (Hebrew); R. de Vaux, "Les Hurrites de l'histoire et les Horites de la Bible", *RB* 74 (1967), pp. 497–503; North, *Bib* 54 (1973), pp. 52–62. On the other hand,

It is patent that the theme of the six-name lists is the legitimation of the Israelite seizure of the Promised Land from the indigenous population. Although the process of dispossession began with the Israelite settlement in Palestine, this sort of list could not be compiled before the process had been finally completed. It has been argued that the last entry in the lists, the Jebusites, fixes the *terminus ad quem* of the list at David's taking of Jerusalem from the Jebusites, its original inhabitants.[25] But we must object to this opinion, since the process of dispossession was completed only when every foreign element had been totally absorbed into the Israelite society; and there is evidence that several foreign communities still kept their politico-ethnical identities in the kingdom of David. For instance, David compensated the Gibeonites, a branch of the Hivites,[26] for the damage which had been inflicted upon them by Saul owing to their being foreigners (2 Sam 21:1–9). Similarly, in taking a census of the population of the kingdom, Joab included "all the cities of the Hivites and Canaanites" (24:7). "The cities of the Hivites and Canaanites" here doubtless the foreign communities in the kingdom of David.

According to 1 Kgs 9:20–22 (cf. 2 Chr 8:7–9), those whom Solomon made slave-labourers were not Israelites but descendants of the indigenous population. However, we are told elsewhere that Solomon actually imposed a forced levy on all Israelites (1 Kgs 5:27–32; 11:28; 12:4; cf. 4:6).[27] Accordingly, it is possible to assume that the former

---

Mendenhall, *The Tenth Generation*, pp. 154–163, maintains that the Hivites were Luwians who came from Cilicia, on the basis of the phonetic identification of "Hivite" with "Quwe" (= Cilicia); Cf. also Na'aman, in *From Nomadism to Monarchy*, p. 240.

[25] North, *Bib* 54 (1973), p. 45.

[26] Josh 9:7 and 11:19 identify the Gibeonites with the Hivites, while they were "Amorites" according to 2 Sam 21:2. This seeming contradiction can be solved by interpreting the term "Amorites" here as a general designation for the whole population of pre-Israelite Palestine, see J. Blenkinsopp, *Gibeon and Israel. The Role of Gibeon and the Gibeonites in the Political and Religious History of Early Israel* (The Society for Old Testament Study Monograph Series 2), Cambridge, 1972, pp. 21 f.

[27] Some scholars find a difference between the types of servitude to which the Israelites and the Canaanites were severally subjected, that is, the corvée (*mas*) for the former and the state slavery (*mas ʿōḇēḏ*) for the latter, see I. Mendelsohn, "State Slavery in Ancient Palestine", *BASOR* 85 (1942), pp. 14–17; J. Gray, *I & II Kings. A Commentary* (OTL), London, 1977[3], pp. 155 f. However, this argument seems inconclusive, see A.F. Rainey, "Compulsory Labour Gangs in Ancient Israel", *IEJ* 20 (1970), pp. 191–202; J.A. Soggin, "The Davidic-Solomonic Kingdom", in J.H. Hayes and J.M. Miller (eds.), *Israelite and Judaean History* (OTL), London, 1977, p. 378; idem, "Compulsory Labor under David and Solomon", in T. Ishida (ed.), *SPDS*, Tokyo/Winona Lake, 1982, pp. 259–267.

narrative stemmed from a claim of Solomon's regime, which alleged no Israelite involvement in its compulsory labour service. This may have been a forced excuse for Solomon. Still, this sort of allegation could be made only to defend in theory a society such as the Solomonic one, in which in fact the distinction between the Israelites and the non-Israelite elements had become more and more ambiguous as a result of a mass assimilation of the native populations to the social structure of the United Monarchy.[28]

It is understandable that the ideological struggle to establish the national identity of the Israelites became acute under these circumstances. Without such an ideological struggle, the Israelites would have lost their identity, like the Philistines, in the process of the rapid absorption of many foreign elements into their society. We can assume, therefore, that the original formula of the six-name lists was produced out of efforts made in the days of Solomon to establish the people of Israel by legitimatizing the Israelite seizure of the Promised Land from the indigenous populations. In any case, thereafter, we never hear of any independent foreign entity living among the Israelites. This fact shows that the process of the assimilation of the indigenous inhabitants to Israelite society was complete by the time of Solomon.[29]

[28] Clear evidence for a policy of integrating the foreign elements into the Solomonic state can be found in the structure of Solomon's twelve administrative districts (1 Kgs 4:7–19), which were formed by following Israelite tribal boundaries and also by incorporating former Canaanite regions, see A. Alt, "Israels Gaue unter Salomo" (1913), in *Kleine Schriften zur Geschichte des Volkes Israel* II, München, 1953, pp. 76–89; N. Na'aman, *Borders and Districts in Biblical Historiography. Seven Studies in Biblical Geographical Lists* (JBS 4), Jerusalem, 1986, pp. 167–201. T.N.D. Mettinger, *Solomonic State Officials. A Study of the Civil Government Officials of the Israelite Monarchy* (CBOTS 5), Lund, 1971, pp. 119 f., maintains that Solomon's subdivision of the districts was based on a policy directed against the house of Joseph. According to Na'aman's analysis, ibid., p. 169, however, "the inclusion of the 'Canaanite' districts in the inheritances of Ephraim and Manasseh is the result of a literary process. . . . . It has no basis in actual fact".

[29] Some scholars contend that the descendants of the Gibeonites survived as the *nᵉṯînîm* without losing their ethnic identity even after the Exile, see Y. Kaufmann, *The Religion of Israel from its Beginnings to the Babylonian Exile* (tr. and abr. by M. Greenberg), New York, 1972, p. 251. However, it is more likely that the *nᵉṯînîm* were descended from a mixture of alien peoples, cf. G.H. Davies, "Nethinim", in *IDB* III, Nashville/New York, 1962, p. 541. On the other hand, Soggin, in *Israelite and Judaean History*, p. 379, assumes that the Canaanites were granted autonomy within the kingdom of Solomon and recovered their independence from the Northern Kingdom of Israel after the division of the United Kingdom. But we can hardly find any explicit evidence in biblical sources for this assumption.

We must deal here with the problem of the omission of the entry "Canaanites" from the list of the descendants of the original nations whom Solomon conscripted as slave-labourers (1 Kgs 9:20). We might well classify this list as belonging to the group in which the Amorites occupy the first position, as "A H-P V J". But we are convinced that we should place the missing entry not in the third but in the first position on the list. First of all, our thesis regarding the Solomonic origin of the formula governing the six-name lists requires this list to belong to the original formula, in which the Canaanites occupy the first position. The parallelism between v. 20 and v. 21 shows that the compiler of this list excluded the Canaanites from it because he understood this term as a general appellation for the land with all its foreign populations. The text reads: "All the people who were left of the Amorites, the Hittites, the Perizzites . . ." (v. 20) // "Their descendants who were left after them in the land . . ." (v. 21). "The land" in v. 21 clearly implies the Land of Israel, which was formerly called the Land of Canaan. In other words, the compiler of the list omitted the entry "Canaanites" from his list because he regarded the other five nations as sub-divisions of the Canaanites.

We are now able to come back to our earlier question: Why were the Hittites in the original formula included among the three major nations, though they were in reality only a minor element of the population in pre-Davidic Palestine? Information about two Hittites among the heroes of David, Ahimelech (1 Sam 26:6) and Uriah (2 Sam 11:3, etc.), testifies to the fact that there existed a community of Hittite origin in Judah in the time of David.[30] On the other hand, as mentioned above, David put the kingdom of Hamath, one of the Neo-Hittite kingdoms, under his sway. This was the first contact between the Israelites and the Neo-Hittites, a contact which continued down to the eighth century B.C. It thus becomes clear that two originally different implications of the term "Hittites" were superimposed one upon the other in the days of David. Subsequently, the compiler of the original formula for the six-name lists in the days of Solomon regarded the Palestinian Hittites, it seems, as a branch of the Neo-Hittites in Syria. Hence the inclusion of the Hittites

[30] Gibson, *JNES* 20 (1961), p. 226, thinks that Ahimelech and Uriah came from Neo-Hittite kingdoms in Syria. It is not easy to suppose, however, that such remote foreigners were included among those who were discontented with Saul's regime and gathered to David (1 Sam 22:2), cf. Delaporte, in *DBSup* IV, col. 109.

among the major nations in the original formula, though in the third position. This assumption also explains the peculiar fact that the original formula is preserved only in two lists (II:1, 2), while the second formula "C H A P V J" is the prevailing one, being found in five cases out of fourteen (II:5–9). It is likely that the insignificant Palestinian Hittites and all other foreign elements ceased to exist in the United Kingdom by the end of the time of Solomon. So, as regards the use of the term "Hittites", the reference to the more important "Neo-Hittites" overshadowed that of "Palestinian Hittites", and the second formula, elevating the Hittites in the second position, had already been compiled perhaps by the end of the time of Solomon.

To sum up, the formulae "C A H P V J" and "C H A P V J" were compiled successively one after the other in the days of Solomon, while the third formula "H A C P V J" appeared in the seventh century B.C. On the other hand, the formulae "A C H P V J" and "A H C P V J" were formed as secondary modifications of the first and second formulae, respectively, in the ninth or the eighth centuries B.C.[31]

We have no intention of discussing here the relationship between these formulae and the entirely different problem of "sources" in the Pentateuch. Still, mention must be made of one thesis that has been maintained; viz., as a general designation for the pre-Israelite nations of the Promised Land, the Yahwist employed the term Canaanites, the Elohist preferred the name Amorites, while the Priestly source made habitual use of Hittites.[32] However, the foregoing investigation into the six-name lists has made the thesis questionable. We have shown that the first position on the six-name lists shifted from the Canaanites to the Amorites, and then to the Hittites, as the applications of these terms developed in the ancient Near East. It is likely that the choice of one of these appellations in preference to the others is likewise not characteristic of a specific "source" but simply reflects the use of these terms in a particular period. Moreover, it is impossible to determine the age of a certain passage on the basis

[31] Richter, *Die Bearbeitungen*, p. 42, assumes that the six-name lists arose as a mnemonic device for teaching historical geography. However, it is difficult, on this assumption, to explain the great diversity in the order of C, A and H in the first half of these lists.

[32] E.g., M. Noth, *The Old Testament World*, London, 1966, p. 77.

of the simple presence there of one of the formulae of the six-name lists, for there was a clear tendency to regard the second formula "C H A P V J" as quasi-canonical after its compilation. Indeed, it is retained in passages regarded as Deuteronomistic or post-Deuteronomistic (Josh 3:10; Judg 3:5)[33] as well as in later sources (Ezra 9:1; Neh 9:8; 2 Chr 8:7). In other words, it was always possible for a "source" to choose one formula from the formulae transmitted as common tradition.

In addition, it is important to note that the term "Hittites" is, contrary to the prevailing view, never used in biblical sources as a general designation for all the inhabitants of pre-Israelite Palestine. The Hittites in all the passages where they allegedly stand as a generic name for the entire population (e.g., Gen 23) should be regarded as Palestinian Hittites. Unlike the terms Canaanites and Amorites, which sometimes stood for the whole population of the country (e.g., Gen 12:6; 15:16), the appellation Hittites continued to have a specific meaning in the Hebrew Bible, referring either to the Palestinian Hittites or to the Neo-Hittites. This fact shows that the terms Canaanites and the Amorites had been fixed as general designations for the original nations in biblical tradition before the term Hittites had lost its specific sense completely with the destruction of Hamath, the last Neo-Hittite kingdom, in 720 B.C. By the end of the eighth century B.C., as we have mentioned above, the term Hittites had in biblical sources been given the position of representative of the pre-Israelite nations in the place of the Canaanites and the Amorites under the influence of the expanded significance of the term Ḫatti, signifying the entire population of Syria-Palestine, in Neo-Assyrian inscriptions. But it was too late for the term Hittites to become another general designation for the indigenous population of the Promised Land.

---

[33] For the Deuteronomistic character of Josh 3:10 see Noth, *Das Buch Josua*, p. 33; cf. also Langlamet, *Gilgal et les récits*, p. 109; J.A. Soggin, *Joshua. A Commentay* (OTL), London, 1972, pp. 51 f. Judg 3:5 is regarded as post-Deuteronomistic by G. Fohrer, *Introduction to the Old Testament*, London, 1970, p. 213.

3. *Lists of Representative Nations*

There are three two-name lists, which consist of the Canaanites and the Perizzites (Gen 13:7; 34:30; Judg 1:4–5). Since the Perizzites are, together with the Girgashites, the most obscure of the "seven nations",[34] it is not easy to find the implication of this combination of peoples. From the context we may understand that the two peoples are mentioned here as the two main population groups in pre-Israelite Palestine. Hence, on the basis of the meaning of the term *p^erāzî* as "rural country", it has been suggested that "the Canaanites" and "the Perizzites" here stand for "those living in fortified cities" and "those living in unwalled towns or hamlets".[35] It is by no means clear, however, whether we can regard the names of the "seven nations" as exclusively political and social, not ethnic, designations.[36] Rather they seem to be ethno-geographic as well as ethno-linguistic, as in the case of the criteria for classifying the nations in the "Table of Nations", i.e., "by their families, their languages, their lands and their nations" (Gen 10:20, 31; cf. 10:5).[37]

From a comparison of the two-name lists with the six-name lists, we may assume that "Canaanites" and "Perizzites" are employed as terms for a broader division of population groups, which include not just the Canaanites and the Perizzites but other ethnic elements as well. In that case, by applying the rules for charting the six-name lists, we can put the two-name list into the following diagrammatic form: C- -P- -. So it is possible to regard the term "Canaanites" as representative of the major nations, and the name "Perizzites" of the minor. It is unlikely, however, that the two-name list was compiled as a variation of the six-name lists, since this sort of list could not have been formulated like the six-name lists according to an ideological scheme reflecting the changing importance of peoples. They

---

[34] See R.F. Schnell, "Perizzite", in *IDB* III, Nashville/New York, 1962, p. 735; S.A. Reed, "Perizzite", in *ABD* V, New York, 1992, p. 231.

[35] Schnell, in *IDB* III, p. 735; du Buit, in *DBSup* VIII, col. 120; cf. KB, p. 777; *HALOT* III, p. 965.

[36] Mendenhall, *The Tenth Generation*, p. 155, takes the "seven nations" to be exclusively socio-political groups, but the purely socio-political approach makes it difficult to explain the ethno-linguistic diversity of Syria-Palestine in the biblical period.

[37] Although recognizing language as a criterion, Speiser, in *IDB* III, p. 236, holds that the principal criteria in biblical traditions were nation and country, i.e., ethno-geographic ones.

are too simple: they reflect blocks of some kind. Therefore it is difficult to say exactly what ethno-geographic or linguistic groups are included in the names of the two nations. Still, the above diagrammatic form "C--P--" suggests the hypothesis that the grouping of the two-name list was based on an ethno-linguistic criterion, that is, "the Canaanites" stand for Semitic populations, and "the Perizzites" for non-Semitic.[38] It is generally assumed that the Perizzites, the Hivites and the Jebusites were non-Semitic.[39] On the other hand, the Canaanites and the Amorites were definitely Semitic. In addition, the Hittites in Palestine must have been classified by the Israelites as members of the Semitic group, since they had been, as mentioned above, completely assimilated to their Semitic surroundings.

We have regarded two of the five-name lists, one omitting the Canaanites and the other the Perizzites (II:2, 8), as variations of the six-name lists, and the problem of the lack of the entry "Canaanites" has already been dealt with. Now, our analysis of the two-name lists has made it clear that the Perizzites could stand as representatives of the minor ethnic groups. Accordingly, it is also possible to assume that, in the list in Exod 13:5, from which the entry "Perizzites" is missing, thus giving it the form "C H A – V J", the entries "Hivites" and "Jebusites" stand for two subdivisions of the "Perizzites".

The sole three-name list, "the Hivites, the Canaanites, the Hittites" (Exod 23:28), is also to be classified among the "lists of representative nations". If we chart it again following the same rules as in the case of the diagram of the six-name lists, it can be schematized as "V – C – H – ". This schematization allows us to assume that the Jebusites, the Amorites and the Perizzites are subsumed in the entries "Hivites", "Canaanites" and "Hittites", respectively. Although this assumption remains hypothetical, these three appellations undoubtedly stand for three representatives of three different ethic groups. The criterion of classification seems rather ethno-geographic than ethno-linguistic, unlike the two-name lists, for the order of the entries suggests a north-south direction (cf. the order of the Hivites and the Canaanites in 2 Sam 24:7 and the Hittite settlements in southern Palestine in the Book of Genesis).

It seems that both the two-name and three-name lists of representative nations served as an earlier form for the first formula of

[38] Cf. Speiser, in *IDB* III, pp. 237, 241; idem, in *WHJP* I/I, p. 169.
[39] Speiser, in *IDB* III, p. 242, links all three with the Hurrians.

the six-name lists "C A H P V J", since it is hardly incidental that combinations of nations like C+(A+H) P+(V+J) or C+(A) H+(P) V+(J) can be detected in both the lists.[40]

4. *Geographical Lists*

Of the twenty-seven lists of nations, four lists (I:3, 12, 16, 18) can be categorized under the heading "geographical lists". In these lists, the nations are arranged geographically, as indicated by the accompanying geographical notes. The following chart gives a general view of the composition of the "geographical lists". The list in Gen 15:19–21 will be placed last as it has a different character from the others.

Table III

No.	Nations in order as found, classified by groups according to the geographical notes	No. of nations	Biblical passages
1	a) Amalek (in the land of Negeb) b) H J A (in the hill country) c) C (by the sea and along the Jordan)	5	Num 13:29
2	a) A (beyond the Jordan to the west) b) C (by the sea)	2	Josh 5:1
3	a) C (in the east and the west) b) A H P J (in the hill country) c) V (under Hermon in the land of Mizpah)	6	Josh 11:3
4	a) Kenites, Kenizites, Kadmonites b) H P, Rephites, A c) C d) G J	10	Gen 15:19–21

The first three lists give us a consistent picture of the geographical distribution of the pre-Israelite nations in Palestine, that is, the Canaanites dwell by the sea coast and in the Jordan valley, while the Amorites live, together with the Hittites, the Jebusites, and the Perizzites, in the hill country.[41] This situation is summed up in the briefest way in the list in Josh 5:1 (cf. Deut 1:7), while the two lists

[40] N. Na'aman, "Canaanites and Perizzites", *BN* 45 (1988), pp. 42–44, is of the opinion that the pair, Canaanites and Perizzites, stemmed from a late strutum in the biblical tradition and "the concept of the Perizzites as a name for the rural population of the country emerged due to popular etymologization of the ethnic name Perizzites".

[41] For the regions of the Amorites and those of the Canaanites, see Maisler (Mazar), *Untersuchungen* I, pp. 39–53, 67–74; cf. also Speiser, in *WHJP* I/I, p. 169.

in Num 13:29[42] and in Josh 11:3 particularize the various ethnic elements dwelling in the hill country. In addition, the former mentions an ethnic group in the southernmost region, while the latter adds one in the northernmost. These additions accord with the particular point of interest of each list. The former is part of a report made by spies in the wilderness of Paran, at Kadesh (Num 13:26). The speakers, residing in a locality to the south of Palestine, were doubtless interested in Amalek in the Negeb, but the Hivites in the northern region were beyond their horizon. It is also natural that they should have put the names of the inhabitants in order of south to north direction, i.e., from close by to far off. The latter list is part of the story of the appeal of Jabin king of Hazor to all the kings and the inhabitants of Palestine (Josh 11:1–3). Evidently, the Hivites "under Hermon in the land of Mizpah" were specially included in the list because of the northern location of Hazor. It is also conceivable, however, that this list was formed on the basis of the first formula for the six-name lists "C A H P V J", with a slight modification in the order of the last two entries. It is quite clear that the reversal of the order of the Hivites and the Jebusites was carried out according to the principle of geographical grouping.

Accordingly, the structure of the list in Josh 11:3 is doubtless schematic rather than geographical in the real sense of the term. Nevertheless, we have reason to believe that both the geographical lists in the Book of Joshua were compiled from authentic historical tradition based on experiences undergone when the Israelites came to Palestine; and such experiences must be reflected in the spy story and the list contained therein (Num 13).[43]

The list in Gen 15:19–21 has neither geographical notes attached nor grouping of ethnic elements, but gives a general definition of the ideal border of Israel (Gen 15:18bβ). However, an analysis of its structure shows that this list belongs to the category of "geographical lists". This list is incorporated in the story of Abraham, who

---

[42] "The descendants of Anak" in the preceding verse (v. 28) cannot be included in the list, since the term Anak is not used as an ethnic designation here, see M. Noth, *Numbers* (OTL), London, 1968, pp. 105–107; cf. E.C.B. MacLaurin, "ANAK/'ANAΘ", *VT* 15 (1965), pp. 468–474.

[43] Cf. Richter, *Die Bearbeitungen*, p. 42; Lohfink, *Die Landverheissung als Eid*, p. 66; Cf. also Aharoni, *The Land of the Bible*, p. 66. But there is also a skeptical view about the historicity of the geographical division between the Canaanites and the Amorites, e.g., de Vaux, *Histoire ancienne d'Israël*, p. 130.

dwelt, presumably, in Hebron at that time; that is, it is composed from the viewpoint of a person residing in the South, as in the case of the list in Num 13:29. We can assume, accordingly, that the nations are lined up here in order of south to north direction. In fact, the first three tribes were populations living in the Negeb.[44] The Hittites, who are mentioned as the first entry in the second group, were, as has been discussed above, inhabitants of the Judaean hills. The following pair, the Perizzites and the Rephites, can be positioned in the forest country between Judah and Ephraim according to the tradition about them in Josh 17:15; cf. also "the valley of Rephaim" in the vicinity of Jerusalem (Josh 15:8; 2 Sam 5:18, etc.). The Rephites are followed by the Amorites, apparently owing to traditions which locate both of them in the Transjordan, or even regard them as one and the same nation.[45] It thus becomes clear that the second group is made up of four ethnic elements living in the hill country and the Transjordan. And then, as the third group, the Canaanites are referred to as the inhabitants of the sea coast and the Jordan valley.

Up to this point, there is an exact correspondence between the two lists in Num 13:29 and Gen 15:19–21, from a structural point of view.

Gen 15:19–21	Num 13:29
Kenites, Kenizites, Kadmonites	Amalek
H P, Rephites, A	H J A
C	C
G J	

But the last group, which consists of the Girgashites and Jebusites, does not fit into this structure. Geographically speaking, the Jebusites should have been placed after the Hittites, as in the list in Num

[44] We do not know who the Kadmonites were, since they are mentioned only here. They are sometimes identified with "the People of the East" (*bᵉnê-qedem*) (Gen 29:1, etc.), see KB, p. 824; but "the People of the East" is understood as a general designation of the nomads in the desert east of Palestine (Judg 6:3, etc.), see I. Ephʿal, *The Ancient Arabs. Nomads on the Borders of the Fertile Crescent 9th–5th Centuries B.C.*, Jerusalem/Leiden, 1982, pp. 9 f., 62 f.

[45] For the traditions about the Rephites and the Amorites see J.R. Bartlett, "Sihon and Og, Kings of the Amorites", *VT* 20 (1970), pp. 268 f.

13:29. This positioning of the Jebusites at the end of the list reminds us of the identical position they have in the formulae of the six-name lists. On the other hand, we have observed that the Girgashites only play the role of an additional entry to make the number of nations up to seven in the seven-name lists, as a variation of the six-name lists. It seems, therefore, that the last two nations were added here under the influence of the six-name lists. This does not mean this was a late addition, however.

It has been suggested that we can find some echoes of the Davidic Empire in the divine promise of land made to Abraham and his descendants in Gen 15.[46] This view clarifies the significance of the first three tribes, whose presence makes our list unique. With regard to the Kenites and Kenizites, we have demonstrated elsewhere that they were integrated into "greater Judah" together with other southern tribes, such as the Calebites, Jerachmeelites, and Simeon, in the days of David.[47] In that case, the Kadmonites stand, in our opinion, for all the other southern tribes apart from the Kenites, Kenizites, and Simeon. (Simeon must have been excluded from this list because of its membership in the twelve-tribe system of Israel). It follows, therefore, that the first three names represent the foreign elements in the South whose absorption into the tribe of Judah was complete by the time of David. This interpretation enables us, in turn, to assume that the position of the Jebusites at the end of the list implies David's conquest of Jebus-Jerusalem completing the Israelite seizure of the land from the indigenous population.[48]

From the above we may conclude that this list was composed with the intention of showing the completeness of David's achievements in changing the Land of Canaan into the Land of Israel. According to the view of the compiler of the list, the process began with the incorporation of the southern tribes into the tribe of Judah and was crowned by the conquest of Jerusalem.[49] The Girgashites and the Jebusites were added at the end of the list in order to emphasize

---

[46] Cf. R. Clements, *Abraham and David. Genesis 15 and its Meaning for Israelite Tradition* (SBTS 5), London, 1967.

[47] T. Ishida, *The Royal Dynasties in Ancient Israel. A Study on the Formation and Development of Royal-Dynastic Ideology* (BZAW 142), Berlin/New York, 1977, pp. 65 f.

[48] Cf. U. Cassuto, "Jerusalem in the Pentateuch" (1951), in *Biblical and Oriental Studies* I: *Bible*, Jerusalem, 1973, p. 74.

[49] Lohfink, *Die Landverheissung als Eid*, pp. 75 f., has suggested that the expression "River (*nahar*) of Egypt" in the definition of the ideal border of Israel (v. 18bβ) may be regarded as a "hyperbole" from the period of David and Solomon.

the completeness of the process, though this addition disturbed the structure of the list. The role of the Girgashites is understood here also as a supplementary entry to make the number of components in the list up to ten, a symbolic figure for completeness.[50]

5. *The List in the Table of Nations*

Another lineup of pre-Israelite nations is found in a list in the Table of Nations (Gen 10:15–18a; 1 Chr 1:13–16). This list consists of the following three parts, which are distinguished from each other by the distinctive nature of the components.

a) Canaan, Sidon, Heth
b) J A G V
c) Arkites, Sinites, Arvadites, Zemarites, Hamathites

The first group consists of Canaan, with two subdivisions in the form of a quasi-genealogy, a common way of representation of ethnogeographical principles of classification in the Table of Nations. As has been assumed for a long time, the continuation of this passage (Gen 10:15) is surely to be found in vv. 18b–19, in which the later expansion of the Canaanites to southern Phoenicia and Palestine is described.[51] It thus becomes clear that Sidon is regarded here as the homeland of the Canaanites, from which they spread later to the Land of Canaan. It is remarkable, however, that Heth is also included within the Canaanite sphere. It is not easy to determine what the term Heth stands for here. It is widely accepted that the association

[50] Clements, *Abraham and David*, p. 21, n. 25, holds that "the reference to 'the land of the Kenites, the Kenizites and the Kadmonites' was the original identification of the land, which a later editor has expanded" by adding the other seven names to indicate the range of the Davidic Empire. Similarly, Lohfink *Die Landverheissung als Eid*, pp. 72–76, argues that the list dates from the time of the settlement of the tribe of Judah, but the definition of the ideal border from the period of David and Solomon; de Vaux, *Histoire ancienne d'Israël*, p. 420, also thinks that this list stemmed from times before the Kenites and the Kenizites had been absorbed into Judah. However we have tried to show that lists of this sort were compiled only after the complete absorption of all the foreign elements into the United Kingdom. About the view of the Deuteronomistic origin of the list see M. Anbar, "Genesis 15: A Conflation of Two Deuteronomic Narratives", *JBL* 101 (1982), pp. 53 f.

[51] See C. Westermann, *Genesis* I. *Kapitel 1–11* (BKAT 1/1), Neukirchen-Vluyn, 1976², pp. 694–699. Maisler (Mazar), *Untersuchungen* I, p. 74, has held a different view, according to which Canaan is referred to as the *hērōs epōnymos* of all the northern neighbours of Israel and of the pre-Israelite inhabitants of Palestine, but v. 19 is a late gloss.

of Canaan with Ham (Gen 10:6) designates its status as an ex-province of Egypt.[52] By analogy it is then possible to understand that Heth stands here for the part of Syria over which the Egyptians established their rule under the Eighteenth and Nineteenth Dynasties. Admittedly, in that case, the use of the term Heth for Syria is not correct from the historical point of view, since the Egyptians lost their control over Syria after the Hittites had penetrated there in the thirteenth century B.C.[53] It is not surprising, however, though anachronistic, that the compiler of the Table of Nations should have called Syria "Heth", taking the name from the occupants of Syria ("Neo-Hittites") in his own days.[54]

The second group consists of four pre-Israelite nations. It is extremely difficult to regard them as subdivisions of Canaan, corresponding to Sidon and Heth in the preceding verse, as has been generally recognized.[55] In our opinion, these four nations were added here in later times in an attempt to form a quasi-seven-name list composed of these and the preceding three terms, taken as the names of nations. The presence of the entry Girgashites also suggests the secondary nature of this lineup of nations. The order of the nations was, presumably, determined on the basis of the grouping of the geographical lists. A sequence of nations like "H J A" is found nowhere but in the list in Num 13:29 (III:1), while the Hivites are given the last position only once, in the list in Josh 11:3 (III:3).

The third group is made up of four cities on the coast of northern Phoenicia and a Neo-Hittite inland city, located not far from the preceding Phoenician cities.[56] It is clear that these five cities had nothing to do with southern Phoenicia and Palestine, the region treated in the following passages (Gen 10:18b–19). Therefore, we may regard them as a second addition to the list.[57] It would then

[52] See Aharoni, *The Land of the Bible*, p. 8.

[53] For the Egyptian rule over Syria in this period see Helck, *Die Beziehungen Ägyptens*, pp. 109 ff.

[54] For the view that the Table of Nations was composed during the period of the United Kingdom, see B. Mazar, "The Historical Background of the Book of Genesis" (1969), in *The Early Biblical Period. Historical Studies*, Jerusalem, 1986, pp. 57–59; cf. also Aharoni, *The Land of the Bible*, p. 8.

[55] See Westermann, *Genesis* I, pp. 694 ff.

[56] For the identification and location of these cities see Westermann, *Genesis* I, p. 697.

[57] The theory of a double expansion of the list has been advanced by J. Simons, "The 'Table of Nations' (Gen. X): Its General Structure and Meaning", *OTS* 10 (1954), p. 168.

follow that this second expansion was made with the intention of making the number in the list up to twelve. We may also assume that in this twelve-name list the four pre-Israelite nations (J A G V) were given as subdivisions of Canaan (Palestine), the four cities of northern Phoenicia as subdivisions of Sidon (Phoenicia) and the Hamathites as representatives of Heth (Syria).[58]

6. *Lists in Later Sources*

In the following diagram, the three lists found in later sources (I:24, 25, 27)[59] are charted according to the same rules and with the same signs as employed in Table II.

The diagram clearly shows that all three were composed, with some modifications, on a pattern based on the second formula of the six-name lists "C H A P V J". This fact implies, as we have suggested above, that the second formula was accepted as a quasi-canonical pattern of the list of pre-Israelite nations. It is worth noting that the order A+H in 1 Kgs 9:20 is reversed in the parallel list in 2 Chr 8:7. The precedence of the Amorites over the Hittites must have been felt to be strange in the Chronicler's time, when the term Amurru had lost its significance as representative of the whole population of Syria-Palestine. Instead, it denoted the Arabs, as the reference to "the kings of Amurru who live in tents" in an

Table IV

No.	Nations in order as found	No. of nations	Biblical passages
1	C H * P – J, Ammonites, Moabites, Egyptians, A	8	Ezra 9:1
2	C H A P – J G	6	Neh 9:8
3	– H A P V J	5	2 Chr 8:7

[58] J. Skinner, *A Critical and Exgetical Commentary on Genesis* (ICC), Edinburgh, 1930², p. 215, asks: "Is it possible that the last five names were originally given as sons of Heth, and the previous four as sons of Zidon?"

[59] The list given in 1 Chr 1:13–16 (I:26) is excluded from this category, since it is identical with the list in the Table of Nations (Gen 10:15–18a).

inscription of Cyrus, king of the Persian Empire, indicates.[60] This is the implication of the term "Amorites" in the list of nations in Ezra 9:1, of which the Amorites were, together with the Ammonites, the Moabites, and the Egyptians, the real enemies of the Jews at that time.[61] In contrast, the first four nations in this list are mentioned here only rhetorically. They were known by the Jews as the peoples dispossessed in ancient times, as is testified in Ezra's prayer (Neh 9:6–8).

It is interesting to note that the order C+A+H is found in Ezekiel's words on Jerusalem's origin: "By origin and birth you belong to the land of Canaan. Your father was an Amorite and your mother a Hittite" (16:3; cf. 16:45). It has been widely held that the prophet's statement was based on a historical reminiscence.[62] However, the whole context of the disgraceful origin of Jerusalem implies that the mention of these nations is rhetorical and pejorative.[63] We are inclined to hold that the prophet has made use of the major trio in the six-name lists of the doomed nations for underlining the inherent sinfulness of Jerusalem. Otherwise, we cannot explain the reference to the Hittites. Historically speaking, Ezekiel should have mentioned the Jebusites instead of the Hittites.[64] But the prophet, who had no intention of telling history of Jerusalem, chose these nations simply because of the notoriety of their past. It seems hardly incidental that he employed the oldest formula of the six-name lists, "C A H". Undoubtedly, it invested his words with an archaic aura.

---

[60] F.H. Weissbach, *Die Keilinschriften der Achämeniden* (VAB 3), Leipzig, 1911, p. 6, line 29; but *CAD* K, p. 601, renders *šarrāni māt Amurrî* as "the kings of the West"; cf. also Liverani, in *POTT*, p. 122.

[61] Cf. van Seters, *VT* 22 (1972), p. 76.

[62] E.g., A. Jirku, "Eine hethitische Ansiedlung in Jerusalem zur Zeit von El-Amarna", *ZDPV* 43 (1920), pp. 58 f.; Maisler (Mazar), *Untersuchungen* I, pp. 80 f.; W. Zimmerli, *Ezekiel* I (BKAT 13/1), Neukirchen-Vluyn, 1958, pp. 347 f.

[63] Cf. van Seters, *VT* 22 (1972), p. 80.

[64] There are explicit references to the Amorites in pre-Davidic Jerusalem in Josh 10:1–27, but we find no reference to the Hittites there. Attempts to identify the Jebusites with the Hittites or to regard the former as a branch of the latter are unconvincing. On the contrary, the mention of the Jebusites and the Hittites side by side in most of the lists of the pre-Israelite nations shows that they were different ethnic groups; cf. S.A. Reed, "Jebus", in *ABD* III, New York, 1992, pp. 652 f.

7. *Conclusions*

From the foregoing study we may summarize the historical development of the lists of pre-Israelite nations as follows:

a) From the period of the settlement down to the establishment of David's Empire, the Israelites considered the indigenous population as composite. This recognition was expressed first in the "geographical lists" as well as in the "lists of representative nations". The former were composed on ethno-geographic principles, while the latter were based on ethno-linguistic as well as ethno-geographic criteria.

b) Both the geographical lists and the lists of representative nations served as prototypes for the six-name lists and provided them with their general framework, when they were compiled in the days of Solomon as an expression of the legitimation of the Israelite seizure of the Promised Land from the indigenous nations. After that, the first formula of the six-name lists "C A H P V J", underwent several modifications, corresponding to the shift in implication of the terms Canaanites, Amorites, and Hittites, up to the time of compilation of the Book of Deuteronomy, i.e., the second half of the seventh century B.C.

c) The fact that the second formula of the six-name lists "C H A P V J", was employed by the authors in later times suggests that it was accepted as the quasi-canonical formula of the lists of nations in biblical traditions.

d) Besides the lists in the main stream of development outlined above, other lists were composed as modifications of the basic patterns or formulae, such as the five- or seven-name lists or the lists in the Table of Nations and Gen 15.

Admittedly, many problems remain to be solved. We have not dealt with the question of the identification of the minor nations, such as the Perizzites, the Hivites, the Jebusites, or the Girgashites. Nor are our theses on the Amorites and the Hittites in pre-Davidic Palestine proved. We have intentionally left these problems on one side, since our source material is, at the moment, not adequate to solve them. Nor have we attempted to verify the attribution of the passages in which the lists of nations are found to Pentateuchal "sources". For, the fluid character of the source-analysis of the Pentateuch aside, we assume that independent material such as the lists of nations transmitted on its own.

Despite all these problems, we are convinced that our study has shown that the complicated structure of the lists of pre-Israelite nations can be explained neither by a static acceptance of their historicity[65] nor by a categorical rejection of it,[66] but by a dynamic approach to their historical development, with a general reliance on the historical consistency of the biblical traditions.[67]

[65] E.g., Mendenhall, *The Tenth Generation*, p. 155, regards the "seven nations" as exclusively socio-political groups.

[66] E.g., Richter, *Die Bearbeitungen*, p. 41, attributes all the six-name lists to the Deuteronomists and does not find any geographical or ethnical connotation in the names of these nations, while van Seters, *VT* 22 (1972), pp. 68–71, suggests a post-Deuteronomistic dating during the Exilic period for the lists in the so-called JE passages.

[67] In this connection, the judgement of Speiser, in *WHJP* I/I, p. 169, seems sound: "The lists may be stereotyped, but they rest on reliable traditions".

ŠŌPĒṬ: THE LEADERS OF THE TRIBAL LEAGUES "ISRAEL" IN THE PRE-MONARCHICAL PERIOD*

1. *A Critical Reconsideration of the Theory of "Minor Judges"*

The Hebrew sentence *wayyišpōṭ* (or *šāpaṭ*) *'eṭ-yiśrā'ēl*, which is generally translated as "he judged Israel", is mentioned seventeen times in the Books of Judges and 1 Samuel concerning the following eleven persons: Othniel, Deborah, Tola, Jair, Jephthah, Ibzan, Elon, Abdon, Samson, Eli, and Samuel.[1] In the period of the monarchy they were called *šōp̄ᵉṭîm* and were regarded as the leaders of Israel in the premonarchical period,[2] but oddly enough the title *šōp̄ēṭ* was given none of them in the narratives concerning their deeds.[3] As is well known, the term *šōp̄ēṭ* is generally used in the sense of a "judge" particularly in the Book of Deuteronomy and the Deuteronomistic historical works referring to the judicial functionaries who were either tribal elders, the appointees of the king, or the priests.[4] But it is extremely

---

* This essay is a revised version of the study which appeared in *RB* 80 (1973), pp. 514–530.

[1] Judg 3:10; 4:4 (*šōp̄ᵉṭāh*); 10:2, 3; 12:7, 8, 9, 11a, 11b, 13, 14; 15:20; 16:31 (*šāpaṭ*); 1 Sam 4:18 (*šāpaṭ*); 7:15, 16 (*šāpaṭ*), 17 (*šāpaṭ*); cf. 1 Sam 7:6 (*wayyišpōṭ 'eṭ-bᵉnê yiśrā'ēl*).

[2] In the Deuteronomistic survey of the period of the Judges (Judg 2:11–19), see M. Noth, *Überlieferungsgeschichtliche Studien. Die sammelnden und bearbeitenden Geschichtswerke im Alten Testament*, Tübingen, 1943, 1957², pp. 6, 53, 91; 2 Sam 7:7 (read *šōp̄ᵉṭê* instead of *šiḇᵗê*, see *BHK*, despite P. de Robert, "Juges ou tribus en 2 Samuel vii 7?", *VT* 21 [1971], pp. 116–118; but see below n. 36), 11 = 1 Chr 17:6, 10; 2 Kgs 23:22; Ruth 1:1. J. Lust, "The Immanuel Figure: A Charismatic Judge-Leader", *ETL* 47 (1971), pp. 464–470, argued that Isaiah had in mind the judge-rulers in the pre-monarchical period by *šōp̄ᵉṭayiḵ kᵉḇārīš'ōnāh* (1:26).

[3] Othniel and Ehud: *môšîaᶜ* (Judg 3:9, 15), Deborah: *nᵉḇî'āh* (4:4), Gideon: *gibbôr ḥayil* (6:12), Jephthah: *gibbôr ḥayil* (11:1) and *rō'š* and *qāṣîn* over all the inhabitants of Gilead (11:11), Samson: *nᵉzîr 'ᵉlōhîm* (13:5, 7; 16:17), Eli: *kōhēn* (1 Sam 1:9), and Samuel: *nāḇî'* (3:20), *'îš-'ᵉlōhîm* (9:6, 7, 8, 10), or *rō'eh* (9:11, 18, 19); cf. *šōp̄ᵉṭāh* for Deborah (Judg 4:4), the participle feminine instead of a third person feminine perfect in MT, suggests an office of judge.

[4] See R. de Vaux, *Ancient Israel. Its Life and Institutions*, London, 1961, pp. 152 ff.; M. Weinfeld, *Deuteronomy and the Deuteronomic School*, Oxford, 1972, p. 234.

difficult to find in the biblical narratives that these pre-monarchical leaders called *šōp̄ᵉṭîm* acted as judges in the court of justice.[5]

The difficulty of seemingly non-judicial *šōp̄ᵉṭîm* is well known. Modern scholarship has tried to solve this problem on the basis of the customary division of the *šōp̄ᵉṭîm* into "major" and "minor judges".[6] According to O. Grether the designation for the "major judges" was originally *môšîaʿ*, but, when the term came to be reserved for God, it was substituted by *šōp̄ēṭ* which was already the designation for the "minor judges" in the same period.[7] M. Noth proposed that the traditions of the "minor judges" (Judg 10:1–5; 12:7–15) were formerly independent from those of the charismatic heroes called the "major judges", but the Deuteronomistic historian, when joining these traditions in the Book of Judges, called the latter by the original title of the former, i.e., *šōp̄ᵉṭîm*, influenced by the tradition of Jephthah who was a charismatic hero as well as a "minor judge".[8] Furthermore, Noth incorporated the theory of the "minor judges" as the "proclaimers of the law", as advanced by A. Klostermann[9] and A. Alt,[10] into his thesis of the Israelite amphictyony[11] and maintained that the "minor judges" held the central office of the amphictyony as the proclaimers of its fundamental law; this office was administered by *one* judge elected for life by the tribal confederation and was succeeded by another without interruption.[12]

---

[5] Eli the priest most probably exercised some judicial functions, since priests are sometimes mentioned along with judges in court proceedings (Deut 17:9, 12; 19:17, etc.). Opinions are divided on the interpretation of the passages which might indicate judicial acts of Deborah (Judg 4:5) as well as those of Samuel (1 Sam 12:3–5).

[6] About the division of the *šōp̄ᵉṭîm* into "major" and "minor judges" see O. Eissfeldt, *The Old Testament. An Introduction*, Oxford, 1965, pp. 258 f.; J.A. Soggin, *Introduction to the Old Testament. From its origins to the closing of the Alexadrian canon*, London, 1980², pp. 175 f. About a short survey of the history of criticism see A. Malamat, "The Period of the Judges", in B. Mazar (ed.), *WHJP* I/III: *Judges*, Tel-Aviv, 1971, pp. 130 ff. For an extensive bibliogrphy on *šōp̄ᵉṭîm* see H. Niehr, "שפט", in *TWAT* VIII, Stuttgart, 1994–95, cols. 408–412.

[7] O. Grether, "Die Bezeichnung 'Richter' für die charismatischen Helden der vorstaatlichen Zeit", *ZAW* 57 (1939), pp. 110–121; cf. W. Beyerlin, "Gattung und Herkunft des Rahmens im Richterbuch", in *Tradition und Situation. A. Weiser Festschrift*, Göttingen, 1963, p. 7.

[8] Noth, *Überlieferungsgeschichtliche Studien*, pp. 47 ff.

[9] A. Klostermann, *Der Pentateuch*, Leipzig, 1907², pp. 418 ff.

[10] A. Alt, "Die Ursprünge des israelitischen Rechts" (1934), in *Kleine Schriften zur Geschichte des Volkes Israel* I, München, 1953, pp. 300 ff.

[11] M. Noth, *Das System der zwölf Stämme Israels* (BWANT 4/1), Stuttgart, 1930.

[12] M. Noth, "Das Amt des 'Richters Israels'" (1950), in *Gesammelte Studien zum Alten Testament* II, München, 1969, pp. 71–85; idem, *The History of Israel*, London,

This thesis found great approval among the scholars,[13] and many theories have been developed upon it. In the opinion of R. Smend the "major judges" were the leaders of the War of Yahweh, whereas the "minor judges" were the representatives of the amphictyony, both offices never being mixed up.[14] According to the analysis of W. Richter the tradition of the deliverers, i.e., the charismatic heroes, as well as that of the *šōpᵉṭîm*, who were, in his opinion, the so-called "minor judges" including Samuel, had already been edited separately so completely that despite the attempt of combining both traditions in his work the Deuteronomistic historian could no longer assimilate the deliverers to the *šōpᵉṭîm* except in the "introduction" (Judg 2:7–19*) and the "*Beispielstück*" (3:7–11).[15] It is interesting to note that these studies sharpened the distinction between "major" and "minor judges", which is the foundation of Grether-Noth's theory, while other scholars were to bring ambiguity to it. Thus, H.W. Hertzberg blurred the picture by adding the six Othniel, Deborah, Gideon, Abimelech, Eli, and Samuel to the six "minor judges" already counted by M. Noth.[16] J. Dus, who thought that pre-monarchical Israel was a republic ruled by a *suffete* holding a central authority as a political-military leader, completely denied the above distinction.[17] On the other hand, this distinction was ignored from the beginning, or was minimized by those who tried to explain the term *šōpēṭ* for the pre-monarchical leaders by means of the semantic interpretation of the term. According to L. Koehler the term *šōpēṭ* as a deliverer is derived from a meaning

1960², pp. 101 f. While Klostermann and Alt supposed that the law proclaimed by the "minor judges" was the Canaanite casuistic law adopted by the people of Israel, Noth thought that it was the characteristic law of the Israelite amphictyony. According to H.-J. Kraus, *Die prophetische Verkündigung des Rechts in Israel* (TS 51), Zürich, 1957, p. 18, *šōpᵉṭîm* were the prophetic-charismatic proclaimers of the law of the amphictyony as the successors of Moses and Joshua. *Mazkîr* was regarded as another office of the Israelite amphictyony by H.G. Reventlow, "Das Amt des Mazkir", *TZ* 15 (1959), pp. 161–175.

[13] E.g., J. Bright, *A History of Israel* (OTL), London, 1960, p. 151, 1972², p. 166; de Vaux, *Ancient Israel*, p. 151; but see now idem, *Histoire ancienne d'Israël* II. *La période des Juges*, Paris, 1973, pp. 19–36.

[14] R. Smend, *Jahwekrieg und Stämmebund. Erwägungen zur ältesten Geschichte Israels* (FRLANT 84), Göttingen, 1963, pp. 33–55.

[15] W. Richter, *Die Bearbeitungen des "Retterbuches" in der deuteronomischen Epoche* (BBB 21), Bonn, 1964, pp. 128 ff.

[16] H.W. Hertzberg, "Die kleinen Richter", *TLZ* 79 (1954), cols. 285–290.

[17] J. Dus, "Die 'Sufeten Israels'", *ArOr* 31 (1963), pp. 444–469; cf. also K.-D. Schunck, "Die Richter Israels und ihr Amt", in *Congress Volume*, Genève 1965 (VTSup 15), Leiden, 1966, pp. 252–262.

of the verb *šāpaṭ* "to help a person to his right"; accordingly, *šōpᵉṭîm* were those who helped the people to gain justice by liberating them from foreign oppressions.[18] H.C. Thomson held that, owing to their charisma by which they could express the divine will (*mišpāṭ*) in some situation of importance to the amphictyony, both "major" and "minor judges" were called *šōpᵉṭîm*, though the former acted in military whereas the latter perhaps in civil affairs.[19]

While the latter studies did undermine Grether-Noth's theory, apart from the hypothesis of the Israelite amphictyony,[20] the theory of the "minor judges" merited critical reconsideration in the 1960s. Y. Kaufmann argued that it is quite unlikely that the "minor judges", about whom traditions tell at most about their numerous descendants, held a central office recognized by all Israel, while no charismatic heroes, whose great achievement of the deliverance of the nation was in circulation in folk tales and poems, could achieve the national unity. Moreover, it is difficult to find any essential difference between "major" and "minor judges". The fact that both Tola and Jair, who belong to the so-called "minor judges", "arose (*wayyāqom*)" (Judg 10:1, 3) shows that they were also deliverers like other "major judges" (cf. 2:16, 18; 3:9, 15). Indeed, as for Tola it is written: "He arose to save (*lᵉhôšîaᶜ*) Israel" (10:1). It is also to be pointed out that the expression "after (*ʾaḥᵃrê*) so-and-so" in the formula of the "minor judges" does not mean that the succession of the same office took place without interruption as in the case of the royal succession where it is expressed in the term "instead of (*taḥaṯ*)". From this expression we may rather suppose that the "minor judges" were also charismatic leaders who sporadically arose one after another.[21]

---

[18] L. Koehler, "Die hebräische Rechtsgemeinde" (1931), in *Der hebräische Mensch*, Tübingen, 1953, pp. 151 f.; "judge (who settles a cause, helps to one's right)" in KB, p. 1003.

[19] H.C. Thomson, "SHOPHEṬ and MISHPAṬ in the Book of Judges", *TGUOS* 19 (1961–62), pp. 74–85. According to J. van der Ploeg, "ŠĀPAṬ et MIŠPĀṬ", *OTS* 2 (1943), pp. 144–155, Deborah, Eli, and Samuel were the "charismatic judges" and the major judges were the "charismatic chiefs", and both of them had the authority to be consulted in difficult cases which were brought in by the members of the amphictyony; cf. also D.A. McKenzie, "The Judges of Israel", *VT* 17 (1967), pp. 118–121.

[20] About the critical discussions on the hypothesis of the Israelite amphictyony see G. Fohrer, *Geschichte der israelitischen Religion*, Berlin, 1969, pp. 78–83; de Vaux, *Histoire ancienne d'Israël* II, pp. 19–36; N.K. Gottwald, *The Tribes of Yahweh. A Sociology of the Religion of Liberated Israel, 1250–1050 B.C.E.*, Maryknoll, N.Y., 1979, pp. 345–386, 748–754; A.D.H. Mayes, "Amphictyony", in *ABD* I, New York, 1992, pp. 212–216.

[21] Y. Kaufmann, *The Book of Judges*, Jerusalem, 1962, pp. 46 ff. (Hebrew).

According to A. Malamat the essential difference between "major" and "minor judges" can be found not in the character of their office but in that of the literary sources drawn from, folk narratives for the former whereas family chronicles for the latter.[22]

2. *The Meanings of the Word* špṭ *in the West Semitics*

However, a decisive argument against Grether-Noth's theory came from the investigation into the West Semitic word *špṭ* especially in the light of the texts from Mari (18th century B.C.) and Ugarit (14th century B.C.).[23] In the Mari documents so far we have *šapāṭum* (verb), *šāpiṭum* (participle), *šipṭum* and *šāpiṭūtum* (abstract nouns) as the derivatives of *špṭ*, which correspond to the Hebrew words *šāp̄aṭ, šōp̄ēṭ* and *mišpāṭ*, respectively.[24] The usage of these words made clear that the term *špṭ* has no judicial meaning as its primary connotation, but rather it is to be translated as "to issue orders, to exercise authority, to rule, to govern, to administer" or the like. In the Mari documents *šāpiṭum* appears to be a person with the administrative authority like a distric governor or a high administrative official.[25] In the texts from Ugarit, while *ṯpṭ* is sometimes used as a synonym for *dyn* in the king's

[22] Malamat, in *WHJP* I/III: *Judges*, p. 131.

[23] F.C. Fensham, "The Judges and Ancient Israelite Jurisprudence", *OTWSA* 2 (1959), pp. 15–22; A. van Selms, "The Title 'Judge'", *OTWSA* 2 (1959), pp. 43–46; A. Malamat, "מארי", in *Encyclopaedia Biblica* IV, Jerusalem, 1962, cols. 576 f. (Hebrew); idem, "The Ban in Mari and in the Bible", *OTWSA* 9 (1967), p. 45; idem, "Mari", *BA* 34 (1971), p. 19; idem, in *WHJP* I/III: *Judges*, p. 131; idem, *Mari and the Early Israelite Experience* (The Schweich Lectures 1984), Oxford, 1989, pp. 33 f., 77; M.S. Rozenberg, *The Stem špṭ. An Investigation of Biblical and Extra-Biblical Sources* (Diss.), Pennsylvania, 1963, pp. 170–222; W. Richter, "Zu den 'Richtern Israels'", *ZAW* 77 (1965), pp. 59–71; W.H. Schmidt, *Königtum Gottes in Ugarit und Israel zur Herkunft der Königsprädikation Jahwes* (BZAW 80), Berlin, 1966², pp. 36–43, 78; H. Cazelles, "Institutions et terminologie en Deutéronome i 6–17", in *Congress Volume,* Genève 1965 (VTSup 15), Leiden, 1966, pp. 108 f.; E.A. Speiser, "The Manner of the King", in B. Mazar (ed.), *WHJP* I/III: *Judges*, Tel-Aviv, 1971, pp. 281 f. On an extensive bibliography on the root *špṭ* and its derivatives in the Semitic languages see A. Marzal, "The Provincial Governor at Mari: His Title and Appointment", *JNES* 30 (1971), p. 188, n. 1.

[24] J. Bottéro and A. Finet, *Répertoire analytique des Tomes I à V des Archives Royales de Mari* (ARM XV), Paris, 1954, pp. 264 f.; *AHw*, pp. 1172 f., 1247; *CAD* Š/1, pp. 450 f., 459 f.; *CAD* Š/3, pp. 91–93; Cf. KB, pp. 579 f., 1002 f.

[25] See A. Marzal, *JNES* 30 (1971), pp. 186–217. Marzal, ibid., esp. pp. 202 f., made it also clear that in Mari *šāpiṭum*, together with *merḫum*, was not the administrator within the tribal system, but the governor of a province (*ḫalṣum*) appointed by the king.

dispensing justice for widows and orphans,[26] it is also found in the parallelism with *mlk* and *zbl*.[27] In the latter case, it is very likely that this term implies "ruler" or "sovereign".[28] In the Phoenician inscription of Ahiram of Byblos (10th century B.C.) the "staff of *mšpṭ*" stands in parallelism to the "throne of the king".[29] It is also likely that *mšpṭ* here signifies "royal" rather than "judicial".[30] In the Punic and Neo-Punic inscriptions *špṭ* stands for the title "*suffete*", which was originally translated as *iudex* meaning Roman consul but later as *rex* when he held the military as well as the civil leadership.[31]

Before finding the West Semitic parallels in extra-biblical sources H.W. Hertzberg maintained that the verb *šāpaṭ* in the biblical Hebrew has a double meaning, "to rule" and "to judge", and the latter is derived from the former.[32] On this assertion opinions have been sharply divided.[33] By analogy with the usages of *špṭ* in the other West Semitic languages, however, scholars have inclined increasingly to think that the meaning "to rule" for the term *špṭ* cannot be

---

[26] *UT* 127:45–50 (p. 194); 2 Aqht: v 7 f. (p. 248).

[27] *ṯpṭn // mlkn* (*UT* 51: iv 43 f. [p. 171]; ʿnt: v 40 [p. 255]); *mṯpṭk // mlkk* (*UT* 49: vi 28 f. [p. 169]); *ṯpṭ nhr // zbl ym* (*UT* 68:14 f., 16 f., 22, 24 f. [p. 180]).

[28] J. Aistleitner (ed. by O. Eissfeldt), *Wörterbuch der ugaritischen Sprache*, Berlin, 1963, p. 342; Rozenberg, *The Stem špṭ*, pp. 215 ff.; C.H. Gordon, *Ugaritic Textbook* (AnOr 38), Roma, 1965, pp. 505 f.; Schmidt, *Königtum Gottes in Ugarit und Israel*, pp. 36 ff.

[29] *tḥtsp ḥṭr mšpṭh tḥtpk ksʾ mlkh* (*KAI* 1:2); a close parallel can be found in a Ugaritic text, *lyhpk ksa mlkk lyṯbr ḫṭ mṯpṭk* (*UT* 49: vi 28 f. [p. 169]); cf. already H.L. Ginsberg, "The Rebellion and Death of Baʿlu", *Or* 5 (1936), p. 179.

[30] (The staff) "of his authority", F.M. Cross and D.N. Freedman, *Early Hebrew Orthography. A Study of the Epigraphic Evidence* (AOS 36), New Haven, 1952, p. 14; "son sceptre judiciaire (seigneurial)", C.F. Jean and J. Hoftijzer, *DISO*, p. 171; "der Stab seiner Herrschaft", W. Röllig, *KAI* II, p. 2; "the scepter of his rule", J. Hoftijzer and K. Jongeling, *DNWSI*, p. 365; but "his judicial staff", F. Rosenthal, "Canaanite and Aramaic Inscriptions", in *ANET*, Princeton, 1969³, p. 661. Cf. Rozenberg, *The Stem špṭ*, pp. 217 f.; Richter, *ZAW* 77 (1965), pp. 68 f.

[31] About "*suffete*" see *DISO*, p. 316; *DNWSI*, pp. 1182 f.; Richter, *ZAW* 77 (1965), p. 70.

[32] H.W. Hertzberg, "Die Entwicklung des Begriffes משפט im AT", *ZAW* 40 (1922), pp. 256–287; 41 (1923), pp. 16–76.

[33] Against the assertion of Hertzberg argued L. Koehler, in *Der hebräische Mensch*, pp. 151 f., n. 9, that the original meaning of the verb *šāpaṭ* is "entscheiden zwischen". From the examination of around 200 cases of the verb *šāpaṭ* in the Hebrew Bible Grether, *ZAW* 57 (1939), pp. 111 ff., came to the conclusion that most of them have the meanings "rechtsprechen, Urteil fällen, Recht schaffen, zum Recht verhelfen, urteilen, strafen", while the meaning "regieren" may be found only three times (Amos 2:3; Dan 9:12, twice). I.L. Seeligmann, "Zur Terminologie für das Gerichtsverfahren im Wortschatz des biblischen Hebräisch", in *Hebräische Wortforschung. W. Baumgartner Festschrift* (VTSup 16), Leiden, 1967, pp. 273 ff., maintained that the verb *šāpaṭ* in the meaning "herrschen" cannot be found in the Hebrew Bible except once (Dan 9:12), and in all the cases where *šōpēṭ* signifies ruler non-Israelite rulers are referred to.

excluded from its usage, though the meaning "to judge" is doubtless dominant in the Hebrew Bible.[34] It is unlikely that in the case of Jotham who *šōpēṭ* the "people of the land" in the place of the leprous Azariah (2 Kgs 15:5 = 2 Chr 26:21) his activity was confined only to "judging". Therefore, *šōpēṭ* here must have the meaning "governing".[35] In the same way, *šōpᵉṭê*[36] *yiśrāʾēl* whom Yahweh commanded to shepherd (*lirʿôṯ*) the people of Israel (2 Sam 7:7 = 1 Chr 17:6) cannot be "judges" in a narrow sense of the term but "rulers" because their activity "to shepherd the people".[37] *Šōpēṭ* standing in the parallelism with either *meleḵ* (Hos 7:7; Ps 2:10; 148:11; cf. Isa 33:22), *śar* (Exod 2:14; Amos 2:3; Mic 7:3; Zeph 3:3; Prov 8:16; 2 Chr 1:2) *meleḵ* and *śar* (Hos 13:10; cf. Ps 148:11), or *rōzēn* (Isa 40:23) also appears to imply a "leader", a "ruler", a "sovereign", or the like. Besides, there are some cases where *šōpēṭ* standing alone is generally regarded as a "ruler" in accordance with the context (Mic 4:14; Dan 9:12). Moreover, when the elders of Israel asked Samuel to appoint

---

[34] Cf. Fensham, *OTWSA* 2 (1959), pp. 17 ff.; Rozenberg, *The Stem špṭ*, pp. 16 ff.; Richter, *ZAW* 77 (1965), pp. 58 f.; Schmidt, *Königtum Gottes in Ugarit und Israel*, pp. 38 f. J. Jeremias, "*Mišpāṭ* im ersten Gottesknechtslied (Jes. XLII 1–4)", *VT* 22 (1972), pp. 31 ff., suggested that *mišpāṭ* in Isa 42:1 refers to the royal function of the servant of Yahweh; cf. also W.A.M. Beuken, "*Mišpāṭ*: The First Servant Song and its Context", *VT* 22 (1972), pp. 1 ff.

[35] Cf. J. Gray, *I & II Kings. A Commentary* (OTL), London, 1977³, pp. 618 f. J.A. Montgomery and H.S. Gehman, *A Critical and Exegetical Commentary on the Books of Kings* (ICC), Edinburgh, 1951, p. 448, suggests that the title "Judge of the people of the land" is a technical term for regency. However, M. Cogan and H. Tadmor, *II Kings. A New Translation with Introduction and Commentary* (AB 11), New York, 1988, p. 167, find here special obligations of the Davidic king to the People of the Land in judicial matters.

[36] *Šiḇᵉṭê yiśrāʾēl* in 2 Sam 7:7 is generally emended into *šōpᵉṭê yiśrāʾēl* on the basis of 1 Chr. 17:6, see Richter, *Bearbeitungen*, p. 118, n. 20. But Z.W. Falk, "Šōpēṭ wᵉšēḇeṭ", *Lešonénu* 30 (1966), pp. 243–247 (Hebrew), held that the emendation is unnecessary, since the term *šēḇeṭ* here is a synonym for *šōpēṭ* in the sense "ruler". This view was accepted by S.E. Loewenstamm, "Ruler and Judge. Reconsidered", *Lešonénu* 32 (1967/68), pp. 272–274 (Hebrew), though he denied Falk's suggestion that the term *šbṭ* is derived from *špṭ*, and made it clear that these two terms are derived from two different proto-Semitic words; cf. also E.Y. Kutscher, "A Marginal Note to S.E. Loewenstamm's Article", *Lešonénu* 32 (1967/68), p. 274 (Hebrew). P.V. Reid, "*šbṭy* in 2 Samuel 7:7", *CBQ* 37 (1975), pp. 17–20, suggested the reading *šōbᵉṭê* for MT *šibᵉṭê*, a denomitative *Qal* participle from *šēbeṭ*, standing for "staff bearers", i.e., tribal leaders like elders. Notwithstanding all the suggestions, the emendation based on 1 Chr 17:6 seems most tenable, cf. H. Niehr, *TWAT* VIII, col. 425.

[37] "Shepherd" is a designation of king in the ancient Near East, cf. 2 Sam 5:2 = 1 Chr 11:2; Isa 44:28; Jer 3:15; 23:2, 4; Mic 5:4; Ps 78:72, etc.; see also M.-J. Seux, *Épithètes royales akkadiennes et sumériennes*, Paris, 1967, pp. 243 ff.; *AHw* pp. 977 f.; cf. also *HALOT* III, pp. 1259 f.; J.W. Vancil, "Sheep, Shepherd", in *ABD* V, New York, 1992, pp. 1187–1190.

for them a king *lᵉšopṭēnû* (1 Sam 8:5, 6, 20), it is quite probable that they expected the king not as a mere judge but as a ruler.[38] In this connection, it is worth noting that the Hall of the Throne (*ʾûlām hakkissēʾ*) in Solomon's palace is called also *ʾûlām hammišpāṭ* (1 Kgs 7:7). On the analogy of the Ugaritic and Phoenician inscriptions mentioned above where *ḥṭr mšpṭ* stands in parallelism with *ksʾ mlk*,[39] in my opinion, the meaning of the words should imply the Hall of the "Government" rather than the "Judgement" as generally understood,[40] because the throne-room was not used only for the judicial court (cf. Isa 16:5).

3. *The Deliverer-Rulers of Israel*

For all the peoples in the ancient Near East, judgement was one of the important royal functions, but, needless to say, it was only one of the royal responsibilities. The above examples appear to show that the West Semitic word *špṭ* primarily implies this sort of government. We may thus conclude that *šāpaṭ* in *wayyišpōṭ ʾeṯ-yiśrāʾēl* in the Books of Judges and 1 Samuel also signifies not "to judge" in a narrow sense of the term but "to rule" in which the function "to judge" is included. From this meaning of the term *špṭ* as well as the analysis of the formula of the judges (Judg 10:1–5; 12:7–15) and of Samuel (1 Sam 7:15–17 + 25:1) W. Richter came to the conclusion that *šōpᵉṭîm* were the non-military, administrative-judicial rulers over a city and its environs, appointed by the tribal elders in the transitional period from tribal to city government.[41] Therefore, Richter did not find any relationship between the *šōpᵉṭîm* and the amphictyony, but he followed the Grether-Noth's theory in assuming that the

---

[38] About the term *šōpēṭ* in association with *śar*, *yōʿēṣ*, *mᵉḥōqēq*, *meleḵ*, and *rōzēn*, see Rozenberg, *The Stem špṭ*, pp. 64 ff.; about "a king *lᵉšopṭēnû*" see Rozenberg, ibid., pp. 26 and 239; Speiser, in *WHJP* I/III, p. 282; cf. also Hertzberg, *ZAW* 40 (1922), p. 257.

[39] See above n. 29.

[40] Z.W. Falk, "Two Symbols of Justice", *VT* 10 (1960), pp. 72 f.; Gray, *I & II Kings*, p. 179. Rozenberg, *The Stem špṭ*, pp. 26 f., thought that "this was the hall where the king rendered decisions", and the translation of *špṭ* here is either "to give decision", or "to administer justice". M. Noth, *Könige* I. *I. Könige 1–16* (BKAT 9/1), Neukirchen-Vluyn, 1968, p. 137, held that the comment on the throne-room as royal tribunal is a secondary addition.

[41] Richter, *ZAW* 77 (1965), pp. 59, 70 ff.; cf. G. Fohrer, *Introduction to the Old Testament*, London, 1970, pp. 207 f.

Deuteronomistic historian added the formula of the judges to the narratives of the charismatic heroes, who had originally nothing to do with the above local administrative-judicial functionaries.[42] However, the figure of the deliverer-šōp̄eṭîm is already found in the prophecy of Nathan (2 Sam 7:7*, 11 = 1 Chr 17:6, 10)[43] originating in the time of David and Solomon.[44] It is also worth noting that Richter's theory, according to which Jephthah and Samuel belong to non-deliverers, i.e., "minor judges", is irreconcilable with the farewell speech of Samuel which explicitly mentions these two together with Jerubaal and Bedan[45] as the deliverers of Israel (1 Sam 12:11).[46] Since the charismatic heroes are called šōp̄eṭîm in various traditions, it is difficult to assume that the figure of the deliverer-šōp̄eṭîm is a pure invention of the Deuteronomist. Rather, if the term šōp̄ēṭ has the meaning "ruler", the very deliverers deserve to be called šōp̄eṭîm.[47]

If we assume that the pre-monarchical leaders called šōp̄eṭîm were

---

[42] Richter, ZAW 77 (1965), p. 47.

[43] According to Grether, ZAW 57 (1939), p. 119, the earliest evidence for the term šōp̄eṭîm as the name of the charismatic heroes is found in the prophecy of Nathan. Against this view, Richter, Bearbeitungen, pp. 119 f.; idem., ZAW 77 (1965), p. 59, n. 64. But his argument seems untenable.

[44] On the Solomonic origin of the prophecy of Nathan see M. Tsevat, "Studies in the Book of Samuel III. The Steadfast House: What was David promised in II Sam. VII 11b–16?", HUCA 34 (1963), pp. 71–82; A. Weiser, "Die Tempelbaukrise unter David", ZAW 77 (1965), p. 156; N. Poulssen, König und Tempel im Glaubenszeugnis des Alten Testamentes (SBM 3), Stuttgart, 1967, pp. 43 ff.; T. Ishida, The Royal Dynasties in Ancient Israel. A Study on the Formation and Development of Royal-Dynastic Ideology (BZAW 142), Berlin/New York, 1977, pp. 81–99; see also below pp. 137 ff.

[45] Since the name Bedan is not mentioned in the Book of Judges, various emendations have been suggested. Y. Zakovitch, "bdn = ypṭḥ", VT 22 (1972), pp. 123–125, held that Bedan is none other than Jephthah's second name, like Gideon-Jerubaal; cf. P.K. McCarter, I Samuel. A New Translation with Introduction, Notes and Commentary (AB 8), Garden City, N.Y., 1980., p. 211. But it is possible to regard him as an unknown deliverer from any other source, see Malamat, in WHJP I/III: Judges, p. 315, n. 15.

[46] On the origin of the farewell speech of Samuel opinions are divided; according to Noth, Überlieferungsgeschichtliche Studien, pp. 59 ff., this was written by the author of the Deuteronomistic history; cf. H.J. Boecker, Die Beurteilung der Anfänge des Königtums in den deuteronomistischen Abschnitten des I. Samuelbuches (WMANT 31), Neukirchen-Vluyn, 1969, pp. 61 ff. But Eissfeldt, The Old Testament, p. 262, allocated it to the source E.A. Weiser, Samuel: seine geschichtliche Aufgabe und religiöse Bedeutung (FRLANT 81), Göttingen, 1962, pp. 88 f., held that this chapter originated in the Gilgal tradition which tells of Samuel's role at the establishment of the monarchy. McCarter, I Samuel, pp. 14–20, 217–221, proposed that Samuel's address in chapter 12 came from the prophetic narrative of the rise of kingship with Deuteronomistic additions in vv. 6–15, 19b(?), 20b–22, 24–25.

[47] Against the view of Richter that šōp̄eṭîm had no function of the military leader, see Schunck, in Congress Volume, Genève 1965 (VTSup 15), pp. 259 f.

the "deliverer-rulers" of Israel, we may ask why the formula *wayyišpōṭ ʾeṯ-yiśrāʾēl* is missing in the narratives of Ehud, Shamgar, Gideon, and Abimelech, though any essential difference cannot be found between these and the other *šōp̄ᵉṭîm*. As for Ehud, we might suppose on the basis of the addition of LXX to Judg 3:30, καὶ ἔκρινεν αὐτοὺς Ἀὼδ ἕως οὗ ἀπέθανεν, that this formula was omitted from the original text in the course of transmission.[48] Since there is reason to believe that Shamgar was a non-Israelite,[49] it is natural that his "rule" over Israel is not told (Judg 3:31). In the story of Abimelech *wayyaśar ʿal-yiśrāʾēl* (9:22) clearly substitutes for this formula, because *śrr* is a synonym for *špṭ* here as has been shown in the parallel between *śar* and *šōp̄ēṭ* (see above p. 43; but see also below p. 52). Most puzzling is Gideon's case, since, despite his clear refusal of the hereditary rulership offered by the men of Israel (8:22–23), the biblical story reveals that he was *de facto* one of the most powerful "rulers" in the pre-monarchical Israel.[50] In my opinion, this formula was omitted from the original text when the episode of his refusal of the rulership was inserted into the story of Gideon,[51] because his answer: "I will not rule (*lōʾ-ʾemšōl*) over you, and my son will not rule (*lōʾ-yišmōl*) over you" (8:23), made an obvious contradiction to the formula: "He ruled (*šāp̄aṭ*) Israel".

4. *The Tribal Leagues "Israel"*

What is then the concept of "Israel" which *šōp̄ᵉṭîm* ruled? M. Noth asserted that "Israel" as in the "judge of Israel" (Mic 4:14) was noth-

---

[48] Cf. Grether, *ZAW* 57 (1939), p. 113, n. 3; R.G. Boling, *Judges. Introduction, Translation, and Commentary* (AB 6A), Garden City, N.Y., 1975, p. 87; but J. Schreiner, *Septuaginta-Massora des Buches der Richter* (AnBib 7), Roma, 1957, p. 49, regarded it as an addition made by LXX.

[49] B. Maisler (Mazar), "Shamgar ben Anat", in *Palestine Exploration Fund Quartely Statement*, London, 1934, pp. 192–194; A. van Selms, "Judge Shamgar", *VT* 14 (1964), pp. 294–309; O. Eissfeldt, "The Hebrew Kingdom", in *CAH* II, ch. XXXIV, Cambridge, 1965, p. 22; Malamat, in *WHJP* I/III, p. 137; cf. also R.G. Boling, "Shamgar", in *ABD* V, New York, 1992, pp. 1155 f.

[50] See Malamat, in *WHJP* I/III: *Judges*, p. 148.

[51] Apart from the question whether this episode reflects the situation in the pre-monarchical period or originated in the late monarchy, it is generally recognized that these passages originally did not belong to the old tradition of Gideon, see C.F. Whitley, "The Sources of the Gideon Stories", *VT* 7 (1957), pp. 161 f.; W. Beyerlin, "Geschichte und heilsgeschichtliche Traditionsbildung im Alten Testa-

ing but the "confederation of the twelve tribes of Israel".[52] According to W. Richter, however, "Israel" in the formula of the judges (Judg 10:1–5; 12:7–15) and of Samuel (1 Sam 7:15–17 + 25:1) could be understood as the political-geographical term for the Northern Kingdom and the United Kingdom, respectively, as it was employed in the royal annals of the Israelite monarchies. But Richter concluded that we can hardly know the precise meaning of this "Israel" in the premonarchical period.[53] While Noth's assertion of a tribal confederation of all Israel that could appoint *one šōpēṭ* for its central office is difficult to accept especially in the light of the evaluation of the period by the biblical tradition (Judg 17:6; 21:25), Richter's conclusion is untenable. It seems necessary to make a re-examination of the name of "Israel" in the narratives of the *šōpᵉṭîm* to reveal the nature of the concept "Israel".

To begin with, let us examine the term "Israel" in case of Deborah and Barak. According to the prose version (Judg 4) ten thousand men from Zebulun and Naphtali under the command of Barak inspired by Deborah defeated the Canaanites, whereas in the Song of Deborah (Judg 5) another four tribes, Ephraim, Benjamin, Machir, and Issachar, joined with Zebulun and Naphtali. From this information we may conclude that Deborah and Barak formed a six-tribe league against the Canaanites the nucleus of which was Zebulun and Naphtali.[54] The Song version mentions additional four tribes which are rebuked for not joining the battle (5:15b–17). It is therefore to be supposed that there existed a community consisting of, at least, these ten tribes which were linked by a sort of national consciousness.[55]

ment. Ein Beitrag zur Traditionsgeschichte von Richter vi–viii", *VT* 13 (1963), pp. 19 ff.; B. Lindars, "Gideon and Kingship", *JTS* 16 (1965), pp. 315–326; cf. also Noth, *The History of Israel*, pp. 164 f.

[52] Noth, in *Gesammelte Studien* II, p. 81.

[53] Richter, *ZAW* 77 (1965), pp. 46, 49, 50 ff., 55.

[54] Noth, *The History of Israel*, p. 150, n. 3, regarded the mention of four tribes in addition to Zebulun and Naphtali as participants in war in the Song as a secondary extension. According to A. Weiser, "Das Deboralied", *ZAW* 71 (1959), pp. 67–97, the enumeration of tribes in Judg 5:14–18 has nothing directly to do with the campaign of Deborah and Barak, which was fought only by Zebulun and Naphtali, but a tribal roll-call on the occasion of a feast of the amphictyony. But we may rather interpret these two sources as complementary, see Kaufmann, *The Book of Judges*, pp. 113 ff.; Smend, *Jahwekrieg und Stämmebund*, pp. 10 f., n. 3; Malamat, in *WHJP* I/III: *Judges*, pp. 137 ff.

[55] "The ten-tribe confederation of Israel" is often supposed on the basis of the Song of Deborah, see S. Mowinckel, "'Rahelstämme' und 'Leastämme'", in *Von*

It is clear that this tribal community was called "Israel", because its common God, Yahweh, is called "God of *Israel*" (4:6; 5:3, 5). On the other hand, it is also self-evident that the concept of "Israel" in the "warriors with long hair of *Israel*" (5:2)[56] and in the "commanders of *Israel* who offered themselves willingly" (5:9) refers only to the six tribes which joined the battle. It is likely that "Israel" in the "peasantry in *Israel*" (5:7, 11) and in "fourty thousand in *Israel*" (5:8) had to do only with the same six tribes which formed a league because of the common suffering from the Canaanite oppression. And the "people of *Israel*" who defeated the Canaanites (4:23, 24) obviously refer to the six tribes only. When the poet says: "Until you arose, Deborah, arose as a mother in *Israel*" (5:7), it appears that he intends "Israel" to mean the community consisting of ten tribes; in reality, though Deborah's authority was recognized only by the members of her six-tribe league. It seems that the four tribes which did not participate in the league are not included among the "people of *Israel*" who came to Deborah for *mišpāṭ* (4:5). The above observation shows that the name "Israel" is used here in a double sense, i.e., on the one hand, it is applied to the large unit of all ten tribes, on the other, it is a limited sense to a part thereof. In other words, "Israel" can be the name of a large community including ten tribes; as well as the designation of a league consisting of six tribes which gathered together under the leadership of Deborah and Barak. From this observation we can come to the conclusion that "Israel" in *hîʾ šōp̄ᵉṭāh ʾeṯ-yiśrāʾēl* (4:4) is not the name of the ten-tribe community but the designation of the six-tribe league against the Canaanites organized by Deborah and Barak.[57]

Ugarit nach Qumran. O. Eissfeldt Festschrift (BZAW 77), Berlin, 1958, pp. 137 f.; Weiser, *ZAW* 71 (1959), p. 87; K.-D. Schunck, *Benjamin. Untersuchungen zur Entstehung und Geschichte eines israelitischen Stammes* (BZAW 86), Berlin, 1963, pp. 70 ff.

[56] About *bip̄ᵉrōaʿ pᵉrāʿôṯ* see C.F. Burney, *The Book of Judges with Introduction and Notes*, London, 1918, pp. 107 f.; E. Täubler (ed. by H.-J. Zobel), *Biblische Studien* I. *Die Epoche der Richter*, Tübingen, 1958, p. 154, n. 1; de Vaux, *Ancient Israel*, p. 467.

[57] In the analysis of the Song of Deborah Smend, *Jahwekrieg und Stämmebund*, pp. 10 f., maintained that "neben dem Israel in der Aktion steht also ein Israel in der Potenz, und nur dieses zweite trägt überhaupt den Namen Israel". Kaufmann, *The Book of Judges*, pp. 36 f., emphasized that, since the tribes of Israel were associated in the common ethnical, cultural, and religious ground in the pre-monarchical period, though they had no political unity, every attack on a tribe from outside was always regarded not as a tribal but as a national event. From the analysis of the boundary list in the Book of Joshua Y. Aharoni, *The Land of the Bible. A Historical Geography*, London, 1966, p. 233, came to the conclusion that there existed a covenant

This double meaning of "Israel" can be discovered also in the narratives of other *šōpᵉṭîm*. "Israel" as the greater tribal community is found in the expression "liberation of Israel" in the story of Gideon's call (6:14, 15; cf. 6:36, 37), whereas the "Israel" called up by him against the Midianites (7:15; cf. 7:2, 8, 14, 23) consisted of at most the tribes Manasseh, Asher, Zebulun and Naphtali with the family Abiezer as its nucleus (6:34–35; 7:23). But the absence of Ephraim, the important member of the tribal community "Israel" (7:24–8:3), did not hinder Gideon's league from calling itself the "camp of Israel" (7:15). In the story of Jephthah, "Israel" often signifies "all the inhabitants of Gilead" (10:17; 11:4, 5, 26, 27, 33) who appointed him *rōʾš* and *qāṣîn* (10:18; 11:11). "Israel" here appears to have included a league of the tribes east of the Jordan in which at least Gilead and Manasseh participated (cf. 11:29).[58] On the other hand, the "history of the settlement of Israel" which he told the king of the Ammonites (11:15–23) is doubtless the history of the great tribal community of which the inhabitants of Gilead were a part. It is also probable that a custom of the lamentation over his daughter was observed in greater Israel (11:39–40). But it is difficult to assume that Jephthah, who repelled the Ephraimites with many casualties (12:1–6), was appointed *šōpēṭ* by all Israel in which Ephraim was included. Hence, "Israel" which Jephthah ruled (12:7) was the tribal league of Gilead upon which he presided as *rōʾš* and *qāṣîn*. In the same way, the "people of Israel" whom Ehud called up against the Moabites were the Ephraimo-Benjaminite league (3:15, 27), while "Israel" which Eli ruled (1 Sam 4:18) appears to have been a league formed by the tribes of central Palestine (cf. 4:1–18).[59] It is likely that the same tribes were lately re-organized by Samuel who led the resistance against the Philistines after the downfall of Shiloh (1 Sam 7:3–17).[60]

of the six northern tribes: Ephraim, Manasseh, Benjamin, Zebulun, Asher, and Naphtali, in the period of the Judges, and this covenant was "Israel in the limited sense of the term".

[58] M. Ottosson, *Gilead. Tradition and History* (CBOTS 3), Lund, 1969, pp. 155 ff., 169 ff., 246.

[59] Noth, *The History of Israel*, p. 166, suggested that in the first battle at Ebenezer a part of Israel fought, but in the second the whole confederation of the tribes, i.e., the amphictyony, participated in the war against the Philistines. It is clear that this suggestion was based on the hypothetical theory of the Israelite amphictyony.

[60] Since part of the chapter clearly reflects the situation after the victories of Saul and David, the historicity of 1 Sam 7 as a whole has been generally regarded as doubtfull. However, a number of scholars found some ancient traditions in this chapter, see Weiser, *Samuel*, pp. 5–24; W.F. Albright, *Samuel and the Beginnings of the*

In the story of Samson, "Israel" under the Philistine rule (Judg 13:5; 14:4) doubtless refers to the greater tribal community, but "Israel" which he ruled (15:20; 16:31) was evidently no more than the tribe Dan, certainly excluding neigbouring Judah (15:9–13). As for Tola (10:1–2) his formula: "After Abimelech there arose to deliver Israel Tola", and the fact that he lived in Ephraim, though he was a man of Issachar, would show that he also organized an Ephraimo-Issachar league against unknown enemies. From the other tradition about Jair (Num 32:41; Deut 3:14) we may suppose that he was also a war leader,[61] but his "Israel" was nothing more than sixty towns in Gilead (Judg 10:4; cf. Num 32:41; Deut 3:14; Josh 13:30; 1 Kgs 4:14; 1 Chr 2:22). The tradition about Ibzan's thirty sons and daughters (Judg 12:9) shows that he made many connections with other clans.[62] From this fact we may hold that Ibzan's "Israel" was a coalition formed by clans around Bethlehem, the town of Ibzan.[63] It is possible to assume a similar situation for Abdon (12:13–15) who had also forty sons and thirty grand-sons. Lastly, we may also suppose that "Israel" which Elon the Zebulunite ruled was the same sort of coalition of the clans in the land of Zebulun (12:11–12). Owing to the nature of the sources it is difficult to prove positively that "Israel" ruled by these *šōp̄ᵉṭîm* designated a tribal league or a coalition of clans. But this is the most suitable explanation for the term "Israel" here, if we accept neither the hypothesis of the Israelite amphictyony, nor regarded it as an anachronistic usage of the term.

The account of Othniel (3:9–11) preserves the act of the deliverer-*šōp̄ᵉṭîm* in the briefest form[64] as follows:

Prophetic Movement, Cincinnati, 1961, p. 14; H. Seebass, "Traditionsgeschichte von I Sam 8, $10_{17\,\text{ff.}}$ und 12", *ZAW* 77 (1965), pp. 292 ff.; idem, "Die Vorgeschichte der Königserhebung Sauls", *ZAW* 79 (1967), pp. 155 ff.; B. Mazar, "The Philistines and their Wars with Israel", in B. Mazar (ed.), *WHJP* I/III: *Judges*, Tel-Aviv, 1971, pp. 177 f.; cf. also F. Langlamet, "Les récits de l'institution de la royauté (I Sam., VII–XII). De Wellhausen aux travaux récents", *RB* 77 (1970), p. 170; Ishida, *The Royal Dynasties*, pp. 33 f.; McCarter, *I Samuel*, pp. 148–151.

[61] Malamat, in *WHJP* I/III: *Judges*, p. 131.

[62] Burney, *The Book of Judges*, p. 289.

[63] For the international treaties which were generally concluded by marriage between royal houses, see A. Malamat, "Aspects of the Foreign Policies of David and Solomon", *JNES* 22 (1963), pp. 8 ff., who particularly dealt with the foreign marital ties of David and Solomon; cf. also J.D. Levenson and B. Halpern, "The Political Import of David's Marriages", *JBL* 99 (1980), pp. 507–518.

[64] According to Noth, *Überlieferungsgeschichtliche Studien*, pp. 50 f., Judg 3:7–11 came from the Deuteronomistic historian. Richter, *Bearbeitungen*, pp. 23 ff., 52 ff., 90 f., 114 f., held that this section was composed as "*Beispielstück*" by Rdt_2 under the

a) the deliverer received Yahweh's spirit (charisma);
b) *wayyišpōṭ ʾeṯ-yiśrāʾēl*;
c) he went out war, and Yahweh gave his enemy into his hand;
d) the land rested until his death.

What was, then, *wayyišpōṭ ʾeṯ-yiśrāʾēl* which took place between receiving Yahweh's spirit and going out to war? Since the meaning "to judge" in judicial proceedings for the term *šāp̄aṭ* does not fit well for the context, either this verb has been understood as a synonym for *hôšîaʿ* standing in the previous verse[65] or the whole sentence has been omitted as a gloss.[66] But while H.C. Thomson interpreted it as asking the will of God,[67] Y. Kaufmann explained it as "to muster Israel", i.e., "to organize them for war".[68] In my opinion, Kaufmann's elucidation is correct, fitting the situation as corroborated by other cases of the deliverer-*šōp̄ᵉṭîm*. As is well known, in the narrative on Saul's campaign against the Ammonites (1 Sam 11:1–11), he behaves according to the tradition of the deliverer-*šōp̄ᵉṭîm*.[69] After being infused with God's spirit, he sent a call-up throughout all the territory of Israel, and at Bezek those who answered his call were organized into a tribal league called "Israel" (11:5–8).[70] It is clearly told that Gideon

influence of Deuteronomy before the final redaction of the Deuteronomistic history; cf. J.A. Soggin, *Judges. A Commentary* (OTL), London, 1981, pp. 45 f. However, though the narrative is highly schematic, it is hardly true that this is a pure Deuteronomistic composition, see Burney, *The Book of Judges*, pp. 64 f.; H.W. Hertzberg, *Die Bücher Josua, Richter, Ruth* (ATD 9), Göttingen, 1959², pp. 163 f.; J. Gray, *Joshua, Judges and Ruth* (NCB), London, 1967, pp. 213 ff.; Boling, *Judges*, pp. 82 f.; cf. A. Malamat, "Cushan Rishathaim and the Decline of the Near East around 1200 B.C.", *JNES* 13 (1954), pp. 231–242.

[65] G.F. Moore, *A Critical and Exegetical Commentary on Judges* (ICC), Edinburgh, 1898², p. 88; Burney, *The Book of Judges*, p. 66; Gray, *Joshua, Judges and Ruth*, p. 261.

[66] Richter, *Bearbeitungen*, pp. 25, 61.

[67] Thomson, *TGUOS* 19 (1961–62), p. 78. Referring to Samuel's action (1 Sam 7:5–6), Boling, *Judges*, p. 83, found in it that "he (= Othniel) presided over a confessional reaffirmation of ultimate loyalties".

[68] Kaufmann, *The Book of Judges*, p. 104; cf. according to Fensham, *OTWSA* 2 (1959), p. 18, the meaning of *špṭ* here is "to act as a charismatic leader".

[69] A. Alt, "Die Staatenbildung der Israeliten in Palästina" (1930), in *Kleine Schriften zur Geschichte des Volkes Israel* II, München, 1953, pp. 17 ff.; W. Beyerlin, "Das Königscharisma bei Saul", *ZAW* 73 (1961), p. 188.

[70] "The men of Judah..." (11:8) is clearly a secondary insertion which reflects the dualism in the period of the kingdom, see Richter, *ZAW* 77 (1965), p. 52. According to Schunck, *Benjamin*, p. 90, the whole verse is a late addition except *wayyip̄qᵉḏēm bᵉḇāzeq*. Opinions are divided on the extent of the tribal league "Israel" organized by Saul at that time. Noth, *The History of Israel*, p. 169, held that the whole confederation of the twelve tribes participated in the campaign, while K. Möhlenbrink, "Sauls Ammoniterfeldzug und Samuels Beitrag zum Königtum

acted after the same pattern, i.e., receiving Yahweh's spirit and organizing a tribal league before going to war (Judg 6:34–35). In the case of Deborah, who was also divinely inspired as indicated by her title "prophetess" (4:4), her attempt to organize a tribal league against the Canaanites was recorded, it seems, in general (4:4–5) as well as in detail (4:6–10). After having fulfilled his divine ordination by assassination of the Moabite king (3:15–25), Ehud succeeded in organizing a tribal league in the hill country of Ephraim (3:27). Although it appears that the Gilead league had been organized before Jephthah was invited (10:17–18), in reality, the league could not function until he took office. Moreover, it is also told that after having received Yahweh's spirit he organized a league of Gilead and Manasseh before going to war (11:29).

These examples clearly show that *šōp̄ᵉṭîm* were military leaders who rose up when Yahweh's spirit came upon them, organized local tribal confederations called "Israel" (*wayyišpōṭ ʾeṯ-yiśrāʾēl*), and went to war as the commander of the army of their confederations. Deborah also follows this pattern in going to war as the supreme commander, though Barak was her chief of staff (4:8–9; 5:15). After having established their charismatic ordination through victories in the field, these military leaders assumed the rulership of the tribal leagues which they organized (*wayyišpōṭ ʾeṯ-yiśrāʾēl*). Their office was for life, but their authority was not extended to their descendants. An exception was Abimelech, who succeeded Gideon (Judg 9). But his kingdom was established outside Israel, and his control over "Israel" was not regarded as the rule of *šōp̄ēṭ* as the different verb *śārar* instead of *šāp̄aṭ* for his rule may indicate (9:22).[71]

5. *From the* Šōp̄ēṭ-*Regime to Monarchy*

With the ever increasing pressure of the Philistines in the mid–11th century B.C., the Israelite tribes realized that the tribal leagues organ-

des Saul", *ZAW* 58 (1940/41), pp. 57–70, thought that only Benjamin and the tribes east of the Jordan came to fight under Saul's command; cf. G. Wallis, "Die Anfänge des Königtums in Israel", *WZ Halle* 12 (1963), pp. 242 f. In my opinion, in addition to the tribes of central Palestine and from east of the Jordan, of whom Saul's main force consisted, the other tribes from "all the territory of Israel" (v. 7) sent contingents to the campaign, see Ishida, *The Royal Dynasties,* pp. 36 f.

[71] Malamat, in *WHJP* I/III: *Judges*, p. 151.

ized occasionally by charismatic leaders and dissolving with their death could not defend them against this new, better organized and equipped enemy. Thereupon, it appears that the tribes of central Palestine organized a league centered around the shrine at Shiloh and appointed Eli the priest as its leader. Thus he became a "priest-*šōpēṭ*" (cf. 1 Sam 4:18). This move must be regarded as an attempt to establish the stable system of the tribal league. Since the priesthood belonged to certain families as hereditary office in ancient Israel,[72] it appears that the intention was to establish the hereditary succession of the office of the leader of the league through Eli's house. The institutional change can also be found in the fact that Eli, though he was a ruler of the league, no longer took command in battle but entrusted the elders of "Israel", i.e., the representatives of the league, with the responsibility for the military operations (4:3). In the catastrophe after the defeat at Ebenezer it was Samuel who made a great effort to re-establish the unity of the tribes of central Palestine to offer resistance against the Philistine rule. It is not surprising that Samuel, whose charisma had been revealed as a "prophet of Yahweh" at Shiloh in his youth (3:19–4:1a), became the rebuilder of the league of Shiloh destroyed by the Philistines. Thus we may call him "prophet-*šōpēṭ*" (cf. 7:15–17).[73] It is interesting to note that his confederation took over the institutional change which had begun

[72] de Vaux, *Ancient Israel*, pp. 359 f.; A. Cody, *A History of Old Testament Priesthood* (AnBib 35), Rome, 1969, p. 60; M. Haran, *Temples and Temple-Service in Ancient Israel. An Inquiry into Biblical Cult Phenomena and the Historical Setting of the Priestly School*, Winona Lake, 1985, pp. 58 ff.

[73] M. Newman, "The Prophetic Call of Samuel", in *Israel's Prophetic Heritage. Essays in Honor of J. Muilenburg*, London, 1962, pp. 86–97, held that Samuel the prophet took over the functions of the covenant mediator of the amphictyony formerly exercised by Eli the priest and transmitted them to the charismatic prophets. M.A. Cohen, "The Role of the Shilonite Priesthood in the United Monarchy of Ancient Israel", *HUCA* 36 (1965), pp. 65 ff., maintained that Samuel's authority was derived from his position as the Shilonite seer-priest; cf. H.M. Orlinsky, "The Seer-Priest", in B. Mazar (ed.), *WHJP* I/III: *Judges*, Tel-Aviv, 1971, p. 273. According to the analysis of M. Noth, "Samuel und Silo", *VT* 13 (1963), pp. 390–400, 1 Sam 3 was composed by an author who wanted to show the close relation of Samuel to Shilo by combining the Shilonite tradition (1 Sam 1; 2:11, 18–21) and the Jerusalemite tradition (2:12–17, 22–36). Although a Jerusalemite polemic against Shiloh is clearly found in 1 Sam 2:35, it appears to me that the narratives on the sins of Eli's sons and the punishment of his house (2:12–17, 22–36; 3:1–18) were originally composed as Samuel's apology against the descendants of the house of Eli, when Samuel took over the league of the central tribes; cf. J.T. Willis, "An Anti-Elide Narrative Tradition from a Prophetic Circle at the Ramah Sanctuary", *JBL* 90 (1971), pp. 288–308.

at Shiloh. Accordingly, he did not take command in war, though he played a priestly role as the leader of the confederation (7:5–11). In addition, he made clear the hereditary character of his office by appointing his sons to *šōpᵉṭîm lᵉyiśrāʾēl* (8:1).[74]

But the fact that Samuel had to change the center of his league from place to place instead of the permanent center like Shiloh (7:16–17) shows that his activity was limited to a high degree under the Philistine supremacy. It is very likely that the Philistines succeeded in paralysing Samuel's league even though they had been unexpectedly defeated near Mizpah (cf. 7:10–11 and 9:16). It is possible, however, that the Philistines preferred indirect rule and therefore allowed Samuel to continue to act as the leader of the league.[75] Indeed, if Samuel had been a "deliverer-*šōpēṭ*", who was capable of mobilizing his tribal league, the elders of Jabesh besieged by the Ammonites would have sent their messengers directly to him (cf. 11:1–4). It was only Saul's spontaneous heroic action after the traditional manner of the charismatic leaders called *šōpᵉṭîm*, which was able to muster the Israelite army for the relief of Jabesh (11:5–7).[76] Now realizing the limitations of the old *šōpēṭ*-regime, Samuel, the last "*šōpēṭ*", finally gave in to the elders of "Israel", who had asked him to appoint a king (8:5, 6, 20), and took the initiative to establish the first monarchy in Israel.[77]

From the foregoing study we can come to the conclusion that the formula *wayyišpōṭ* (or *šāpaṭ*) *ʾeṯ-yiśrāʾēl* is used as a sort of *terminus technicus* signifying the charismatic leaders who spontaneously rose up, organized tribal leagues called "Israel", and ruled over them until their death. This government of *šōpēṭ* corresponds exactly to the socio-

---

[74] A note on the appointment of Samuel's sons as *šōpᵉṭîm* in Beer-sheba (1 Sam 8:2) would show that Samuel's tribal league tried to invite the southern tribes. It is possible that the name of another town in which the second son was appointed was found in the original text, see McKenzie, *VT* 17 (1967), p. 121. Richter, *ZAW* 77 (1965), p. 59, pointed out that among a triple accusation against Samuel's sons: turning aside after gain, taking bribes, and perverting justice (8:3), while the last two belong to the *Richterspiegel*, the first can be referred to every ruler.

[75] Albright, *Samuel and the Beginnings of the Prophetic Movement*, p. 14.

[76] "Samuel" in 1 Sam 11:7 is generally regarded as an addition, see J.A. Soggin, *Das Königtum in Israel. Ursprünge, Spannungen, Entwicklung* (BZAW 104), Berlin, 1967, p. 44. But some scholars do not accept the omission of the name "Samuel", see H.W. Hertzberg, *I & II Samuel. A Commentary* (OTL), London, 1964, p. 90, n. b; Weiser, *Samuel*, pp. 26, 70, 75. It is possible to assume that Samuel co-operated with Saul by supporting the latter's charismatic action.

[77] For the historical process of the establishment of the monarchy see Ishida, *The Royal Dynasties*, pp. 31 ff.

political conditions of the Israelite tribes which occasionally formed tribal leagues for reasons of self-defense in the period prior to the formation of the monarchy.[78] The largest league was organized by Deborah-Barak with six tribes, but generally only several tribes came together to make a local league.

Then, when did this term take root in Israel? It is unlikely that this terminology was current in the time of the charismatic leaders called *šōp̄ᵉṭîm*, because none of them had this title in their own narratives. A. van Selms suggested that the editor of the Book of Judges borrowed the title *šōp̄ᵉṭîm* from city-states at the coast in the period of Hezekiah,[79] but, as has been pointed out, they were already called *šōp̄ᵉṭîm* in Nathan's prophecy (2 Sam 7:7 = 1 Chr 17:6) originating in the early monarchical period. In addition, since it is very clear that the term *šōp̄ēṭ* generally referred to a "judge" in the judicial sense of the term in the late monarchical period, it is difficult to imagine that the editor of the Book of Judges, or the Deuteronomistic historian, as Noth, Richter and others think, chose exactly this term for indicating the leaders of pre-monarchical Israel.[80] In my opinion, the earliest evidence for the word *šōp̄ēṭ* as a leader of the tribal league can be found in the appointment of Samuel's sons as *šōp̄ᵉṭîm lᵉyiśrā'ēl* (1 Sam 8:1). It is not incidental that this terminology appears in Samuel's last years, because it is very likely that the people, who were looking for a king "governing them like all the nations", keenly felt the necessity of a terminology for the earlier system of the government and its leader in order to differentiate it from the terminology of the newly established monarchy.[81]

---

[78] Cf. Malamat, in *WHJP* I/III: *Judges*, pp. 129 f.

[79] van Selms, *OTWSA* 2 (1959), pp. 49 f.

[80] Prof. A. Malamat suggested to me that the West Semitic word *špṭ* might have originally a double connotation, i.e., "to judge" and "to govern, to rule", of which the first was dominant in urban society like Ugarit, while the second originated in the tribal society like Mari. In Israel co-existed both tribal and sedentary traditions from the beginning. It is interesting to note that Kutscher, *Lešonénu* 32 (1967/68), p. 274, suggested that the term *špṭ* might be a latecomer to biblical Hebrew, since it does not occur in early biblical poetry.

[81] Rozenberg, *The Stem špṭ*:, pp. 88 f., thought that the reason why the term *šōp̄ēṭ* as a title does not appear in the early period is to be found in the transitory nature of the regime of the *šōp̄ēṭ*; see also idem, "The *Šōfᵉṭīm* in the Bible", in B. Mazar (ed.), *Nelson Glueck Memorial Volume* (Eretz-Israel 12), Jerusalem, 1975, pp. 85* f.; cf. E.A. Speiser, "Background and Function of the Biblical Nāśī'", *CBQ* 25 (1963), p. 117. It may look strange, however, that there was no definite terminology for the regime of *šōp̄ēṭ* when it was fully functioning. But, since this was not common established regime in the ancient Near East like, for instance, monarchy, the designations of

As for the name "Israel", in the pre-monarchical time it simultaneously indicated the whole as well as part of the tribal community. Similarly, the same usage is found in the narratives about the United Kingdom, where "Israel" refers to the United Kingdom, to the northern tribes, or to a part thereof.[82] Hence the people who did find fundamental difference between the government of *šōpēṭ* and monarchy could on the other hand apply the same term "Israel" in its general and particular senses.

---

the regime and its leader could be fixed only after a long experience. B. Halpern, *The Emergence of Israel in Canaan* (SBLM 29), Chico, 1983, p. 207, dare not "determine when the judge-titulature arose", although he inclines "to concede the existence of some national structures before Saul's time, one of which was the position of the Judge".

[82] "Israel" for the United Kingdom or all the tribes of Israel: 2 Sam 6:1; 10:9; 11:1; 17:11, etc.; for the northern tribes: 2 Sam 3:10; 5:1–3; 1 Kgs 1:35, etc.; for a part of the northern tribes: 2 Sam 2:9 (Gilead, Asher?, Jezreel, Ephraim, and Benjamin); 2:28 (Benjamin, cf. 2:25); 3:19 (the northern tribes except Benjamin); cf. H.-U. Nübel, *Davids Aufstieg in der frühe israelitischer Geschichtsschreibung* (Diss.), Bonn, 1959, pp. 109 f.; Richter, *ZAW* 77 (1965), pp. 50 ff.

CHAPTER THREE

NĀḠÎḎ: THE TERM FOR THE LEGITIMIZATION OF THE KINGSHIP*

1. *Four Theses on the Title Nāḡîḏ*

The title *nāḡîḏ* is sometimes applied to royalty in the Hebrew Bible. Although many suggestions have been made about the function of the title, its exact meaning still remains undecided.[1] The suggestions made may be grouped under the following four categories:

a) A sacral title from pre-monarchical times: a charismatic war-leader,[2] a title connected with the Israelite amphictyony;[3]

b) A future king: a king designate,[4] an heir apparent,[5] a crown prince;[6]

c) A synonym for the term *meleḵ*: a Deuteronomistic term for the national leader;[7]

d) A politico-administrative title: a prefect.[8]

---

* This essay is a revised version of the study which appeared in *AJBI* 3 (1977), pp. 35–51.

[1] For an extensive bibliography and a summary of various views see G.F. Hasel, "נגיד", in *TWAT* V, Stuttgart, 1984–86, cols. 203–219.

[2] A. Alt, "Die Staatenbildung der Israeliten in Palästina" (1930), in *Kleine Schriften zur Geschichte des Volkes Israel* II, München, 1953, p. 23; W.F. Albright, *Samuel and the Beginnings of the Prophetic Movement*, Cincinnati, 1961, pp. 15 f.; W. Richter, "Die *nāḡīd*-Formel. Ein Beitrag zur Erhellung des *nāḡīd*-Problems", *BZ* 9 (1965), pp. 71–84; L. Schmidt, *Menschlicher Erfolg und Jahwes Initiative. Studien zu Tradition, Interpretation und Historie in Überlieferungen von Gideon, Saul, und David* (WMANT 38), Neukirchen-Vluyn, 1970, pp. 152 ff.

[3] M. Noth, "David und Israel in 2. Samuel 7" (1957), in *Gesammelte Studien zum Alten Testament*, München, 1960², pp. 335 f.; H. Gese, "Der Davidsbund und die Zionserwählung", *ZTK* 61 (1964), p. 23.

[4] M. Noth, The History of Israel, London, 1960², p. 169, n. 1.

[5] T.C.G. Thornton, "Charismatic Kingship in Israel and Judah", *JTS* 14 (1963), p. 8.

[6] E. Lipiński, "*Nāgîd*, der Kronprinz", *VT* 24 (1974), pp. 497–499; T.N.D. Mettinger, *King and Messiah. The Civil and Sacral Legitimation of the Israelite Kings* (CBOTS 8), Lund, 1976, pp. 151–184.

[7] R.A. Carlson, *David the chosen King. A Traditio-Historical Approach to the Second Book of Samuel*, Stockholm/Göteborg/Uppsala, 1964, pp. 52 ff.; cf. T. Veijola, *Die ewige Dynastie. David und die Entstehung seiner Dynastie nach der deuteronomistischen Darstellung*, Helsinki, 1975, pp. 52 ff., 129, 139, 141.

[8] G.C. Macholz, "NAGID—der Statthalter, 'praefectus'", in *Sefer Rendtorff. R. Rendtorff*

Since the etymology of the term has not yet been clarified satisfactorily,[9] the validity of each theory can be confirmed only through examination of its aptness to the context of the passages in which the term is used as a royal title. The texts in question are as follows:

Saul

1) Now the day before Saul came, Yahweh had revealed to Samuel, "Tomorrow about this time I will send to you a man from the land of Benjamin, and you shall anoint him to be *nāḡîḏ* over my people Israel. He shall save my people from the hand of the Philistines" (1 Sam 9:15–16).

2) Then Samuel took a vial of oil and poured it on his head, and kissed him and said, "Has not Yahweh anointed you to be *nāḡîḏ* over his people Israel? And you shall reign over the people of Yahweh and you will save them from the hand of their enemies round about" (10:1 LXX).

David

3) And Samuel said to Saul, "You have done foolishly . . . . . for now Yahweh would have established your kingdom over Israel for ever. But now your kingdom shall not continue; Yahweh has sought out a man after his own heart; and Yahweh has appointed him to be *nāḡîḏ* over his people" (13:13–14).[10]

4) When Abigail saw David . . . . . she fell at his feet and said, "Upon me alone, my lord, be the guilt . . . . . and when Yahweh has done to my lord according to all the good that he has spoken concerning you, and has appointed you *nāḡîḏ* over Israel, my lord shall have no cause of grief . . . . ." (25:23–24, 30–31).

5) Then all the tribes of Israel came to David at Hebron, and said,

---

Festschrift (Dielheimer Blätter zum Alten Testament 1), Dielheim, 1975, pp. 59–72.

[9] On the basis of an assumed connection with the preposition *neḡeḏ*, the original meaning of the term is generally explained as "one who stands in front" (active form) or "one placed in front" (passive form); but we cannot even decide whether the form is active or passive; see Richter, *BZ* 9 (1965), p. 72, n. 6; J. Liver, "נגיד", in *Encyclopaedia Biblica* V, Jerusalem, 1968, col. 753 (Hebrew). An attempt to relate the term *nōqēḏ* by J.J. Glück, "Nagid-Shepherd", *VT* 13 (1963), pp. 144–150, has been judged unsuccessful, see Richter, *BZ* 9 (1965), pp. 72 f., n. 7. Another suggestion was made by Mettinger, *King and Messiah*, pp. 158–162, 182, according to which the word *nāḡîḏ* is "understood as a Qal passive participle of the root *n-g-d*": to proclaim (*lᵉhaggîḏ*). "The sense of the term is then 'the one proclaimed', 'the one designated'" (p. 182). As he observaed, there seems to be a word play between the word *lᵉhaggîḏ* and the term *nāḡîḏ* in the biblical narratives. Then is it a *Volksetimologie* in the biblical time? See B. Halpern, *The Emergence of Israel in Canaan* (SBLM 29), Chico, 1983, p. 200, n. 50.

[10] The name David is implicit in this passage; see H.W. Hertzberg, *I & II Samuel* (OTL), London, 1964, p. 105; P.K. McCarter, *I Samuel. A New Translation with Introduction, Notes and Commentary* (AB 8), Garden City, N.Y., 1980, p. 229.

"Behold, we are your bone and flesh. In times past, when Saul was king over us, it was you that led out and brought in Israel; and Yahweh said to you: You shall be shepherd of my people Israel, and you shall be *nāğîḏ* over Israel" (2 Sam 5:1–3; cf. 1 Chr 11:1–2).

6) And David said to Michal, "It was before Yahweh, who chose me above your father, and above all his house, to appoint me as *nāğîḏ* over Israel, the people of Yahweh" (2 Sam 6:21).

7) Thus says Yahweh of hosts, "I took you from the pasture, from following the sheep, that you should be *nāğîḏ* over my people Israel (2 Sam 7:8; cf. 1 Chr 17:7).

8) And he said, "Blessed be Yahweh, the God of Israel, who with his hand has fulfilled what he promised with his mouth to David my father, saying: Since the day that I brought my people out of the land of Egypt, I chose no city in all the tribes of Israel in which to build a house, that my name might be there, and I chose no man as *nāğîḏ* over my people Israel; but I have chosen Jerusalem that my name may be there and I have chosen David to be over my people Israel" (2 Chr 6:4–6).[11]

Solomon

9) King David said, "Call to me Zadok the priest, Nathan the prophet, and Benaiah the son of Jehoiada". So they came before the king. And the king said to them, "Take with you the servants of your lord, and cause Solomon my son to ride on my own mule, and bring him down to Gihon; and let Zadok the priest and Nathan the prophet there anoint him king over Israel; then blow the trumpet, and say: Long live King Solomon! You shall then come up after him, and he shall come and sit upon my throne; for he shall be king in my stead; and I have appointed him to be *nāğîḏ* over Israel and over Judah" (1 Kgs 1:32–35).

10) And they made Solomon the son of David king the second time, and they anointed him as *nāğîḏ* for Yahweh, and Zadok as priest (1 Chr 29:22b).

Abijah

11) And Rehoboam appointed Abijah the son of Maacah as chief, as *nāğîḏ* among his brothers, for he intended to make him king (2 Chr 11:22).

Jeroboam the son of Nebat

12) Thus says Yahweh, the God of Israel, "Because I exalted you from among the people, and made you *nāğîḏ* over my people Israel, and

[11] The name David is implicit also in the following text: "Though Judah became strong among his brothers and a *nāğîḏ* was from him . . ." (1 Chr 5:2). In a similar context the tribe Judah is called *nāğîḏ*: "Then King David rose to his feet and said: . . . Yahweh, the God of Israel, chose me from all my father's house to be king over Israel for ever; for he chose Judah as *nāğîḏ* . . ." (1 Chr 28: 2, 4).

tore the kingdom away from the house of David and gave it to you . . . . ." (1 Kgs 14:7–8).

Baasha
13) And the word of Yahweh came to Jehu the son of Hanani against Baasha, saying, "Since I exalted you out of the dust and made you *nāgîḏ* over my people Israel . . . . ." (16:1–2).

Hezekiah
14) And before Isaiah had gone out of the middle court, the word of Yahweh came to him, "Turn back, and say to Hezekiah *nāgîḏ* of my people, thus says Yahweh, the God of David your father: I have heard your prayer . . . . . behold, I will heal you . . . . ." (2 Kgs 20:4–5).

Hereafter we will refer to these texts by the numbers given here.

2. *A Critical Reconsideration of the Previous Theses*

Apparently, the first suggestion, which regards *nāgîḏ* as a sacral title originating in pre-monarchical Israel, has enjoyed the widest approval. This thesis is based mainly on the fact that the title *nāgîḏ* appears in most cases in connection with Yahweh's designation of a future ruler over Israel, his people. But difficulties arise for this thesis in the cases of both Solomon (no. 9) and Abijah (no. 11) who were appointed to be *nāgîḏ* not by Yahweh but by the reigning monarch.[12] Accordingly, the advocates of this thesis dismiss these cases as exceptional and settle the problem by speaking of a misuse of the term.[13] Even if this explanation were to be accepted, the thesis of the pre-monarchical Israelite origin of the title is hardly convincing. The most serious argument against it is the complete absence of evidence of its attribution to anybody prior to Saul.[14]

As to the second thesis, it is not easy to apply the meaning "crown prince" or "heir apparent" to five monarchs (Saul, David, Jeroboam, Baasha and Hezekiah) out of the seven kings whose designation as *nāgîḏ* is reported, since four of them were founders of their own dynasties and Hezekiah was by no means a future king, but had long been a reigning king when called "*nāgîḏ* of my people" (no. 14).

---

[12] In text no. 10, Solomon was anointed as *nāgîḏ* by the people; this text must be dealt with separately, see below p. 67.

[13] Alt, in *Kleine Schriften* II, p. 62, n. 1; cf. Richter, *BZ* 9 (1965), p. 77.

[14] Cf. Liver, in *Encyclopaedia Biblica* V, cols. 753 f. (Hebrew); Lipiński, *VT* 24 (1974), p. 498; B. Halpern, *The Constitution of the Monarchy in Israel* (HSM 25), Chico, 1981, pp. 3–6.

Moreover, Jotham the son of Azariah really deserved the title "crown prince" when he acted as regent for his leprous father, but he was called simply "the king's son" (2 Kgs 15:5); this expression doubtless corresponds to *mār šarri* in Akkadian, which denotes "crown prince, designated successor".[15] The more general definition "king designate" fits the whole situation better. Still, we can hardly explain Hezekiah's case on the basis of this assumption. In addition, it is worth asking why the title *nāḡîḏ* was borne by only seven monarchs out of the 42 kings of Israel and Judah.

The third theory that takes the term *nāḡîḏ* to be a Deuteronomistic synonym for the term *meleḵ* seems unjustified. We should again draw our attention to the fact that the title was applied to only one sixth of all the kings of Israel and Judah. If the term had been Deuteronomistic, this title would have been borne by every king, since the Deuteronomists were, as is accepted, responsible for the compilation of the Books of the Kings.[16] Admittedly, it seems to be a synonym for the term *meleḵ* in many instances. However, it is definitely not so in the case of Solomon (no. 9) and Abijah (no. 11). In both the cases, the term must have an implication other than *meleḵ*. Otherwise, these sentences do not make sense.

In the opinion of Macholz, who has advanced the last theory, the term *nāḡîḏ* signifies the politico-administrative function of "praefectus" in Latin, i.e., the possessor of the ruling power. He derives it from the passages concerning David's appointment of Solomon as *nāḡîḏ* (no. 9), where, according to his interpretation, the former entrusted the latter with the governance over Israel and Judah. He maintains further, that in all the other instances, where Yahweh designated a king as *nāḡîḏ*, the original implication of the term was adapted to a theological explanation of the structure of the Israelite kingship, which was actually Yahweh's kingship entrusted to a human king.[17] The thesis seems unwarranted, since it is precisely in those

[15] *AHw*, p. 615b; *CAD* Š/2 pp. 105–109. F.M. Cross, "The Stele Dedicated to Melcarth by Ben-Hadad of Damascus", *BASOR* 205 (1972), p. 41, reads בר מלך ארם in the Melcarth Stele and translates the words as "crown prince of Aram", but this reading remains a tentative suggestion; cf. J.C.L. Gibson, *Textbook of Syrian Semitic Inscriptions* II: *Aramaic Inscriptions*, Oxford, 1975, pp. 3 f.

[16] From the fact that a priest of the Temple in Jerusalem had the title *nāḡîḏ* in the last days of the kingdom of Judah (Jer 20:1) we may suppose that this title was applied not only to royalty but also to any appointee as the head in the days of the Deuteronomists.

[17] Macholz, in *Sefer Rendtorff*, pp. 65 ff.

texts where the relation between Yahweh's kingship and the Israelite monarchy is dealt with in the most serious manner, as in the narrative on Samuel's choosing of Saul as king by lot at Mizpah (1 Sam 10:17–27) and Samuel's farewell speech (1 Sam 12), that the term *nāḡîḏ* is not used. On the other hand, it is unlikely, as I will discuss presently, that the problem of Yahweh's kingship is the main theme of the narrative about Samuel's anointing of Saul as *nāḡîḏ* (1 Sam 9:1–10:16). Nor is it easy to assume that the same problem is dealt with in "the History of David's Rise" in which the term *nāḡîḏ* is used most frequently.[18] We are also skeptical of Macholz's method, according to which he sets as the starting-point Solomon's designation as *nāḡîḏ*, by assuming the function of *nāḡîḏ* in other instances to be secondary.[19] The function of *nāḡîḏ* must have been the same, at least in contemporary sources.

3. *The Situations in which the Title* Nāḡîḏ *is mentioned*

From the observations of the fourteen texts cited above, together with the foregoing examination of the four theses on *nāḡîḏ*, it seems possible to draw the following conclusions:

a) The title *nāḡîḏ* was introduced into ancient Israel only with the establishment of Saul's monarchy.

b) It was applied solely to the kings from the period of the early monarchies, i.e., from Saul to Baasha, with the sole exception of Hezekiah. Accordingly, it seems justifiable to deal with Hezekiah's case separately.

c) It was a royal title, but not an exact synonym for the term *meleḵ*.

d) It was mentioned in connection only with the designation as rulers of the following six kings: Saul, David, Solomon, Jeroboam, Baasha and Abijah.

e) Four kings from the same period did not bear the title; they are Ishbaal, Rehoboam, Nadab and Asa.

---

[18] For "the History of David's Rise" see Mettinger, *King and Messiah*, pp. 33 ff.; T. Ishida, *The Royal Dynasties in Ancient Israel. A Study on the Formation and Development of Royal-Dynastic Ideology* (BZAW 142), Berlin/New York, 1977, pp. 55 ff.; McCarter, *I Samuel*, pp. 27 ff.

[19] Macholz, in *Sefer Rendtorff*, pp. 59 ff., adopted this method from Lipiński's study in *VT* 24 (1974), pp. 497–499; cf. also Mettinger, *King and Messiah*, pp. 158–171.

Under these circumstances, it appears important to make clear the situations in which these six monarchs were appointed to be *nāgîḏ*. In comparing them with the other four, who did not bear the title, one circumstance immediately stands out. All of the six monarchs had serious problems in one way or another, when they ascended the throne, whereas the other four kings succeeded to their own fathers' thrones without having any difficulty over the legitimacy of their kingship. To be specific, Saul, David, Jeroboam and Baasha were founders of their own dynasties; Solomon barely succeeded in getting the designation as king (1 Kgs 1:5–53); and Abijah was chosen as successor to the throne out of 26 brothers (2 Chr 11:21–22), although he seems not to have been the eldest son.[20]

This argument is supported by an examination of each of the texts concerning the designation of these six kings as *nāgîḏ* (nos. 1–13). I have demonstrated elsewhere, that the theme of the narrative about Samuel's anointing of Saul as *nāgîḏ* (nos. 1, 2) should be regarded as Saul's claim to the divine election of his kingship, in order to limit the voice of the people of Israel, who had originally elevated him to the kingship.[21] Then, the main concern of this narrative is to be found in Saul's attempt to legitimatize his kingship. All the texts about David's designation as *nāgîḏ* (nos. 3–8) are obviously connected with the theme of the defense of the legitimacy of his kingship against the house of Saul by underlining Yahweh's election of him instead of Saul.[22] Yahweh's designation of Jeroboam, the son of Nebat, is told side by side with his election from among the people and his acquisition of part of the kingdom which had been ruled under the house of David (no. 12). We may assume that this passage was originally Jeroboam's legitimization to the people of his monarchy as against that of the house of David, although the present text was written in the form of a prophetic accusation against him. Similarly, Baasha's appointment as *nāgîḏ* is combined with his divine election "out of the dust" (no. 13). It seems that the expression "out of the dust" corresponds to the Akkadian phrase *mār lā mammānim* "son of nobody", which denotes a usurper.[23] Therefore,

[20] The principle of primogeniture was fundamental to the royal succession of the throne of David, but it was often overruled; see Ishida, *The Royal Dynasties*, pp. 155 ff.

[21] See ibid., pp. 49 f.

[22] About the legitimization of the kingship of David, see ibid., pp. 55 ff.

[23] *AHw*, p. 601a; *CAD* M/1 pp. 200 f. W. Brueggemann, "From Dust to Kingship",

we can find here also the legitimization of a king who usurped the throne.

In contrast to these dynastic founders, both Solomon (no. 9) and Abijah (no. 11) were appointed to be *nāgîḏ* not by Yahweh but by David and Rehoboam, respectively. This fact reflects a situation in which legitimization in the framework of the dynastic succession was based mainly on the authorization of the reigning monarch, while the founders of dynasties could derive their legitimization solely from their divine election.[24] It is also worth noting that, in the appointment of both Solomon and Abijah, the appointment as *nāgîḏ* clearly took place prior to the accession to the throne. This order shows a logical procedure: first, the reigning king's designation of his successor, then, the latter's enthronement. In other words, the designation as *nāgîḏ* was the precondition for enthronement.

The situation was quite different in the case of the appointment of the founders of dynasties as *nāgîḏ* by Yahweh. For them, it was not an actual condition for their elevation to the kingship. The tradition that Saul was "a handsome young man" (1 Sam 9:2) when designated as *nāgîḏ* shows that his title *nāgîḏ* stemmed from a retrospective interpretation of the historical facts, which brought about his monarchy. David had other circumstances. The term *nāgîḏ* is not used in the story of Yahweh's election of David in his youth (16:1–13).[25] This story emphasizes that Yahweh had already chosen David as king instead of Saul while the latter was still reigning. David was already king (cf. 5:1) while he was keeping the sheep (5:11). Accordingly, he had no need to be first designated as *nāgîḏ*, at least in this highly ideological story, before he was anointed king. In all the six texts about David's designation as *nāgîḏ* (nos. 3–8), the title *nāgîḏ* has noth-

ZAW 84 (1972), pp. 2 f., maintains that this royal formula of enthronement lies behind the creation formula in Gen 3:19 and finds a parallel between the downfall of Baasha and his house (1 Kgs 16:3) and Yahweh's sentence on Adam: "to dust you will return". It is unlikely, however, that the prophecy about the destruction of the royal house was included in the original formula of enthronement.

[24] Mettinger, *King and Messiah*, pp. 151 ff., maintained that the theological use of the term *nāgîḏ* to express divine designation of the king derived from the secular use of the term of which the oldest occurrence is found in David's designation of Solomon (1 Kgs 1:35). However, the divine election and the reigning king's designation are not mutually exclusive for the legitimization of the kings who succeeded to their own fathers' thrones; cf. Ishida, *The Royal Dynasties*, pp. 6 ff.

[25] There is a suggestion to emend *neḡeḏ YHWH* (1 Sam 16:6) to *n^eḡîḏ YHWH*, but it is not acceptable; see J.H. Grønbaek, *Die Geschichte vom Aufstieg Davids (1.Sam. 15–2.Sam.5). Tradition und Komposition*, Copenhagen, 1971, p. 70.

ing to do with any precondition for his enthronement, but only testifies to the legitimacy of his rule over Israel. Similar circumstances are to be found in the short notes on the rise to power of Jeroboam and Baasha (nos. 12, 13).

From the above, we may assume that the term *nāḡîḏ* was originally the title of a person who was designated to be ruler either by Yahweh or by the reigning monarch. If our assumption is correct, it is likely that the other kings of this period were also actually appointed as *nāḡîḏ* by their fathers before their accession to the throne, perhaps with the exception of Ishbaal because of the state of emergency at his enthronement (1 Sam 31:1–7; 2 Sam 2:8–9), although their appointment as *nāḡîḏ* is not mentioned explicitly. However, when the legitimacy of the kingship was disputed, and only then, the kings expressly mentioned their designation as *nāḡîḏ* in order to demonstrate that their appointment as ruler had been legitimately confirmed by human or divine authority. A similar phenomenon can be found in the specific mention of a king's anointing in the Hebrew Bible, which is made only in instances of founders of dynasties or of contested successions, although it is very likely that all the kings of Israel and Judah were actually anointed at their enthronement.[26]

4. *Later Development*

As to the expression "*nāḡîḏ* of my people" in Yahweh's words to Hezekiah through Isaiah (no. 14), we must suppose a different situation. Since it reminds us of the common expression "*nāḡîḏ* over my/his people" referring to the kings from the early monarchies (nos. 1–3, 7, 8, 12, 13; cf. no. 6), it is certain, that this title of Hezekiah originated in the early usage, which showed Yahweh's designation of each king as the ruler of Israel, the people of Yahweh. But Hezekiah had no special reason to emphasize his divine designation as the ruler of Israel at this juncture. The whole story tells us about Hezekiah's miraculous recovery from a fatal sickness, which was connected with the deliverance of Jerusalem from the Assyrian invasion "for my (i.e., Yahweh's) own sake and for my servant David's

[26] See A. Malamat, "The Last Kings of Judah and the Fall of Jerusalem", *IEJ* 18 (1968), p. 140.

sake" (2 Kgs 20:6). Therefore, the central theme of this story is not the fate of Hezekiah himself, but the existence of Jerusalem and the house of David. In fact, Yahweh is called here "the God of David your father" (20:5). This context shows that the expression "*nāḡîḏ* of my people" serves here as a sign of Yahweh's support of the rule of David's house over the people of Israel. (However, the term *nāḡîḏ* is omitted from the parallel passage in Isa 38:5).

If our interpretation of Hezekiah's title "*nāḡîḏ* of my people" is acceptable, we can conclude that the original use of the title *nāḡîḏ* as a term for the legitimization of the kingship ceased with Baasha. Indirect but clear evidence for our assumption can be deduced from the narrative about Jehu's designation as king by a prophet. The text reads: "Thus says Yahweh the God of Israel: I anoint you *meleḵ* over the people of Yahweh, over Israel. And you shall strike the house of Ahab your master . . . . ." (2 Kgs 9: 6–7). If we compare this passage with text no. 2 (Saul), it becomes evident that the term *meleḵ* is here substituted for the term *nāḡîḏ*.

Thereafter, the implication of the term changed in various ways in the course of later development. The main uses of the term in later times may be grouped under the following three categories:

a) A synonym for the term *meleḵ*: "Who cuts off the spirit of *nᵉḡîḏîm*, who is terrible to *malḵê-ʾāreṣ*" (Ps 76:13); "*nāḡîḏ* of Tyre" (Ezek 28:2); other passages in which the term seems to imply king or ruler are: Isa 55:4; Job 29:10; 31:37; Prov 28:16; Dan 9:25–26; 11:22; 1 Chr 5:2 (implicitly David); 28:4 (the tribe Judah).

b) The title of the chief priests of the Temple of Jerusalem: "*nāḡîḏ* in the temple of Yahweh" (Jer 20:1); "*nāḡîḏ* of the temple of God" (Neh 11:1 = 1 Chr 9:11; 2 Chr 31:13; 35:8).

c) The title of various chief officials: those in charge of religious matters (1 Chr 9:20; 26:24; 2 Chr 31:12), over the tribes (1 Chr 27:16), in charge of royal matters and the palace (2 Chr 19:11; 28:7) and of the army (1 Chr 12:28; 13:1; 27:4; 2 Chr 11:11).[27]

In short, the title *nāḡîḏ*, in later times, came to stand for king, ruler, chief priests and chief officials of the Temple, chief officers, governors and military commanders. Although their functions are quite different one from another, we may give a common definition to all the uses of the word: the appointee as the head of a certain group or organization. In this sense, the original meaning of the

[27] The meaning of *nᵉḡîḏîm* in Prov 8:6 is unclear. Perhaps the text is corrupt.

term as "one who is designated as ruler of the people" was preserved, but its use in legitimization of the kingship was completely lost.

The various later uses of the term are found mostly in the Books of the Chronicles. We must assume, therefore, that most of them, particularly those under categories b) and c), stemmed from the Chronicler's special terminology. The question then arises, whether we can include texts no. 8 (David), no. 10 (Solomon) and no. 11 (Abijah) in the source material for our investigation of the early use of the term, since they come from the Chronocler's texts without parallels in any other books. In these cases, we may still maintain that texts no. 8 and no. 11 can be utilized safely, since the original use of the term is obviously reflected in them. By contrast, text no. 10 must be excluded from the source material for the early period. Solomon was anointed here a *nāğîḏ*, after he had already become king (1 Chr 23:1). This order is the reverse of what the text in 1 Kings (no. 9) indicates. Moreover, the expression "*nāğîḏ* for Yahweh" stands isolated in the Hebrew Bible, and its implication is unclear. We have the feeling that the Chronicler's own distinctive outlook is mirrored in this text.[28]

Thus we can come to the conclusion that the original use of the term *nāğîḏ* as an expression for the legitimization of the kingship ceased with Baash in the Northern Kingdom and with Abijah in the Kingdom of Judah. It seems that the firm establishment of the monarchy in both the kingdoms by dynastic succession made it unnecessary to emphasize the designation as *nāğîḏ* prior to the accession to the throne.[29]

[28] For a different interpretation see Halpern, *The Constitution*, p. 7.

[29] Halpern, *The Constitution*, pp. 10–11, holds that the title's fall into desuetude came from conceptual atrophy of the divine designation in the period after the division of the United Kingdom. We are of the opinion, however, that the title *nāğîḏ* was not always connected with the deity's designation in the early monarchies in Israel.

CHAPTER FOUR

THE PEOPLE UNDER ARMS IN THE STRUGGLES FOR THE THRONE*

1. *The Military Factors*

According to the biblical narrative in 1 Samuel 8:20, the monarchy was introduced into Israel when the people wanted to be like all the nations by having a king who would govern them and who would lead them in battle. There is a tacit understanding in this narrative that the police and military powers were inherent in kingship. Similarly, the biblical historiographers in the Books of Samuel and Kings generally do not omit to mention the military factors involved in the foundation of new dynasties or in irregular successions to the royal throne in the kingdoms of Israel and Judah, although they are never eager to report on purely political matters. It was not easy for them to explain the course of events without mentioning the military factors that had played the decisive role in the struggles for the throne.

In this chapter the characteristic features of these factors will be examined by classifying them into groups by formulary expressions. In so doing, we shall reach the following two conclusions. First, the biblical historiographers used a definite technical term for king-making as a political action. Secondly, there was a contrasting development between the kingdoms of Israel and Judah concerning the people under arms as a determining factor at establishment of the royal throne.

2. *Two Types of Seizure of the Throne in the Northern Kingdom*

Apart from David's accession, the throne of the Northern Kingdom of Israel, including Saul's monarchy, was seized ten times during its existence for about three centuries. In these dynastic foundations or

---

* This essay is a revised version of the study which appeared in J.A. Emerton (ed.), *Cogress Volume*, Jerusalem 1986 (VTSup 40), Leiden, 1988, pp. 96–106.

changes, two types of seizure are differentiated one from the other in the biblical sources. While the first type was carried out by the people who helped their war-leader to the throne, the second was executed by usurpers who conspired against their lords. Each type is expressed by its set formula.

The first formula is formed by the expression *wayyamlîḵû ʾōṯô*: "And they made him king" or *wayyamlîḵû ʾeṯ*-P.N.: "And they made so-and-so king", with either *kol-hāʿām*: "all the people" or *kol-yiśrāʾēl*: "all Israel" as the subject. The second formula consists of the following four expressions. *wayyiqšōr ʿālāw*: "And he conspired against him", *wayyakkēhû*: "And he struck him down", *wayᵉmîṯēhû*: "And he killed him", and *wayyimlōḵ taḥtāw*: "And he reigned in his stead". We shall call the first the *wayyamlîḵû*-type and the second the *wayyiqšōr*-type.

In addition, some biblical narratives tell us about the divine designation of several founders as future kings by prophets, when these founders were still commoners. These source materials are generally called prophetic narratives. Although they are strongly coloured by a certain theological interpretation of the course of events, with proper analysis we are able to obtain important historical information from these materials too.

According to our sources, the *wayyamlîḵû*-type foundation is recorded in the case of the following three kings: Saul in 1 Samuel 11:15, Jeroboam ben Nebat in 1 Kings 12:20 (cf. 2 Kgs 17:21), and Omri in 1 Kings 16:16. On the other hand, the throne was seized in a *wayyiqšōr*-type *coup d'état* by the following five usurpers: Baasha in 1 Kings 15:27–28, Zimri in 16:9–10, Shallum in 2 Kings 15:10, Pekah in 15:25, and Hoshea in 15:30. The dynastic changes made by Jehu and Menahem cannot be classified at once into either of the two types because of the irregular condition of the source materials. We shall deal with the problems later.

Among the three founders of the *wayyamlîḵû*-type, both Saul and Jeroboam ben Nebat have prophetic narratives, in which Samuel anointed Saul to be *nāḡîḏ* (1 Sam 9:1–10:16) or took him by lot as king (10:17–27), while Ahijah the Shilonite told Jeroboam the latter's designation as king over Israel (1 Kgs 11:26–40). In the meantime, the people remained passive according to the characteristic mode of prophetic narratives. It is striking, however, that the expression *wayyamlēḵ/wayyamlîḵû ʾōṯô*: "And he/they made him king" is missing in these narratives. In other words, the prophets anoint future kings and announce their divine designation, but the expression *wayyamlēḵ/*

wayyamlîkû ʾōtô is not used in connection with the prophets' actions.

In this connection, mention must be made of two narratives in which the verb *himlîk* is used with God as the subject, i.e., in 1 Samuel 15:11, 35 in the narrative of Saul's rejection and 1 Kings 3:7 in the narrative of Solomon's dream. In both narratives the royal investiture is remembered as divine appointment. Evidently, this is a theological reflection about a past event. Therefore, it is legitimate for us to treat these cases separately.[1] Accordingly, in the historical descriptions in the Books of Samuel and Kings, it is always the people who made someone king by the expression *wayyamlîkû ʾōtô*.

Who are the people? The narrative about Saul's enthronement at Gilgal tells us that they are the people called up for military service from *kol-gᵉbûl yiśrāʾēl*: "all the territory of Israel" (1 Sam 11:7). By contrast, *kol-yiśrāʾēl*: "all Israel" who assembled at Shechem to negotiate with Rehoboam on the conditions for their subordination to him in 1 Kings 12:1–15 were no doubt unarmed. However, as soon as the negotiations were broken off, they went back home and rose in rebellion (12:16, 18). At that stage, we can hardly imagine that there was no military confrontation (cf. 2 Chr 11:1). It is probable that "all Israel" who made Jeroboam king (1 Kgs 12:20) were the people under arms.

The brief report about Omri's accession tells us that those who made him king were the people who had been encamped against the Philistines at Gibbethon under his command (16:15–16). Presumably, these troops, called either *hāʿām* or *kol-yiśrāʾēl*, were a part of the army of the kingdom. Another part was under Tibni's command, and they also tried to "make him king" (*lᵉhamlîkô*) just as Omri's people did (16:21).[2] From the above it is clear that the people who acted as the driving force in the *wayyamlîkû*-type foundation were the people under arms from "all the territory of Israel" or the army called "all Israel".

[1] T.N.D. Mettinger finds a "synergism" in the fact that the verb *himlîk* is used with both God and human beings as the subject, *King and Messiah. The Civil and Sacral Legitimation of the Israelite Kings* (CBOTS 8), Lund, 1976, p. 107. This is a different approach from ours.

[2] J.A. Soggin has suggested on the basis of the recensions of the LXX that Tibni was the king elected by the popular assembly but Omri usurped the throne, "Tibnî, King of Israel in the First Half of the 9th Century B.C." (1972), in *Old Testament and Oriental Studies* (BibOr 29), Rome, 1975, pp. 50–55; idem, *A History of Israel. From the Beginnings to the Bar Kochba Revolt, AD 135*, London, 1984, p. 202. However, it is not easy to accept the view, since there is no reason to suspect that "all Israel"

We come now to the *wayyiqšōr*-type seizure of the throne, which was carried out by five usurpers. Unfortunately, the information about their deeds is so scanty and defective that it is extremely difficult to clarify the real state of affairs. Within this limitation, we shall submit the following suggestions. The fact that Zimri (16:9–10) and Pekah (2 Kgs 15:25) succeeded in attacking their lords in the capital cities shows that the former as "commander of half the chariots" and the latter as king's "aide-de-camp" took advantage of their high-ranking military positions at the court. By contrast, in the case of Baasha and Shallum, who assassinated the reigning kings outside the capitals (1 Kgs 15:27; 2 Kgs 15:10), their titles as royal servants are not given. Instead, the texts report their origins: Baasha was from the house of Issachar, and Shallum probably from Jabesh in Gilead.[3] These pieces of information point out that the supporters of Baasha and Shallum came from their own tribes, while Zimri and Pekah recruited rebel forces from their own soldiers. If this assumption is tenable, "the fifty men of the Gileadites" with whom Pekah conspired (15:25) are to be understood as the king's bodyguard, like the Cherethites, the Pelethites, the Gittites, or the Carites in the Jerusalem court.[4]

In the account of Hoshea's usurpation we have virtually no information about his supporters, except the fact that Tiglath-Pileser's invasion of the country served as the background (15:29–30). But we can learn about the situation from Tiglath-Pileser's text, according to which the change of regime was made not by Hoshea but by the Assyrian king.[5] It appears that Hoshea seized the throne with

who made Omri king were the militia of the kingdom of Israel; see Mettinger, *King and Messiah*, p. 117; E. Würthwein, *Das Erste Buch der Könige: Kapitel 1–16* (ATD 11/1), Göttingen, 1977, p. 196.

[3] See R. Althann, "Shallum", in *ABD* V, New York, 1992, p. 1154.

[4] This suggestion does not exclude the thesis of the Gileadite involvement in the power struggles in the Northern Kingdom; see T. Ishida, *The Royal Dynasties in Ancient Israel. A Study on the Formation and Development of Royal-Dynastic Ideology* (BZAW 142), Berlin/New York, 1977, pp. 175 f.; N. Na'aman, "Historical and Chronological Notes on the Kingdoms of Israel and Judah in the Eighth Century B.C.", *VT* 36 (1986), pp. 78 f.

[5] P. Rost, *Die Keilschrifttexte Tiglat-Pilesers III. nach den Papierabklatschen und Originalen des Britischen Museums* I: *Einleitung, Transcription und Uebersetzung, Wörterverzeichnis mit Commentar*, Leipzig, 1893, pp. 80 f.; H. Tadmor, *The Inscriptions of Tiglath-Pileser III King of Assyria. Critical Edition, with Introductions, Translations and Commentary*, Jerusalem, 1994, pp. 140 f. (Summary Inscription 4, 15'–18'); A.L. Oppenheim, "Babylonian and Assyrian Historical Texts", in *ANET*, Princeton, 1969³, p. 284; cf. also R. Borger and H. Tadmor, "Zwei Beiträge zur alttestamentlichen Wissenschaft aufgrund der

Assyrian support. To sum up, the common denominator of all the five usurpers is that not one of them won broad support from *hāʿām* or *kol-yiśrāʾēl*.

We are now in a position to deal with the problem of Menahem. In the narrative about his seizure of the throne in 2 Kings 15:14 we find all the expressions of the *wayyiqšōr*-type formula except the very expression *wayyiqšōr ʿālāw*. A comparison of his action to that of Omri seems to help us to understand the situation. Hearing of Zimri's *coup d'état*, Omri immediately went up from Gibbethon to Tirzah, then the capital, and put an end to the usurper's seven-day rule (1 Kgs 16:15–18). Similarly, Menahem marched from Tirzah against Samaria, the capital, and brought Shallum's one-month reign to an end (2 Kgs 15:13–14). Menahem's delay seems to have been caused by opponents with whom he had to fight before reaching Samaria (15:16).

These actions of Omri and Menahem clearly indicate that there never existed a lord-servant relationship between Zimri and Omri or between Shallum and Menahem. It is then natural that there was no conspiracy on the part of Omri and Menahem. The fact that the formula *qišrô ʾašer qāšār*: "the conspiracy which he made" is found in the stereotyped references only to Zimri (1 Kgs 16:20) and Shallum (2 Kgs 15:15) but not to any other usurper shows that the biblical historiographers regarded Zimri and Shallum as conspirators to be punished. This also reminds us of Jezebel's taunting words to Jehu: "Is it peace, you Zimri, murderer of your lord?" (9:31).

However, there remains a significant difference between Omri and Menahem. Menahem's troops are never called *kol-yiśrāʾēl* as against those who supported Omri. This can be understood as a sign that Menahem's troops were not recognized as the regular army of the kingdom. Was he an independent warlord rather than a commander of the garrison at Tirzah? If so, such an assumption may explain the background of the atrocities which his troops committed against the inhabitants of Tappuah (15:16 LXX). On the other hand, the report of Menahem's imposing a levy on *gibbôrê haḥayil* (15:19–20) shows that he succeeded in gaining the support of the people of the kingdom during his reign.[6] But this can also be regarded as the cause

Inschriften Tiglatpilesers III", *ZAW* 94 (1982), pp. 244–249; Na'aman, *VT* 36 (1986), pp. 71–74.

[6] For *gibbôrê haḥayil* see H. Tadmor, "'The People' and the Kingship in Ancient

of the dynastic change after the two-year rule of Pekahiah, his son (15:23, 25).[7] In any case, Shallum's *coup d'état* and Menahem's seizure of the throne inaugurated the rapid dissolution of the Northern Kingdom. The prophet Hosea also refused to recognize the legitimacy of these last kings in the following words: "They made kings (*hēm himlîḵû*), but not through me. They set up princes, but without my knowledge" (Hos 8:4); "I have given you kings in my anger, and I have taken them away in my wrath" (13:11).

Finally, we shall deal with the problem of Jehu's seizure of the throne. Information about his revolt comes mostly from the prophetic narratives in 2 Kings 9–10, of which the beginning reminds us of the two accounts of Saul's designation as *nāḡîḏ* and king in 1 Samuel 9–10. They especially resemble each other in the prophetic anointing which both the candidates received with a divine commission to destroy the enemies. Another similarity may be seen in comparing the acclamation given to Saul with the proclamation of Jehu's kingship after the announcement or disclosure of their divine designation. It is important to note, however, that those who acclaimed Saul were the people from *kol-šiḇṭê yiśrā'ēl*: "all the tribes of Israel" (1 Sam 10:20), whereas those who proclaimed Jehu's kingship were the commanders of the army who had been stationed in Ramoth-gilead (2 Kgs 9:4–5). Undoubtedly, Saul's elevation was recognized as a legitimate action by all the people. Accordingly, dissenters were called "worthless fellows" (1 Sam 10:27). Despite the prophetic anointing with a divine commission, however, there is no evidence to show that Jehu's revolt was accepted unanimously by "all the people" or "all Israel". On the contrary, his wholesale massacre was remembered in a certain circle as a treacherous deed to be punished by God even about a century later, as the prophet Hosea's following words indicate: "For yet a little while, and I will punish the house of Jehu for the blood of Jezreel, and I will put an end to the kingdom of the house of Israel" (Hos 1:4).

In fact, Jehu's revolt was nothing but a conspiracy against the legitimate king, carried out by a group of commanders under his

---

Israel: The Role of Political Institutions in the Biblical Period", *JWH* 11 (1968), p. 63, n. 33; C. Schäfer-Lichtenberger, *Stadt und Eidgenossenschaft im Alten Testament. Eine Auseinandersetzung mit Max Webers Studie <Das antike Judentum>* (BZAW 156), Berlin/New York, 1983, pp. 313–321; H. Eising, "חיל", in *TWAT* II, Stuttgart, 1974–77, cols. 905 f.

[7] See Ishida, *The Royal Dynasties*, pp. 172 f.

leadership in co-operation with Elisha's prophetic community and other Yahwistic zealots like Jehonadab ben Rechab. Therefore, the historiographer in 2 Kings 9:14 does not forget not only to mention the expression *wayyitqaššēr yēhûʾ . . . ʾel-yôrām*: "Jehu . . . conspired against Joram", though in a slightly different wording from the *wayyiqšōr*-formula, but also to emphasize that *kol-yiśrāʾēl*: "all Israel", were with Joram on guard at Ramoth-gilead.[8]

3. *The People's Role in the Kingdom of Judah*

Now we proceed to examine the problem of the royal succession in the kingdom of Judah. In contrast to the monarchies in the Northern Kingdom, the kingdom of Judah was ruled by the house of David as its sole dynasty throughout its existence, except for a short interruption during Athaliah's usurpation. The normal succession in this kingdom made it a condition that the reigning king designated his first-born or eldest surviving son as his successor.[9] Its procedure is expressed by the formula *wayyimlōḵ* P.N. *bᵉnô taḥtāw*: "And so-and-so his son reigned in his stead" (1 Kgs 11:43; 14:31; 15:8, etc.). The reigning king's designation of the heir is specially mentioned only when the principle of primogeniture or the priority of the surviving eldest son was overruled. The typical example is David's announcement of Solomon's designation (1:35).

From the circumstances we can assume that Ahaziah, Amon, and Josiah were killed and Amaziah was taken captive before they had designated their successors.[10] In all these instances the political powers called either *kol-ʿam yᵉhûḏāh*: "all the people of Judah" or *ʿam hāʾāreṣ*: "the people of the land" intervened in determining the succession

---

[8] M.C. Astour has suggested that Jehu's revolt was a *coup d'état* arranged by the pro-Assyrian faction in the Northern Kingdom, "841 B.C.: The First Assyrian Invasion of Israel", *JAOS* 91 (1971), pp. 383–389. If so, we can regard Jehu's seizure of the throne as a dynastic change supported by Assyria like Hoshea's usurpation. It is also worth noting that Menahem paid tribute to Tiglath-Pileser III to assure his throne with Assyrian backing (2 Kgs 15:19–20); cf. H. Tadmor, "Azriyau of Yaudi", in C. Rabin (ed.), *Studies in the Bible* (Scripta Hierosolymitana 8), Jerusalem, 1961, pp. 251 f. For the Assyrian sources about Menahem's tribute see M. Weippert, "Menahem von Israel und seine Zeitgenossen in einer Steleninschrift des assyrischen Königs Tiglathpileser III. aus dem Iran", *ZDPV* 89 (1973), pp. 26–53; Tadmor, *The Inscriptions of Tiglath-Pileser III*, pp. 68 f. (Ann. 13*), 89 (Ann. 27), 106–109 (Stele III A).

[9] See Ishida, *The Royal Dynasties*, pp. 152, 169.

[10] See ibid., pp. 162–164.

of the throne of David. Their actions are formulated by the expression *wayyamlîkû ʾōṯô*.[11] The expression *kol-ʿam yᵉhûḏāh* and *ʿam hāʾāreṣ* are generally regarded as synonymous, and they represented "the whole body of citizens of Judah", according to the currently prevailing view.[12] Without entering into this much-debated problem, we wish to focus our attention upon the fact that they were the people under arms at the time when they played the decisive role in the succession problems, i.e., they were the people who participated either in the *coup d'état* against Athaliah (2 Kgs 11), in the warfare against Jehoash of Israel (14:11–14, 21), in the counter-revolt against the conspirators against King Amon (21:23–24), or in the warfare against Pharaoh Neco (23:29–30).

It is surprising, however, that the people who determined the succession problems in the last days of the kingdom played only a passive role in the early monarchies. When the kingdom of Judah was founded in Hebron, "the men of Judah came, and there they anointed David king over the house of Judah" (2 Sam 2:4). Similarly, after Ishbaal had been assassinated, "all the elders of Israel came to the king at Hebron . . . and they anointed David king over Israel" (5:3). It is striking that the expression *wayyamlîkû ʾōṯô* is missing in both the texts. Instead, royal anointing is mentioned.[13]

Apart from prophetic anointing of Saul (1 Sam 10:1), David (16:1–13), and Jehu (2 Kgs 9:6), royal anointing is specially mentioned also in the historiographical sources in connection with the accessions of David, as was mentioned above, Solomon (1 Kgs 1:34, 39, 45; cf. 5:15; cf. also 1 Chr 29:22), Joash (2 Kgs 11:12), and Jehoahaz (23:30). Absalom's anointing is also suggested (2 Sam 19:11). Now,

[11] In the account of the accession of Joash and Athaliah's overthrow, the subject of the expression *wayyamlîkû ʾōṯô* is unspecified (2 Kgs 11:12). Accordingly, on the basis of the LXX the emendation of the pl. of the verb into the sing. has been suggested to make the subject Jehoiada; see B. Stade and F. Schwally, *The Book of Kings*, Leipzig, 1904, p. 236; A. Šanda, *Die Bücher der Könige* II (EHAT 9/2), Münster i. Westf., 1912, p. 131; J. Gray, *I & II Kings. A Commentary* (OTL), London, 1977³, p. 571. However, in addition to the context of vv. 12–14, the usage of the expression *wayyamlîkū ʾōṯô* requires that the pl. must remain by taking *hāʿām* in v. 13 as the subject; see also E. Würthwein, *Die Bücher der Könige: 1.Kön. 17–2.Kön. 25* (ATD 11/2), Göttingen, 1984, pp. 344, 349 f.

[12] In my opinion, "the people of Judah" has a broader connotation than "the people of the land"; see below p. 90. For the discussions on "the people of the land" see below pp. 81 ff.

[13] For discussions of royal anointing see Mettinger, *King and Messiah*, pp. 185–232; B. Halpern, *The Constitution of the Monarchy in Israel* (HSM 25), Chico, 1981, pp. 13–19; K. Seybold, "משח" in *TWAT* V, Stuttgart, 1984–86, cols. 46–59, esp. 49–55.

in these texts, Solomon, Joash, and Jehoahaz were given at the same time either the reigning king's designation (Solomon) or the people's appointment indicated by the expression *wayyamlîḵû ʾōṯô* (Joash and Jehoahaz). But royal anointing stands alone in the texts about David and Absalom. This observation suggests that the expression *wayyamlîḵû ʾōṯô* is intentionally avoided for David and Absalom.

According to 2 Samuel 2:3, the military factor that determined the foundation of the dynasty of David was not the men of Judah but David's men whom he brought up with him from Ziklag to Hebron. These soldiers called *ʾanšê dāwīḏ*: "David's men" were, as their appellation suggests, his personal army which consisted of six hundred men, originally four hundred, who had been organized by David from those outside normal society (1 Sam 22:1–2). Besides, foreign mercenaries like the Cherethites, the Pelethites, and the Gittites served as the king's bodyguard. This army was loyal only to the person of David and had nothing to do with the tribal society of Israel.[14] In these circumstances, the only condition required for David to establish the kingdom was the consent of the men of Judah, and they showed it by the rite of anointing. Similarly, the anointing given to David by the elders of Israel is understood as their acknowledgement of David's rule over Israel.[15] At that time the tribes of Israel no longer had any military power to compete with David's army. This time again the determining factor which made David king over Israel was his own personal army.[16]

---

[14] The episode about Ittai the Gittite in Absalom's rebellion (2 Sam 15:19–22) well illustrates the status of David's foreign mercenaries. For David's personal army see R. de Vaux, *Ancient Israel. Its Life and Institutions*, London, 1961, pp. 218–222; L.M. Muntingh, "The Kerethites and the Pelethites. A Historical and Sociological Discussion", in A.H. van Zyl (ed.), *Studies on the Books of Samuel*, Pretoria, 1960, pp. 43–53; B. Mazar, "The Military Élite of King David" (1963), in *The Early Biblical Period. Historical Studies*, Jerusalem, 1986, pp. 83–103; D.G. Schley, "David's Champions", *ABD* II, New York, 1992, pp. 49–52.

[15] Pointing out that anointing has a contractual meaning, Mettinger, *King and Messiah*, p. 228, interprets the rites of anointing given to David by the men of Judah and the elders of Israel as "the people's homage to the king", in other words, "formal public acknowledgement of allegiance".

[16] We are told in 1 Kings 11:23–24 that the kingdom of Aram Damascus was established in a similar way to the kingdom of Judah. In this narrative, the last verb is difficult because of the pl.: *wayyimlᵉḵû*: "and they became kings" (v. 24). W. Rudolph, "Zum Text der Königsbücher", *ZAW* 63 (1951), p. 205, has suggested the reading *wayyamlîḵûhû* "And they made him king", and Würthwein, *Das Erste Buch der Könige*, p. 138, follows him. Criticizing the emendation, M. Noth, *Könige* I: *I. Könige 1–16* (BKAT 9/1), Neukirchen-Vluyn, 1968, pp. 240, 242, rendered: "und herrschten in Damasukus wie ein König". It is not a natural reading. If we apply

In his rebellion against David, Absalom finally succeeded in rallying *kol-ʾîš yiśrāʾēl*: "all the men of Israel" (2 Sam 16:18; 17:14, 25, etc.).[17] However, they were not present at his accession in Hebron. It was carried out as a surprise by his initiative. Then they were told to recognize his kingship (15:10). It was a conspiracy which began in secrecy. Then it gathered strength rapidly, swallowed up all the men of Israel, and finally swept them away like an avalanche (15:11–13). In such a progress of the rebellion, the people had no opportunity to make Absalom king. Although we are not told on which occasion Absalom was anointed, his anointing is also understood as the manifestation of the people's acknowledgement of his kingship.

4. *King-Making by the People*

From the foregoing discussion it has emerged that the expression *wayyamlîḵû ʾōṯô* stands for king-making by the people under arms either at the foundation of new dynasties in the Northern Kingdom or at irregular successions in the kingdom of Judah.[18] In this connection, mention must be made of "all Israel" who assembled at Shechem to make Rehoboam king in 1 Kings 12:1. In this text the expression *lᵉhamlîḵ ʾōṯô*: "to make him king" is used with "all Israel" who were unarmed, as we have noted above. This exceptional use of the expression can be explained by the situation that the objective of

our analysis of the expression *wayyamlîḵû ʾōṯô* to the text, the emendation *wayyamlîḵûhû* is unacceptable. It seems that the verb should be read in the sing. on the basis of the LXX; see J.A. Montgomery and H.S. Gehman, *A Critical and Exegetical Commentary on the Books of Kings* (ICC), Edinburgh, 1951, pp. 241, 246; cf. also W.T. Pitard, *Ancient Damascus. A Historical Study of the Syrian City-State from Earliest Times until its Fall to the Assyrians in 732 B.C.E.*, Winona Lake, 1987, p. 96, n. 50.

[17] For Absalom's supporters see Tadmor, *JWH* 11 (1968), pp. 49–57; idem, "Traditional Institutions and the Monarchy: Social and Political Tensions in the Time of David and Solomon", in T. Ishida (ed.), *SPDS*, Tokyo/Winona Lake, 1982, pp. 241 f., 246 f.; Mettinger, *King and Messiah*, pp. 121 f.; F. Crüsemann, *Der Widerstand gegen das Königtum. Die antiköniglichen Texte des Alten Testamentes und der Kampf um den frühen israelitischen Staat* (WMANT 49), Neukirchen-Vluyn, 1978, pp. 94–101.

[18] According to 2 Chr 22:1, *yôšᵉḇê yᵉrûšālayim*: "the inhabitants of Jerusalem" made Ahaziah king. Since he was the only surviving son of the late king (21:17; 22:1), we cannot imagine that there was any succession problem. Yet it seems that there was a political tension; cf. my analysis of this passage in Ishida, *The Royal Dynasties*, pp. 159 f. At the same time, we must note that the Chronicler's use of the verb *himlîḵ* does not always fit our analysis of the same verb in the Books of Samuel and Kings, see 1 Chr 11:10; 12:32, 39; 29:22.

their assembly was neither founding a new dynasty nor determining a successor of the Davidic dynasty.

Now to elucidate this formulary expression in a broader context let us examine other texts in which it is found in slightly different forms: (a) after the catastrophe at Gilboa, Abner, the commander of Saul's army, took Ishbaal and "made him king (*wayyamlīḵēhû*) . . . over all Israel" (2 Sam 2:8–9); (b) in answer to Jehu's challenge, the royal officials of Samaria, the elders and the tutors said: "We will not make anyone king" (*lōʾ namlîḵ ʾîš*) (2 Kgs 10:5); (c) Pharaoh Neco "made Eliakim . . . king" (*wayyamlēḵ . . . ʾeṯ-ʾelyāqîm*) (23:34); (d) the king of Babylon "made Mattaniah . . . king" (*wayyamlēḵ . . . ʾeṯ-mattanyāh*) (24:17). In these texts those who acted as king-makers were a commander of the army, high officials and leading men of the capital city, though they did not exercise their authority, and foreign conquerors. These examples show that, if there was no normal succession, whoever possessed the strongest power, including the people under arms, could determine the royal successor. At the same time, we may conclude that the formulary expression *wayyamlēḵ*/*wayyamlîḵû ʾōṯô* was used as a definite technical term for king-making as a political action in the sources discussed.[19]

Among these irregular king-makers, the people under arms especially deserve to receive attention as the representatives of the so-called democratic tradition of the Israelite society.[20] Who, then, were the people under arms? This is a big problem with which we cannot deal in detail in the scope of the present study. For the moment, we must be satisfied with pointing out the following three features as a clue to further studies.

---

[19] Judg 9:6 reads: "And *kol-baʿalê šeḵem* and *kol-bêṯ millôʾ* came together, and they went *wayyamlîḵû ʾeṯ-ʾabîmelek lemelek*". The text shows that the assembly, which consisted of the *baʿalê šeḵem* and *bêṯ millôʾ*, possessed power to make Abimelech king. The wording of the expression *wayyamlîḵû ʾeṯ-ʾabîmelk lemelek* is slightly different from the formula *wayyamlîḵû ʾeṯ* P.N. in the Books of Samuel and Kings, but the practice described is the same. For the nature of Abimelech's kingship see H. Reviv, "The Government of Shechem in the El-Amarna Period and in the Days of Abimelech", *IEJ* 16 (1966), pp. 252–257.

[20] For the relationship between the popular assembly and the kingship in Israel see A. Malamat, "Organs of Statecraft in the Israelite Monarchy" (1965), in *The Biblical Archaeologist Reader* III, New York, 1970, pp. 163–198; J.A. Soggin, *Das Königtum in Israel. Ursprünge, Spannungen, Entwicklung* (BZAW 104), Berlin, 1967, pp. 18–20, 44 f., 69 f.; Tadmor, *JWH* 11 (1968), pp. 46–68; idem, in *SPDS*, pp. 239–57; Mettinger, *King and Messiah*, pp. 111–130; Crüsemann, *Der Widerstand gegen das Königtum*, pp. 94–101; Halpern, *The Constitution*, pp. 187–216.

a) We can clearly observe the structural change of *kol-hāʿām* or *kol-yiśrāʾēl* according to the historical development. First, those who made Saul king at Gilgal were irregular tribal league organized *ad hoc* for saving Jabesh-gilead; secondly, those who made Jeroboam king at Shechem were a popular assembly, called *kol-qᵉhal yiśrāʾēl* (1 Kgs 12:3) or *hāʿēdāh* (12:20), which seems a well-organized political body; thirdly, those who made Omri king in the military camp were the militia of the Northern Kingdom.

b) Our historiographers emphasize the unity of Israel achieved on the occasions of king-making by the people, as the following words indicate: "They came out as one man" (1 Sam 11:7); or "There was none that followed the house of David, but the tribe of Judah only" (1 Kgs 12:20). Similarly, the people are called in these contexts *kol-hāʿām* or *kol-yiśrāʾēl.* Is this unity a fiction fabricated by the historiographers? We are of the opinion that the term *kol-* here is to be understood not as quantitative but as qualitative. Omri's case gives a good example. Although *kol-yiśrāʾēl* made him king (16:16), *ḥᵃṣî hāʿām*: "half the people" followed Tibni to make him king (16:21). The term *kol-* here seems to imply the legitimate representation.[21]

c) There was a contrasting development between the kingdoms of Israel and Judah concerning the people's involvement in king-making. In the Northern Kingdom the people even took the initiative twice to establish their monarchy, i.e., with Saul and with Jeroboam ben Nebat. The continuation of this popular initiative can be found also in Omri's elevation to the throne. But this was the last opportunity for the people of Israel to play the active role as a united military factor in establishing their monarchy. This action may be regarded as a popular effort to recover the unity of Israel which had been lost in consequence of the *wayyiqšōr*-type usurpations of Baasha and Zimri. However, the people of Israel could not alter the subsequent historical development in which the dynastic changes made by the *wayyiqšōr*-type usurpation became the characteristic features of the Northern Kingdom.

By contrast, the people of Judah were totally passive in the beginning. From the inception of the kingdom of Judah to the end of David's reign the overwhelming military power of David's personal army acted as the decisive factor in every critical phase. The period of David and Solomon was the formative years of the people of

[21] Cf. Tadmor, in *SPDS*, p. 244.

Judah, centering around the Davidic-Judahite ideology,[22] they emerged for the first time as a significant factor to secure the dynasty of David against Athaliah's usurpation. Their designation *ʿam hāʾāreṣ* suggests that a solid unification of the people was achieved by this period. Finally, it was *ʿam hāʾāreṣ* who acted as the decisive factor in determining the succession to the throne of David in the last days of the kingdom.

[22] The nucleus of this ideology is formed by the doctrine of the joint election of David's house and of Zion, which originated in the covenant of Yahweh with David, see Ishida, *The Royal Dynasties*, pp. 147 f.

CHAPTER FIVE

THE PEOPLE OF THE LAND AND THE POLITICAL CRISES IN JUDAH*

1. *The Judaeans in the Monarchical Period*

In his basic treatment of "the people of the land" (*ʿam hāʾāreṣ*), E. Würthwein defined the expression as "*die zu einem bestimmten Territorium gehörige Vollbürgerschaft*", i.e., the full citizens of a given territory.[1] He further maintained that the expression "people of the land" of Judah is synonymous with "the people of Judah" (*ʿam y^ehûḏāh* or *ʾanšê y^ehûḏāh*) as the designation of the Judaeans in the monarchical period, excluding the inhabitants of Jerusalem.[2] This definition of the term was confirmed by R. de Vaux by distinguishing "the people of the land" from the king or the ruler, his servants, the nobles, the priests, and the prophets, i.e., the monarchical and religious functionaries.[3]

* This essay is a revised version of the study which appeared in *AJBI* 1 (1975), pp. 23–38.

[1] E. Würthwein, *Der ʿamm haʾarez im Alten Testament* (BWANT 66), Stuttgart, 1936, p. 14; cf. L. Rost, "Die Bezeichnungen für Land und Volk im Alten Testament" (1934), in *Das kleine Credo und andere Studien zum Alten Testament*, Heidelberg, 1965, p. 92.

[2] Würthwein, *Der ʿamm haʾarez*, pp. 15 ff. According to S. Talmon *ʿam haʾareṣ libnê yehûdāh* were the Judahites who followed David to Jerusalem, the new capital, from Hebron, "The Judaean *ʿAm Haʾareṣ* in Historical Perspective", in *Fourth World Congress of Jewish Studies* (1965) I, Jerusalem, 1967, pp. 71–76; idem, "עם הארץ", in *Encyclopaedia Biblica* VI, Jerusalem, 1971, cols. 239–242 (Hebrew); cf. C. Schäfer-Lichtenberger, *Stadt und Eidgenossenschaft im Alten Testament. Eine Auseinandersetzung mit Max Webers Studie < Das antike Judentum >* (BZAW 156), Berlin/New York, 1983, p. 395. The late Prof. B. Mazar suggested to me in his letter of March 8, 1974, that we may assume that both the Hittites in the story of Abraham's purchase of Machphelah (Gen 23:7, 12–13) and the inhabitants of the land which Moses made spy out (Num 14:9) are anachronistically called "the people of the land", since they were also the inhabitants of "the land of Judah".

[3] R. de Vaux, *Ancient Israel. Its Life and Institutions*, London, 1961, p. 71; idem, "Le sens de l'expression 'peuple du pays' dans l'Ancien Testament et le rôle politique du peuple en Israël", *RA* 58 (1964), p. 168; cf. J.L. McKenzie, "The 'People of the Land' in the Old Testament", in *Akten des vierundzwanzigsten Internationalen Orientalisten-Kongresses Münchens 28. Aug. bis 4. Sept. 1957*, Wiesbaden, 1959, pp. 207 f.; H. Tadmor, "'The People' and the Kingship in Ancient Israel: The Role of Political Institutions in the Biblical Period", *JWH* 11 (1968), p. 67.

While the thesis has been widely accepted as a working hypothesis, it was also disputed by not a few scholars.[4] It is not our intention to seek another definition of the expression "people of the land" by investigating into all the evidence for the term; rather, we shall re-examine each historical situation of the political crises in the kingdom of Judah to shed light on the roles played by "the people of the land".[5] In so doing, we will try to make clear the intention of the historiographer who employed the expression *ʿam hāʾāreṣ*.

2. *The Rebellion against Athaliah*

The expression "people of the land" appears, for the first time, in the account of the rebellion against Athaliah and the enthronement of Jehoash (2 Kgs 11; 2 Chr 23). The origin of this political crisis can be traced back to Jehoshaphat's alliance with the Omrides (1 Kgs 22:2 ff.; 2 Chr 18:1 ff.), which was sealed by the marriage of Jehoram, his son, and Athaliah, Omri's daughter.[6] By making

---

[4] E.W. Nicholson, "The Meaning of the Expression עם הארץ in the Old Testament", *JSS* 10 (1965), pp. 59–66, rejects to regard "the people of the land" "as a technical term designating a specific class or group within the population of Judah" and concludes that "the term has no fixed and rigid meaning but is used rather in a purely general and fluid manner and varies in meaning from context to context". T.N.D. Mettinger maintains that the *ʿam hāʾāreṣ* who had a role at the royal investitures in the period after Solomon correspond to the *ʿam* as the popular assembly in the previous period, *King and Messiah. The Civil and Sacral Legitimation of the Israelite Kings* (CBOTS 8), Lund, 1976, pp. 124–130. B. Halpern holds that "the term 'the people of the land' is not a technical expression for some fixed sub-group of the tribe or kingedom of Judah", *The Constitution of the Monarchy in Israel* (HSM 25), Chico, 1981, p. 194. On the other hand, S. Talmon, in *Fourth World Congress of Jewish Studies* (1965) I, pp. 71–76, argues that "the *ʿam haʾareṣ* of Judah cannot be viewed as a democratic or otherwise constitutionally circumscribed institution. Rather is it a body of Judaeans in Jerusalem that rose to some power and importance which was ultimately derived from their loyalty to the Davidic dynasty". Moreover, R.M. Good proposes that the expression "the people of the land" belongs to the vocabulary of the time of the Deuteronomistic historian, i.e., the Exilic period, *The Sheep of His Pasture. A Study of the Hebrew Noun ʿAm(m) and Its Semitic Cognates* (HSM 29), Chico, 1983, pp. 109–122. C. Levin comes to the conclusion: "Den *ʿam hāʾāreṣ* im eingeschränkten Sinn hat es nicht gegeben. Er ist ein exegetische Phantom", *Der Sturz der Königin Atalja. Ein Kapitel zur Geschichte Judas im 9. Jahrhundert v. Chr.* (SBS 105), Stuttgart, 1982, p. 69. For an extensive bibliography and discussions see E. Lipiński, "עם", in *TWAT* VI, Stuttgart, 1987–89, cols. 177–194; J.P. Healey, "Am Ha'arez", in *ABD* I, New York, 1992, pp. 168 f.

[5] Cf. T. Ishida, *The Royal Dynasties in Ancient Israel. A Study on the Formation and Development of Royal-Dynastic Ideology* (BZAW 142), Berlin/New York, 1977, pp. 160 ff.

[6] According to one tradition (2 Kgs 8:26; 2 Chr 22:2), Athaliah was Omri's

peace with the Northern Kingdom, with which Judah had been in a state of war for half a century since the division of the United Kingdom, Jehoshaphat brought prosperity to his kingdom (2 Chr 17). His foreign policy, however, was not completely accepted by his people (19:2).

We learn of the critical condition in the last years of Jehoshaphat's reign by his treatment of his sons. He bequeathed the property to his sons, "but gave the kingdom to Jehoram, because he was the first-born" (2 Chr 21:3). This note on Jehoram's designation is conspicuous. It is absolutely superfluous, because the first-born was usually the successor to the throne in Judah.[7] This reveals, therefore, that Jehoshaphat had a special reason in defending his designation of Jehoram. It is likely that Jehoshaphat could appoint Jehoram as his successor only by suppressing the opposing power.

We can assume that Jehoram's purge of his brothers after Jehoshaphat's death (2 Chr 21:4) was caused by the confrontation between his regime and the opposing power, with which his brothers were connected.[8] Undoubtedly, Athaliah, his wife, actively participated in the oppression (cf. 2 Kgs 8:18; 2 Chr 21:6). When he died, Ahaziah, the only surviving son of Jehoram and Athaliah (2 Chr 21:17), ascended the throne with the backing of "the inhabitants of Jerusalem" (22:1). The description of Ahaziah's enthronement is also remarkable because of the special mention of his supporters. Since we never hear of supporters of the new king at the normal accession, it must be assumed that there existed a conflict between the regime supported by "the inhabitants of Jerusalem" and the other Judaeans.

Ahaziah's monarchy was actually Athaliah's regime, since this

---

daughter, while the other tradition (2 Kgs 8:18; 2 Chr 21:6) regards her as Ahab's daughter. But chronological studies show that she could not be Ahab's daughter, see J. Begrich, "Atalja, die Tochter Omris", *ZAW* 53 (1935), pp. 78 f.; H.J. Katzenstein, "Who Were the Parents of Athaliah?", *IEJ* 5 (1955), 194–197; Levin, *Der Sturz der Königin Atalja*, p. 83, n. 3; W. Thiel, "Athaliah", in *ABD* I, New York, 1992, pp. 511 f.; see below pp. 99 f.

[7] When the principle of the primogeniture was overruled, we frequently hear how and why the irregular succession took place. This kind of additional explanation can be found concerning the succession of the following kings: Solomon (2 Sam 9–20 + 1 Kgs 1–2), Abijam (2 Chr 11:21–22), Ahaziah (21:17; 22:1), Azariah (2 Kgs 14:21; 2 Chr 26:1), Jehoahaz (2 Kgs 23:30; 2 Chr 36:1), and Zedekiah (2 Kgs 24:17; 2 Chr 36:10).

[8] Cf. W. Rudolph, *Chronikbücher* (HAT 21), Tübingen, 1955, p. 265; H. Tadmor, "יהורם, יורם", in *Encyclopaedia Biblica* III, Jerusalem, 1958, col. 539 (Hebrew).

young king, who was twenty-two at his enthronement (2 Kgs 8:26),[9] was under the strong influence of the ambitious queen-mother: *g^e^b̂îrāh*[10] (cf. 2 Kgs 8:26–27; 2 Chr 22:2–4). However, Jehu's revolution against the Omrides deprived Athaliah of all her support at one blow. The house of Omri, from which she came, was completely destroyed (2 Kgs 9:21–26, 30–37; 10:1–11, 17). Moreover, Ahaziah, her son, was killed during his involvement in the revolution (2 Kgs 9:27–28; 2 Chr 22:7–9). Naturally, she had to prepare to defend herself and her regime from the counterattack of the opponents before they rose up under the impact of the Yahwistic revolution in the Northern Kingdom. She immediately annihilated all the pretenders to the Davidic throne and usurped it (2 Kgs 11:1–3; 2 Chr 22:10–12). This was her pre-emptive attack against the opposing power which had a long confrontation with the regime since Jehoshaphat allied himself with the Omrides.

Did she really seek the life of Jehoash, her infant grandson, as the biblical source relates? H.L. Ginsberg maintains that it is difficult to assume that she sought to destroy Jehoash, who "constitutes the sole claim of her rule to legitimacy".[11] It seems that she only eliminated some adult members of the house of David who might seek the throne as rivals to the infant Jehoash. It is likely that the biblical historiographer, out of his hatred for this foreign queen, distorted the account presenting her as a ruthless ruler who seeks even the life of her own grandson. In developing this thesis, H. Reviv argued that Jehoash was actually put in the custody of Jehosheba at Athaliah's request. This meant that Athaliah became the queen regent, although never usurping the throne.[12] It is clear that she could not establish her rule without some compromise with the priests of Yahweh headed

[9] According to 2 Chr 22:2, he ascended the throne at the age of forty-two. This figure is clearly corrupted, since Jehoram, his father, died at the age of forty (2 Kgs 8:17; 2 Chr 21:5). In the main texts of LXX stands here the number "twenty", while "twenty-two" in minor texts. J.M. Myers, *II Chronicles. Introduction, Translation, and Notes* (AB 13), Garden City, N.Y., 1965, p. 125, assumes that the number "forty-two" resulted from the conflation of the two traditions.

[10] About the office of queen-mother (*g^e^b̂îrāh*) see G. Molin, "Die Stellung der Gebira im Staate Juda", *TZ* 10 (1954), pp. 161–175; H. Donner, "Art und Herkunft des Amtes der Königinmutter im Alten Testament", in *J. Friedrich Festschrift*, Heidelberg, 1959, pp. 105–145; de Vaux, *Ancient Israel*, pp. 117 ff.; Ishida, *The Royal Dynasties*, pp. 156 ff.; L.S. Schearing, "Queen", in *ABD* V, New York, 1992, pp. 585 f.

[11] H.L. Ginsberg, "The Omrid-Davidid Alliance and its Consequences", in *Fourth World Congress of Jewish Studies* (1965) I, Jerusalem, 1967, p. 92.

[12] H. Reviv, "על ימי עתליה ויואש", *Beth Mikra* 16 (1970/71), pp. 541–548 (Hebrew).

by Jehoiada. It is also probable that Jehoash was fostered by Jehosheba, Jehoram's daughter and Jehoiada's wife (2 Chr 22:11), with Athaliah's consent. However, judging from the fact that Jehoiada eventually plotted against Athaliah claiming that the throne should belong to the house of David (23:3), we can hardly accept the view that she actually did not assume the throne.

The rebellion against Athaliah was organized by Jehoiada the priest and was carried out by the royal mercenaries and guards. In addition, "the people of the land" participated in it.[13] Who were "the people of the land", who were differentiated from captains, the royal mercenaries, guards (2 Kgs 11:19), nobles, and governors (2 Chr 23:20)? From the course of history sketched above we can assume that they were those who were allied with the group which opposed the regime because of its alliance with the Omrides. We can also assume that the designation "people of the land" (*ʿam hāʾāreṣ*), stemmed from classifying them as the opponents to "the inhabitants of Jerusalem" (*yôšᵉḇê yᵉrûšālaym*), the supporters of the regime (22:1).

However, it is misleading to regard these designations as a sign of the antagonism between Jerusalem and Judah. Among the opponents to the regime are mentioned such people as a seer (19:2), Jehoram's brothers, some nobles (21:4), and the royal family (2 Kgs 11:1; 2 Chr 22:10). Most of them were Jerusalemites. Moreover, it seems that those Jerusalemites who were suppressed by the regime acted as the leaders of "the people of the land".[14]

[13] Since B. Stade, "Anmerkungen zu 2 Kö.10–14", *ZAW* 5 (1885), pp. 280 ff., it has been widely held that 2 Kgs 11 is resolved into two sources, i.e., a priestly source (vv. 1–12, 18b–20) and a popular source (vv. 13–18a); cf. J.A. Montgomery and H.S. Gehman, *A Critical and Exegitical Commentary on the Books of Kings* (ICC), Edinburgh, 1951, p. 418; J. Gray, *I & II Kings. A Commentary* (OTL), London, 1977³, pp. 566 ff. According to the analysis of Levin, *Der Sturz der Königin Atalja*, pp. 16 ff., this chapter consists of the following four layers: an early text from the Book of the Chronicles of the Kings of Judah used by the Deuteronomistic historian, a covenant-theological redaction in the late Deuteronomistic period, a priestly redaction, and an early Chronicler redaction. Against the view of separete sources, W. Rudolph argues for the unity of the chapter, "Die Einheitlichkeit der Erzählung vom Sturz der Atalja (2 Kön. 11)", in *A. Bertholet Festschrift*, Tübingen, 1950, pp. 473–478. In his view, however, all references to *ʿam hāʾāreṣ* before v. 20 are secondary (p. 477). Halpern points out that the scholars do not reckon with the problem of simultaneity in this chapter, *The Constitution*, p. 276, n. 88; cf. also M. Liverani, "L'histoire de Joas", *VT* 24 (1974), pp. 438–453.

[14] According to R. Gordis, "Sectional Rivalry in the Kingdom of Judah", *JQR* 25 (1934/35), pp. 237–259, there was always friction concerning the high places

The rebellion against Athaliah confirms this situation. It was Jehoiada the priest who took the initiative. Furthermore, he relied mainly on the royal mercenaries and guards to carry out his plot. By contrast, "the people of the land" played only passive role in the rebellion such as the attendance at the ceremony of Jehoash's enthronement (2 Kgs 11:14, 19; 2 Chr 23:13, 20) and the participation in the covenant-making between Yahweh, the king, and the people through Jehoiada's mediation (2 Kgs 11:17; 2 Chr 23:16). It is true that they destroyed the temple of Baal and slew its priest (2 Kgs 11:18; 2 Chr 23:17). Yet, undoubtedly Jehoiada's initiative was behind the banishment of Baalism from Jerusalem. Therefore, we cannot agree with the view that Athaliah's regime was overthrown by "a national revolution".[15] It was a court rebellion supported by the people. Nor can we find any contrast between "the rejoicing people of the land" and "the quiet city" after the rebellion (2 Kgs 11:20; 2 Chr 23:21), as E. Würthwein and A. Alt maintained.[16] It seems that the implication of the sentence, *hāʿîr šāqᵉṭāh*, is simply that "the city became peaceful" after the rebellion successfully came to an end.[17]

It must be pointed out that "the people of the land" played an important role, though it was passive. The main purpose of the rebellion was the restoration of the Davidic line. From the ideological point of view, it was inseparably connected with the purge of Baalism, since the restoration of the Davidic throne could be legitimatized solely by Yahweh who made a covenant with David by promising the eternal rule of the house of David over Israel (2 Sam 7:5–16; 1 Chr 17:4–14).[18] On the other hand, the house of David was

---

between the Jerusalemites and "the people of the land", who were the representatives of country; the coalition between them came into being only at the rebellion against Athaliah under the leadership of the Jerusalemites.

[15] Würthwein, *Der ʿamm haʾarez*, pp. 24 ff.; de Vaux, *Ancient Israel*, p. 71; Nicholson, *JSS* 10 (1965), p. 62.

[16] Würthwein, *Der ʿamm haʾarez*, p. 25; A. Alt, "Das Königtum in den Reichen Israel und Juda" (1951), in *Kleine Schriften zur Geschichte des Volkes Israel* II, München, 1953, p. 127.

[17] Cf. de Vaux, *Ancient Israel*, p. 71; G. Buccellati, *Cities and Nations of Ancient Syria. An Essay on Political Institutions with Special Reference to the Israelite Kingdoms* (Studi Semitici 26), Roma, 1967, pp. 168 f.

[18] For the covenant of David see M. Weinfeld, "ברית", in *TWAT* I, Stuttgart, 1970–73, cols. 799–801; idem, "Covenant, Davidic", in *IDBSup*, Nashville, 1976, pp. 188–192; Mettinger, *King and Messiah*, pp. 254 ff.; D.J. McCarthy, *Old Testament Covenant. A Survey of Current Opinions*, Oxford, 1973, pp. 45–52; Ishida, *The Royal Dynasties*, pp. 99 ff.; H. Kruse, "David's Covenant", *VT* 35 (1985), pp. 139–164; G.E. Mendenhall and G.A. Herion, "Covenant", in *ABD* I, New York, 1992, pp.

acknowledged as the ruling dynasty over Judah by the covenant which David made with the men of Judah when he established the kingdom of Judah at Hebron (2 Sam 2:4).[19] This ideological structure of the Davidic rule compelled Jehoiada to perform the renewal ceremony of both covenants in the midst of the rebellion.[20] Therefore, the Davidic rule over Judah could not have been restored without the support and participation of "the people of the land".

We must conclude that "the people of the land" who took part in the rebellion against Athaliah were none other than the people of Judah. Judging from the situation, it is reasonable to suppose that only a part of the people participated in it.[21] We do not know whether

---

1188 f., 1191 f. They recommend the term "charter" instead of "covenant"; M.D. Guinan, "Davidic Covenant", in *ABD* II, New York, 1992, pp. 69–72.

[19] The term "covenant" is missing from the text, but we can hardly doubt that a covenant was established between David and the men of Judah at that time, just as between David and the people of Israel, when they offered the kingship to David at Hebron (2 Sam 5:3), see A. Alt, "Die Staatenbildung der Israeliten in Palästina" (1930), in *Kleine Schriften zur Geschichte des Volkes Israel* II, München, 1953, p. 41; cf. also G. Fohrer, "Der Vertrag zwischen König und Volk in Israel" (1959), in *Studien zur alttestamentlichen Theologie und Geschichte (1949–1966)* (BZAW 115), Berlin, 1969, pp. 332 f.

[20] Opinions are variously divided on the parties between whom Jehoiada made the covenant. A single covenant between Yahweh on the one side and the king and the people on the other is maintained by G. von Rad, *Studies in Deuteronomy* (SBT 9), London, 1953, pp. 65 f., while M. Noth holds a single covenant between the king and the people only, "Das alttestamentliche Bundschließen im Lichte eines Mari-Textes" (1955), in *Gesammelte Studien zum Alten Testament*, München, 1957, pp. 151 f.; cf. also Levin, *Der Sturz der Königin Atalja*, pp. 60 f. According to D.J. McCarthy, *Treaty and Covenant. A Study in Form in the Ancinet Oriental Documents and in the Old Testament* (AnBib 21A), Rome, 1978², p. 215, the covenant was twofold, i.e., a covenant of the people and king with Yahweh and one of the people with the king. A double covenant between Yahweh and the king on the one side and between the king and the people on the other is suggested by K. Baltzer, *The Covenant Formulary in Old Testament, Jewish, and Early Christian Writings*, Oxford, 1971, pp. 78 ff., and A. Malamat, "Organs of Statecraft in the Israelite Monarchy" (1965), in *The Biblical Archaeologist Reader* III, New York, 1970, p. 166. A triple covenant between Yahweh and the king, between Yahweh and the people, and between the king and the people is argued by Gray, *I & II Kings*, p. 579, and B. Mazar, "המלוכה בישראל", in *Types of Leadership in the Biblical Period*, Jerusalem, 1973, p. 32 (Hebrew). It seems to us that this was a double covenant between Yahweh and the king and between the king and the people, since the covenant of David gave the position of mediator between Yahweh and the people to the Davidic kings; see also Halpern, *The Constitution*, p. 276, n. 87; M. Cogan and H. Tadmor, *II Kings. A New Translation with Introduction and Commentary* (AB 11), New York, 1988, pp. 132 f. About parallel example for this sort of double covenant in the ancient Near East see Ishida, *The Royal Dynasties*, pp. 115 ff.

[21] Mettinger, *King and Messiah*, p. 124, suggests the possibility that the rebellion took place at a new year feast connected with the year of release of every seven

they were the formal representatives or not.[22] In any case, acting under the name of the whole people, out of loyalty to Yahwism as well as to the house of David, they opposed the regime under the foreign queen supported by "the inhabitants of Jerusalem". The initiative for this revolt was taken by Jehoiada the priest of the temple of Yahweh in Jerusalem.

3. *Regicides in the Kingdom of Judah*

Jehoash, who was enthroned by Jehoiada with the help of "the people of the land", met a violent end as a result of a conspiracy of his servants (2 Kgs 12:20–21). This was the revenge of the priests who were enraged at the king's violence against Zechariah the son of Jehoiada (2 Chr 24:25), which was the culmination of the conflict between the king and the priests caused by the king's intervention in repairing of the temple (2 Kgs 12:4–16; 2 Chr 24:4–14) and his plundering of the temple treasury (2 Kgs 12:18).[23] Amaziah, however, succeeded Jehoash in the normal way (2 Kgs 14:1; 2 Chr 24:27b). There was no Judaean king but Amaziah, whose father died an unnatural death, however, he ascended the throne without any intervention. A. Malamat suggested that the intervention of "the people of the land" was not mentioned on this occasion due to the fact that Amaziah was already an adult, i.e., twenty-five years old, at his accession (2 Kgs 14:2; 2 Chr 25:1).[24] But Jehoahaz was also an adult of twenty-three, when "the people of the land" helped him ascend the throne (2 Kgs 23:30–31; 2 Chr 36:1–2). Therefore, Malamat regards Jehoahaz's case as exceptional on the basis of his assumption that a *coup d'état* had been carried out by "the people of the land".

---

years when the people from the whole country came to Jerusalem (Deut 31:9 ff.). It seems a conjecture based on an indefinite evidence (cf. 2 Kgs 11:4).

22 M. Sulzberger argues that "the people of the land" were nothing but the national council which served as the representative body of the people in the political as well as the judicial spheres, *Am ha-aretz: the Ancient Hebrew Parliament*, Philadelphia, 1910²; idem, "The Polity of the Ancient Hebrews", *JQR* 3 (1912/13), pp. 1–81; cf. N. Sloush, "Representative Government among the Hebrews and Phoenicians", *JQR* 4 (1913/14), pp. 303–310. On the other hand, de Vaux, *RA* 58 (1964), p. 171, is of the opinion that the elders (*zᵉqēnîm*) acted as the representatives of "the people of the land".

23 Cf. de Vaux, *Ancient Israel*, p. 377; Gray, *I & II Kings*, p. 590; Reviv, *Beth Mikra* 16 (1970/71), pp. 545 ff.

24 A. Malamat, "The Last Kings of Judah and the Fall of Jerusalem", *IEJ* 18 (1968), p. 140, n. 6.

We may assume, however, building on this suggestion, that Amaziah had been designated as the heir apparent long before Jehoash was murdered, so that his succession left no room for a question which would bring about intervention. On the other hand, the intervention of "the people of the land" in Jehoahaz's succession to Josiah was caused by lack of the official designation of the successor at Josiah's unexpected death. Josiah was still a young, ambitious king of thirty-nine, when killed in battle (2 Kgs 22:1; 2 Chr 34:1). Apart from his relatively young age, it appears that the political antagonism at the court between the pro-Egyptian party and the anti-Egyptian faction postponed his decision about the appointment of the heir apparent.[25]

It must be mentioned, however, that "the people of the land" perhaps felt no need to intervene in Amaziah's succession because this political crisis (which resulted from the conflict between the Davidic king and the priests of Yahweh) did not affect either Davidic succession or Yahwism. Moreover, "the people of the land", whose power was not strong enough to take the initiative in the political change at that period, could not intervene in Amaziah's succession without an invitation from one of the parties in the capital city.

Amaziah also fell a victim to a conspiracy (2 Kgs 14:19; 2 Chr 25:27). Owing to lack of direct information, the motive of this conspiracy is very obscure. Some scholars assume that the same conflict between the royal and the sacerdotal authorities caused the conspiracy.[26] A closer examination of the biblical sources indicates a different situation, however. Amaziah took revenge for his father's death upon the conspirators, when he consolidated his rule (2 Kgs 14:5; 2 Chr 25:3). Yet, we do not hear of this sort of revenge taken by Azariah, who succeeded Amaziah, his father. It has been suggested, on the grounds of chronological studies, that Azariah ascended the throne not after Amaziah was killed but when Amaziah was taken captive by Jehoash king of Israel at Beth-shemesh (2 Kgs 14:13; 2 Chr 25:23). This took place at least fifteen years before Amaziah's assassination (cf. 2 Kgs 14:17; 2 Chr 25:25).[27] On the basis of these observations we may suppose, as H. Frumstein (Tadmor) has suggested,

[25] About the political conflict at Josiah's court see ibid., p. 140.

[26] See de Vaux, *Ancient Israel*, p. 377; Reviv, *Beth Mikra* 16 (1970/71), p. 548. However, Gray, *I & II Kings*, p. 613, prefers a military uprising.

[27] See J. Lewy, *Die Chronologie der Könige von Israel und Juda*, Giessen, 1927, pp. 11 ff.; H. Frumstein (Tadmor), "הבעיות הכרונולוגיות" in "אמציה, אמציהו", in *Encyclopaedia*

that Amaziah's assassination was caused by a conflict between Azariah, the regent, and Amaziah, the deposed king.[28]

If this is the case, we should reconsider the identity of "all the people of Judah" (*kol ʿam-yᵉhûḏāh*) who helped Azariah ascend the throne instead of Amaziah (2 Kgs 14:21; 2 Chr 26:1). It has been widely held that "all the people of Judah", who intervened in Azariah's enthronement, were none other than "the people of the land".[29] However, if Azariah was made king to fill the vacant throne left by the defeated king who was taken captive, those who elevated him to the throne must have been all the men who were fighting against the enemy. Thus, we must assume that "all the people of Judah", who supported Azariah, included not only "the people of the land" but also the royal officials, the noble men, the military people, and other men of rank and influence. We can conclude, therefore, that the designation "people of Judah" does not always signify "the people of the land", but it was used in the wider sense as the designation of the whole nation of Judah including the officials in Jerusalem.

When Azariah became a leper, Jotham, his son, administered public affairs as the regent. His office is described as "over the palace and governing the people of the land" (2 Kgs 15:5; 2 Chr 26:21). "The people of the land" are contrasted here with "the palace". In a similar way, the offering of "the people of the land" is distinguished from that of king Ahaz (2 Kgs 16:15; cf. Ezek 45:22; 46:9–10). In both cases, it appears that the expression "people of the land" is used simply as a synonym for "the people of Judah" under the monarchical rule. Accordingly, it is difficult to deduce from these passages any specific political role assigned to "the people of the land" in that period.[30] This means we have virtually no information at all on the political activity of "the people of the land" during the two hundred year period from Athaliah's overthrow to Josiah's enthronement.

Biblica I, Jerusalem, 1950, col. 439 (Hebrew); H. Tadmor, "כרונולוניה", in *Encyclopaedia Biblica* IV, Jerusalem, 1962, col. 282 (Hebrew); E.R. Thiele, *The Mysterious Numbers of the Hebrew Kings*, Grand Rapids, 1983³, p. 199.

28 Frumstein (Tadmor), in *Encyclopaedia Biblica* I, col. 439 (Hebrew); cf. also Cogan and Tadmor, *II Kings*, p. 159.

29 Würthwein, *Der ʿamm haʾarez*, p. 15; de Vaux, *Ancient Israel*, p. 71; Alt, in *Kleine Schriften* II, p. 127; Malamat, *IEJ* 18 (1968), p. 140; Tadmor, *JWH* 11 (1968), p. 66. According to Talmon, in *Fourth World Congress of Jewish Studies* I, p. 74, the expressions *ʿam hāʾāreṣ* and *ʿam yᵉhûḏāh* are two different abbreviations of the same full designation of a political body: *ʿam hāʾāreṣ liḇnê yᵉhûḏāh*.

30 Cf. Nicholson, *JSS* 10 (1965), pp. 62 f.

4. *The Last Days of the Kingdom of Judah*

The long reign of Manasseh was followed by Amon's short-lived rule. When Amon was murdered by his servants in the second year of his reign, "the people of the land" slew all the conspirators and elevated Josiah to the throne (2 Kgs 21:19, 23–24; 2 Chr 33:21, 24–25). Since we have only this terse report, it is extremely difficult to clarify the situation.[31]

Both international and domestic conditions must be considered as the background of this political change. As for the international political sphere, it was the time of dramatic changes. About 656 B.C. the Egyptians succeeded in expelling the Assyrians from Egypt.[32] This was the beginning of the rapid decline of the Assyrian empire. At the same time, the Egyptians, as an ambitious heir to the Assyrians, began to influence Syria-Palestine. This situation seems to be reflected in Manasseh's change of religious policy and his fortification of the city of David and the citadels in Judah (2 Chr 33:14–16). This was an attempt to recover the sovereignty from the Assyrian rule. The time was not yet ripe, however. Because of this rebellious attempt, Manasseh was punished by the Assyrians (33:11).[33] We can assume that the Judaean king was caught between the anti-Assyrian movement supported by the awakening people and the Assyrian pressure in the last years of his reign.

A. Malamat once argued that Amon was assassinated by an anti-Assyrian party, but a counter-revolution was achieved by "the people

---

[31] Scholars once regarded the conspirators as the priests of Yahweh who tried to reform the foreign cult supported by Manasseh and Amon, see E. Sellin, *Geschichte des israelitisch-jüdischen Volkes* I, Leipzig, 1924, 1935², p. 282; R. Kittel, *Geschichte des Volkes Israel* II, Stuttgart, 1925⁷, pp. 401 f. But it is difficult to assume that "the people of the land", who opposed the conspirators, were anti-Yahwist.

[32] About the historical vicissitude in this period see F.K. Kienitz, *Die politische Geschichte Ägyptens vom 7. bis zum 4. Jahrhundert vor der Zeitwende*, Berlin, 1953, pp. 11 ff.; idem, "Die Saïtische Renaissance", in *Fischer Weltgeschichte* IV. *Die Altorientalischen Reiche* III. *Die erste Hälfte des 1. Jahrtausends*, Frankfurt a/M., 1967, pp. 256 ff., 265 f.; K.A. Kitchen, *The Third Intermediate Period in Egypt (1100–650 B.C.)*, Warminster, 1973, pp. 400 ff.

[33] See J. Liver, "מנשה", in *Encyclopaedia Biblica* V, Jerusalem, 1968, col. 43 (Hebrew); cf. Y. Aharoni, *The Land of the Bible. A Historical Geography*, London, 1966, p. 346. However, some scholars argue that the fortification was made against Egypt with the Assyrian consent, see W. Rudolph, *Chronikbücher*, p. 317; J. Bright, *A History of Israel* (OTL), London, 1972², p. 313; cf. also J.A. Soggin, *A History of Israel. From the Beginnings to the Bar Kochba Revolt, AD 135*, London, 1984, p. 239.

of the land", who were afraid of Assyrian punitive action.[34] Then, by slightly modifying this theory, he has put the stress on the Egyptian instigation behind the courtier's revolt against Amon.[35] It is very likely that around 640 B.C., when Amon's assassination took place, there was a conflict between a pro-Assyrian group and a pro-Egyptian party at the Judaean court, because in that period the Egyptians tried to take over the Assyrian domination in Western Asia.[36] On the other hand, Amon's yielding to the foreign cult (2 Kgs 21:20–22; 2 Chr 33:22–23) would show his submissiveness to the Assyrian rule. Therefore, it is possible to assume that the Egyptians urged conspirators to murder their pro-Assyrian king.

It seems, however, that this political conflict was interwoven with domestic antagonism. When Manasseh died at sixty-seven, Amon was a young prince of twenty-two (2 Kgs 21:1, 19; 2 Chr 33:1, 21). Amon was born to Manasseh when he was forty-five. Judging from the fact that almost all the Judaean kings were born when their fathers were about twenty,[37] it is likely that Amon was neither the first-born nor the eldest surviving son. If this is the case, we can assume that some court intrigue helped Amon ascend the throne, as is usually the case when the principle of primogeniture is overruled.[38]

---

[34] A. Malamat, "The Historical Background of the Assassination of Amon, King of Judah", *IEJ* 3 (1953), pp. 26–29; cf. idem, "The Last Wars of the Kingdom of Judah", *JNES* 9 (1950), p. 218; cf. also M. Noth, *The History of Israel*, London, 1960², p. 272; F.M. Cross & D.N. Freedman, "Josiah's Revolt against Assyria", *JNES* 12 (1953), p. 56; Bright, *A History of Israel*, p. 315. According to K. Galling, *Die israelitische Staatsverfassung in ihrer vorderorientalischen Umwelt* (AO XXVIII 3/4), Leipzig, 1929, pp. 33 f., 59 f., an ultra-pro-Assyrian party, which doubted Amon's pro-Assyrian stance and tried to replace him by a foreigner, was responsible for his assassination.

[35] A. Malamat, "Josiah's Bid for Armageddon. The Background of the Judean-Egyptian Encounter in 609 B.C.", in *The Gaster Festschrift, JANES* 5 (1973), p. 271. The identity of Amon's assassins with Egyptian agents had been suggested by N.M. Nicolsky, "Pascha im Kulte des jerusalemischen Tempels", *ZAW* 45 (1927), pp. 241 ff.; E. Auerbach, *Wüste und gelobtes Land* II, Berlin, 1936, p. 159; cf. also Gray, *I & II Kings*, pp. 711 f.

[36] According to the study of Malamat, in *The Gaster Festschrift, JANES* 5 (1973), pp. 270 ff., esp. p. 273, while expulsion of the Assyrian rule from Egypt took place between 656 and 652 B.C., the alliance between Egypt and Assyria against the Chaldeans came into being between 622 and 617 B.C.; thus, the Egyptian activity of taking over the Assyrian rule in Palestine must have been limited to the years between 652 and 622 B.C.

[37] Cf. Tadmor, in *Encyclopaedia Biblica* IV, cols. 303 f. (Hebrew); Thiele, *The Mysterious Numbers*, p. 206.

[38] See above p. 83, n. 7.

On the other hand, the biblical source testifies to a bloody antagonism among the inhabitants of Jerusalem under Manasseh (2 Kgs 21:16; cf. 24:4). Although we are not informed of the situation, it is not unlikely that it was the beginning of the clash between the pro-Assyrian party and the pro-Egyptian faction. The former backed Manasseh's rule and Amon's succession, while the latter tried to overthrow the pro-Assyrian regime by supporting Amon's elder brothers under Egyptian instigation.

It appears that "the people of the land" avoided this struggle in Jerusalem. Judging from the political development under Josiah and his successors, it is clear that "the people of the land" belonged neither to the pro-Assyrian party nor to the pro-Egyptian faction. But when Jerusalem fell into chaos at Amon's assassination, they intervened in the conflict on their own accord. By taking advantage of the confusion among the people of the ruling class in the capital city, they were able to carry out "a national revolution", in order to bring about nationalistic reform under a Davidic king.

In contrast to the rebellion against Athaliah, it is remarkable that "the people of the land" played the leading role in this political change. We do not know exactly how they came to dominate in this period. Possibly, the collapse of the military power as a result of the Assyrian invasion at Hezekiah's time weakened the authority of the central government.[39] The severe domestic struggle in Jerusalem under Manasseh and Amon also undermined the control of the central authority. In addition, we can assume that the northern tribes, who took refuge in Judah from the catastrophe of Samaria in 722 B.C. and the subsequent disturbances, brought with them the strong tradition of the popular sovereignty and strengthened the people's voice in political affairs. In any case, "the people of the land" are mentioned most frequently in the Hebrew Bible in the last days of Judah. Moreover, the fact that they are mentioned side by side with people of the ruling class, such as the kings, the royal servants, the nobles, the priests, and the prophets (Jer 1:18; 34:19; 37:2; 44:21; Ezek 7:27; 22:24–29), testifies to the influential position they occupied in this period.

Evidently, "the people of the land" acted as the driving force of Josiah's policy of national independence from foreign rule in the

---

[39] Cf. E. Junge, *Der Wiederaufbau des Heerwesens des Reiches Juda unter Josia* (BWANT 75), Stuttgart, 1937, pp. 24 ff.

political as well as religious spheres. "All the men of Judah" mentioned first together with the inhabitants of Jerusalem and the religious functionaries, who participated in the covenant-making of Josiah's reform (2 Kgs 23:2; 2 Chr 34:30), were doubtless the same "people of the land" who enthroned Josiah.[40] When Josiah was killed during a battle at Megiddo in 609 B.C., "the people of the land" intervened again in the question of the succession to the throne and elevated Jehoahaz, the second son of Josiah, to the throne by overruling the principle of primogeniture (2 Kgs 23:30; 2 Chr 36:1). Apparently, Jehoahaz was connected with the nationalistic party supported by "the people of the land", while Jehoiakim, his elder brother, was backed by the pro-Egyptian faction. It is clear that by this intervention "the people of the land" attempted to continue their nationalistic policy which started with their enthronement of Josiah.[41]

However, Neco, the Egyptian king, who killed Josiah, deposed Jehoahaz and appointed Jehoiakim as his puppet king (2 Kgs 23:33–34; 2 Chr 36:3–4). As Neco's royal vassal, Jehoiakim imposed a heavy tax on "the people of the land" to send tribute to Egypt (2 Kgs 23:35). Naturally, "the people of the land" refused to co-operate with this Egyptian puppet regime. Even when Jehoiakim rebelled against Nebuchadnezzar, king of Babylon, most of "the people of the land" stayed away from besieged Jerusalem, except "the poorest people of the land" (2 Kgs 24:14). Under Zedekiah, "the people of the land" changed this negative attitude towards the regime into the positive support.[42]

Nebuchadnezzar designated Zedekiah, the third son of Josiah, as the king of Judah (2 Kgs 24:17; 2 Chr 36:10). He was Jehoahaz's brother by blood (cf. 2 Kgs 23:31; 24:18), whom "the people of the land" once vainly supported. Although Zedekiah was Nebuchadnezzar's appointee, it is understandable that "the people of the land" set their hope on him to restore their nationalistic policy which was

---

[40] A close relationship between "the people of the land" and the Deuteronomistic reform under Josiah is argued by von Rad, *Studies in Deuteronomy*, pp. 60 ff.; cf. J.A. Soggin, "Der judäische *ʿam haʾareṣ* und das Königtum in Juda", *VT* 13 (1963), pp. 187–195.

[41] Cf. Malamat, *IEJ* 18 (1968), pp. 139 f.

[42] M. Sekine, "Beobachtungen zu der Josianischen Reform", *VT* 22 (1972), pp. 367 f., regards the co-operation of "the people of the land" with Zedekiah's regime as a sign of the decadence of their ethos, which took place after the frustration of Josiah's reform.

frustrated by Neco. We learn of this situation from the impressive presence of "the people of the land" in Jerusalem, when it was besieged again by the Babylonians in the time of Zedekiah (2 Kgs 25:3, 19; Jer 34:19; cf. 2 Kgs 25:12).

Ezekiel also mentions the gathering of "the people of the land" in Jerusalem at that time. However, according to his view, they were gathered to Jerusalem by Yahweh to be punished (Ezek 22:19–22). His equation of "the people of the land" with "the inhabitants of Jerusalem" (12:19) shows that "the people of the land" finally became the dominant power in the capital city. But both Jeremiah (37:2) and Ezekiel (7:27; 22:23–31) directed their severest attacks against "the people of the land" as well as the other national leaders. These prophetic words testify to the tragic fact that the fanatical pursuit of nationalism by "the people of the land" in the last days of the kingdom of Judah only served to contribute to the disastrous end of their country.

5. *Summary*

From the foregoing examination of the historiographical reports and prophetic sayings in which "the people of the land" (*ʿam hāʾāreṣ*) are mentioned we can come to the following conclusions:

a) We cannot but admit that there are texts in which the expression "the people of the land" of Judah seems to be used as synonymous with "the people of Juda" (*ʿam yᵉhûḏāh* or *ʾanšê yᵉhûḏāh*), e.g., "And Jotham the king's son was over the household, governing the people of the land" (2 Kgs 15:5; cf. 2 Chr 26:21); "And King Ahaz commanded . . . . . upon the great altar burn . . . . . the king's burnt offering . . . . . with the burnt offering of all the people of the land" (2 Kgs 16:15). Therefore, we can hardly accept the view that the expression "people of the land" stands for any social class or a small number of the political power.

b) However, there are also other texts which tell about "the people of the land". In all the texts in question "the people of the land" play a certain role in determinig the succession of the Davidic throne, i.e., the overthrow of Athaliah and the enthronment of Joash (2 Kgs 11; 2 Chr 23); the execution of the conspirators against King Amon and the investiture of Josiah (2 Kgs 21:23–24; 2 Chr 33:24–25); the enthronement of Jehoahaz after Josiah' s death in battle (2 Kgs 23:30;

2 Chr 36:1). It is not easy to regard the expression "people of the land" in these texts as a simple synonym for "the people of Juda". Otherwise, it is difficult to answer the question why the historiographer employed the very expression "people of the land" in these texts instead of "the people of Juda". It cannot be by chance, since all the texts report on the same theme: the intervention of "the people of the land" in the political crises to secure the succession of David's throne.

c) It seems legitimate to assume, therefore, that the historiographer indicated by the expression "people of the land" that the people of Judah who took part in determining Judaean kings from the Davidic family acted under the name of the whole people. We can find a similar implication in the expressions *kol-hāʿām*: "all the people" or *kol-yiśrāʾēl*: "all Israel" who took the initiative to designate kings in the Northern Kingdom from Saul to Omri. What the historiographers emphasized in both the expressions was the unity of the people or the legitimate representation of the people who determined their kings.[43]

d) Judging from the situation, *kol-ʿām yᵉhûḏāh*: "all the people of Judah" who helped Azariah ascend the throne (2 Kgs 14:21; 2 Chr 26:1) are regarded as the whole nation who included not only "the people of the land" but also all the royal servants. On the other hand, the whole nation who supported Josiah's reform consisted of *kol-ʾîš yᵉhûḏāh*: "all the men of Judah", all the inhabitants of Jerusalem, i.e., the royal servants, and religious functionaries (2 Kgs 23:2; 2 Chr 34:30). This distinction of the members of the whole nation corresponds to the dichotomy of the kingdom as "Judah and Jerusalem" (2 Kgs 23:1; 2 Chr 34:29).[44]

e) It is very likely that the expression "people of the land" has, at least, double meanings in Judah in the monarchical period: either the people of Judah in general or the people who held power over determining successors to the Davidic throne in cooperation with or in opposition to the inhabitants of Jerusalem, i.e., the royal servants and religious functionaries.

---

[43] See above p. 79.
[44] Cf. Cogan and Tadmor, *II Kings*, pp. 284 f.

CHAPTER SIX

THE HOUSE OF AHAB*

1. *The Prophetic Attack against Ahab*

The royal dynasties of Israel and Judah are usually designated as "founder's house", i.e., Saul's house (2 Sam 3:1, 6, 10, etc.), David's house (3:1, 6; 1 Kgs 12:19, etc.), Jeroboam's house (1 Kgs 13:34; 15:29; 21:22 etc.), Baasha's house (16:3, 7; 21:22 etc.), and Jehu's house (Hos 1:4). Yet the name Omri's house is conspicuously missing from the Hebrew Bible. Instead, the same dynasty is always called Ahab's house, although Omri was the dynastic founder and Ahab was his successor.

Ahab's house (בית אחאב) is mentioned eighteen times in the Hebrew Bible under three categories. First, as a royal house destroyed at Yahweh's command (2 Kgs 9:7–9; 10:10–11, 30; 21:13; 2 Chr 22:7–8); second, as an example of an evil royal house which committed a grave sin against Yahweh (2 Kgs 8:18 = 2 Chr 21:6; 2 Kgs 8:27aα = 2 Chr 22:3a; 2 Kgs 8:27aβ = 2 Chr 22:4a; 2 Chr 21:13; Mic 6:16); third, as the relatives of Ahaziah, the king of Judah (2 Kgs 8:27b).

Since it is legitimate to assume that Ahab's house became an example of a sinful royal dynasty only after it had been overthrown, the second category would derive from the first. In the first category, Ahab's house is, with only one exception (2 Kgs 21:13), mentioned in direct connection with Jehu's rebellion. J.M. Miller assumed that the account of Jehu's rebellion, in which Ahab's house appears as the target of the rebellion, was composed by an author who, according to the principle of the charismatic monarchy, accepted Omri as a legitimate ruler but attacked Ahab and his sons for ascending the throne without charismatic credentials.[1] This is the reason for the extraordinary reference to "Ahab's house", and never to "Omri's house". However, it appears that the ideology of the so-called charismatic

* This essay is a revised version of the study which appeared in *IEJ* 25 (1975), pp. 135–137.

[1] J.M. Miller, "The Fall of the House of Ahab", *VT* 17 (1967), pp. 318–321.

kingship has nothing to do with this phenomenon, and a closer examination of the biblical texts seems to indicate a different source.

The origin of Jehu's rebellion lies in Elisha's confrontation with Ahab. In condemning Ahab, Elisha asserted: "I have not troubled Israel; but you, and your father's house" (1 Kgs 18:18). He also predicted Ahab's doom: "And I will make your house like the house of Jeroboam the son of Nebat, and like the house of Baasha the son of Ahijah" (21:22). Evidently, both "your father's house" and "your house" in these words of Elisha refer not to Omri's but to Ahab's house. Although some scholars interpret "your father's house" here as Omri's house,[2] since a "father's house" is a *terminus technicus* for a fundamental unit in the patriarchal society which disintegrates on the death of the father as the head of the family,[3] the "father's house" of Ahab cannot be Omri's house. The same usage of "house" can be found in the prophet Amos' prediction of the doom of Jeroboam's house (Amos 7:9). This Jeroboam was the fourth king of the Jehu dynasty, but Amos speaks of the fall of Jeroboam's rather than Jehu's house. Both Elijah and Amos intensified the threat of the attack against the reigning kings by calling their dynasties directly after their own instead of the founder's names. It appears, therefore, that the designation "Ahab's house", first coined by Elijah, was transmitted together with the other Yahwistic traditions to the historiographer of Jehu's rebellion.

However, the historiographer may have had another reason for adopting this designation for the Omrides. Jehu's rebellion was a Yahwistic revolution against the Baalism which prevailed in the Northern Kingdom under Jezebel, Ahab's queen consort (1 Kgs 16:31). After Ahab's death she exercised authority over the kingdom as the queen-mother: *g^e^b̲îrāh* (2 Kgs 10:13; cf. 1 Kgs 22:52; 2 Kgs 9:22).[4] The whole account clearly leaves the impression that the arch-enemy against whom Jehu directed his attack was not Jehoram, king of the Omrides, who even carried out a reform agaisnt Baalism (2 Kgs 3:2), but Jezebel and her regime. It is clear that he called actually Jezebel's regime by her husband's name: Ahab's house.

---

[2] S. Timm, *Die Dynastie Omri. Quellen und Untersuchungen zur Geschichte Israels im 9. Jahrhundert vor Christus* (FRLANT 124), Göttingen, 1982, p. 63.

[3] See J. Pedersen, *Israel. Its Life and Culture* I–II, London/Copenhagen, 1926, pp. 51–54; R. de Vaux, *Ancient Israel. Its Life and Institutions*, London, 1961, pp. 7 f.

[4] About the queen-mother's authority in the kingdoms of Israel and Judah see above p. 84, n. 10.

2. *The Symbolic Name of the Most Evil Dynasty*

It appears that Ahab's house became the symbolic name of Israel's most evil dynasty soon after its destruction. In the words of the prophet Micah, who was active about a century after the downfall of the dynasty of Omri, we find that "all the works of the house of Ahab" are paralleled with "the statutes of Omri" (Mic 6:16). From these words we see how quickly the tradition became rooted in Israel. Micah must have known this dynasty under the name "Omri's house", as the Assyrians contemporary with him called it *Bīt-Ḫumri*.[5] But he could no longer change the fixed connotation of Ahab's house as the most sinful dynasty even when mentioning both Omri and Ahab side by side.

As for Ahab's "seventy sons in Samaria" (2 Kgs 10:1), scholars either regard this as a later addition,[6] or interpret "sons" in a general sense as all the family of Ahab, including sons and grandsons.[7] However, because of the expression "his father's throne" in Jehu's letter (2 Kgs 10:3) it is clear that they were Jehoram's sons, i.e., Ahab's grandsons. Then why are they not called the seventy sons of Jehoram? Perhaps the name Ahab here denotes Ahab's house as the royal dynasty to be destroyed and suggests the anticipated doom of these princes.

The crux of Athaliah's double paternity is also to be solved by the same interpretation of "Ahab's house". A biblical tradition refers to Athaliah as Ahab's daughter (2 Kgs 8:18 = 2 Chr 21:6), while another calls her Omri's daughter (2 Kgs 8:26 = 2 Chr 22:2). This inconsistency can seemingly be solved by the use of a Semitic idiom in which the terms son and daughter express not only this precise family relationship, but also membership of a family. Accordingly,

---

[5] S. Parpola, *Neo-Assyrian Toponyms* (AOAT 6), Neukirchen-Vluyn, 1970, pp. 82 f.; *ANET*, pp. 280 f., 284 f. Oddly enough the name *Bīt-Ḫumri* in Assyrian sources, in all cases known to me, never indicates the Omride dynasty but refers to the kingdom of Israel under the rule of Jehu and his successors. But there is no reason to doubt that the Assyrians began to call Israel *Bīt-Ḫumri*, perhaps under the influence of the Aramaeans, when they first encountered her in Ahab's time; cf. also *KAI* 181:4–8; *ANET*, p. 320 (the Moabite stone).

[6] B. Stade, "Anmerkungen zu 2 Kö. 10–14", *ZAW* 5 (1885), p. 275; *BHK*, p. 574.

[7] J.A. Montgomery and H.S. Gehman, *A Critical and Exegetical Commentary on the Books of Kings* (ICC), Edinburgh, 1951, p. 408; J. Gray, *I & II Kings. A Commentary* (OTL), London, 1977[3], p. 553.

in order to smooth over the contradiction, she is generally regarded as Ahab's daughter and Omri's granddaughter.[8] However, chronological studies have shown that Athaliah was Omri's daughter and could not have been Ahab's child.[9]

It is worth noting that Athaliah is called Omri's daughter in the stereotyped introductory formula of the Judaean kings (2 Kgs 8:26), while the epithet Ahab's daughter is mentioned in a Deuteronomistic verdict on Jehoram, king of Judah (8:18). Undoubtedly, the former information, which is believed to originate in official royal records, is more authentic and historically reliable than the latter. Therefore, we can regard the epithet "Ahab's daughter" as a secondary tradition. However, it seems as though this stemmed neither from wrong information[10] nor from her relationship as foster-daughter to Ahab.[11] From the beginning the historiographer's intention was not to use her father's name but to show her membership of "Ahab's house", i.e., the most sinful dynasty in Israel.[12]

A similar Deuteronomistic verdict follows the introductory formula for Ahaziah's reign (2 Kgs 8:25–27; cf. 2 Chr 22:2–4). In the formula, as has been mentioned above, Ahaziah's mother Athaliah is called Omri's daughter (2 Kgs 8:26). In the verdict, however, Ahaziah is referred to as "the son-in-law of the house of Ahab" (2 Kgs 8:27). If we press the literal meaning of Ahab's house here, Ahaziah's mother must be a daughter of Ahab. But it is unlikely that such an obvious inconsistency was allowed between the formula and the verdict, both of which are directly connected. We must conclude that Ahab's house stands here also for the name of the most sinful royal house in Israel as the quasi-designation of the dynasty of Omri.[13]

---

[8] M. Noth, *The History of Israel*, London, 1960², p. 236, n. 4; M. Cogan and H. Tadmor, *II Kings. A New Translation with Introduction and Commentary* (AB 11), New York, 1988, p. 98.

[9] J. Begrich, "Atalja, die Tochter Omris", *ZAW* 53 (1935), pp. 78 f.; H.J. Katzenstein, "Who Were the Parents of Athaliah?", *IEJ* 5 (1955), pp. 194–197; see above pp. 82 f.

[10] Begrich, *ZAW* 53 (1935), p. 79. He also proposes to read מבת instead of בת and אשה instead of לאשה in 2 Kgs 8:18, i.e., "denn *aus dem Hause* Ahabs hatte er *eine Frau*" (my italics).

[11] Katzenstein, *IEJ* 5 (1955), p. 197.

[12] Cf. W. Thiel, "Athaliah", in *ABD* I, New York, 1992, p. 511.

[13] The usage of "Ahab's house" in the first half of the same verse: "And he walked in the way of *the house of Ahab*, and did evil in the sight of Yahweh, as did *the house of Ahab*" (2 Kgs 8:27a; my italics), also supports this interpretation.

PART TWO

THE SUCCESSION NARRATIVE IN HISTORIOGRAPHICAL PERSPECTIVE

CHAPTER SEVEN

SOLOMON'S SUCCESSION TO THE THRONE OF DAVID*

1. *Methodological Problems*

Appreciation of a large literary complex in most of 2 Samuel and 1 Kings 1–2, usually designated the "Succession Narrative" or the "Court History",[1] as one of the earliest, as well as one of the finest, historical works in the Hebrew Bible, composed by an eyewitness or eyewitnesses to events and episodes reported in it, was once established in the scholarly world.[2] Especially the thesis of L. Rost concerning the Succession Narrative, the purpose of which was Solomon's legitimation of his kingship,[3] was widely accepted by the great majority of scholars.[4] But since the 1960's, and especially in the 1970's, this thesis has been attacked by many scholars with different approaches.[5]

* This essay is a revised version of the studies which appeared in T. Ishida (ed.), *SPDS*, Tokyo/Winona Lake, 1982, pp. 175–187; *Biblical Studies* 19 (1985), pp. 5–43 (Japanese); R.E. Friedman and H.G.M. Williamson (eds.), *The Future of Biblical Studies. The Hebrew Scriptures*, Atlanta, 1987, pp. 165–187.

[1] I prefer the designation "Succession Narrative" to "Court History" based on my analysis of the literary complex according to which the theme of the narrative is to be regarded as the legitimation of Solomon's succession to the throne of David. For different opinions see H.O. Forshey, "Court Narrative (2 Samuel 9–1 Kings 2)" in *ABD* I, New York, 1992, pp. 1176–1179.

[2] J. Wellhausen, *Die Composition des Hexateuchs und der historischen Bücher des Alten Testaments*, Berlin, 1899³, 1963⁴, pp. 259 f.; E. Meyer, *Die Israeliten und ihre Nachbarstämme. Alttestamentliche Untersuchungen*, Halle an der Saale, 1906, p. 485.

[3] L. Rost, "Die Überlieferung von der Thronnachfolge Davids" (1926), in *Das kleine Credo und andere Studien zum Alten Testament*, Heidelberg, 1965, pp. 119–253. Rost regards the contents of the Succession Narrative as including: 2 Sam 6:16, 20 ff. . . . 7:11b, 16 . . .; 9:1–10:5, (10:6–11:1); 11:2–12:7a; 12:13–25, (26–31); 13:1–14:24; 14:28–18:17; 18:19–20:22; 1 Kgs 1–2:1; 2:5–10; 2:12–27a, 28–46, ibid., pp. 214 f.

[4] E.g., M. Noth, *Überlieferungsgeschichtliche Studien. Die sammelnden und bearbeitenden Geschichtswerke im Alten Testament*, Tübingen, 1943, 1957², pp. 61–72; G. von Rad, "Der Anfang der Geschichtsschreibung im alten Israel" (1944), in *Gesammelte Studien zum Alten Testament*, München, 1958, pp. 148–188; R.N. Whybray, *The Succession Narrative. A Study of II Samuel 9–20; I Kings 1 and 2* (SBTS 9), London, 1968; J.A. Soggin, *Introduction to the Old Testament. From its origins to the closing of the Alexandrian canon*, London, 1980², pp. 192 f.; cf. idem, *A History of Israel. From the Beginnings to the Bar Kochba Revolt, AD 135*, London, 1984, pp. 43 f.

[5] For bibliographies and various opinions see C. Conroy, *Absalom Absalom! Narrative*

Despite criticisms, however, the thesis of Rost is still held as valid in principle in studies in which historical approaches are employed.[6] In contrast, scholars who take either redaction-criticism[7] or literary-structural analysis[8] as their method assume a critical attitude toward the longstanding thesis about the narrative. The redaction-criticism approach postulates doublets or triplets in the narrative and solves textual difficulties by an assumption of two- or three-fold redactions. In contrast to this diachronic analysis, those who take a literary-structural approach argue for a synchronic understanding of the narrative, describing such patterns as inclusio, chiasmus, concentric

and Language in 2 Sam 13–20 (AnBib 81), Rome, 1978, pp. 1–4; D.M. Gunn, *The Story of King David. Genre and Interpretation* (JSOTSup 6), Sheffield, 1978, pp. 19–34; E. Ball, "Introduction", in L. Rost, *The Succession to the Throne of David*, Sheffield, 1982, pp. xv–l; R.C. Bailey, *David in Love and War. The Pursuit of Power in 2 Samuel 10–12* (JSOTSup 75), Sheffield, 1990, pp. 7–31, 131–142; G.H. Jones, *The Nathan Narratives* (JSOTSup 80), Sheffield, 1990, pp. 179–186.

[6] E.g., T.N.D. Mettinger, *King and Messiah. The Civil and Sacral Legitimation of the Israelite Kings* (CBOTS 8), Lund, 1976, pp. 27–32; F. Crüsemann, *Der Widerstand gegen das Königtum. Die antiköniglichen Texte des Alten Testamentes und der Kampf um den frühen israelitischen Staat* (WMANT 49), Neukirchen-Vluyn, 1978, pp. 180–193; K.W. Whitelam, *The Just King: Monarchical Judicial Authority in Ancient Israel* (JSOTSup 12), Sheffield, 1979, pp. 123–166; idem, "The Defence of David", *JSOT* 29 (1984), pp. 61–87; P.K. McCarter, "'Plots, True or False'. The Succession Narrative as Court Apologetic", *Int* 35 (1981), pp. 355–367; idem, *II Samuel. A New Translation with Introduction, Notes and Commentary* (AB 9), Garden City, N.Y., 1984, pp. 9–16; S. Zalewski, *Solomon's Ascension to the Throne. Studies in the Books of Kings and Chronicles*, Jerusalem, 1981, pp. 11–144 (Hebrew).

[7] E.g., E. Würthwein, *Die Erzählung von der Thronfolge Davids—theologische oder politische Geschichtsschreibung?* (TS 115), Zürich, 1974; idem, *Das Erste Buch der Könige: Kapitel 1–16* (ATD 11/1), Göttingen, 1977, pp. 1–28; T. Veijola, *Die ewige Dynastie. David und die Entstehung seiner Dynastie nach der deuteronomistischen Darstellung*, Helsinki, 1975; F. Langlamet, "Pour ou contre Salomon? Le rédaction prosalomonienne de I Rois, I–II", *RB* 83 (1976), pp. 321–379, 481–528; idem, "Absalom et les concubines de son père. Recherches sur II Sam. XVI, 21–22", *RB* 84 (1977), pp. 161–209; idem, "Ahitofel et Houshaï. Rédaction prosalomonienne en 2 Sam 15–17?", in Y. Avishur and J. Blau (eds.), *Studies in Bible and the Ancient Near East. Presented to S.E. Loewenstamm on His Seventieth Birthday*, Jerusalem, 1978, pp. 57–90; idem, "David et la maison de Saül", *RB* 86 (1979), pp. 194–213, 385–436, 481–513; *RB* 87 (1980), pp. 161–210; *RB* 88 (1981), pp. 321–332; idem, "Affinités sacerdotales, deutéronomiques, élohistes dans l'Histoire de la succession (2 S 9–20; 1 R 1–2)", in A. Caquot and M. Delcor (eds.), *Mélanges bibliques et orientaux en l'honneur de M. Henri Cazelles* (AOAT 212), Neukirchen-Vluyn, 1981, pp. 233–246; idem, "David, fils de Jessé. Une édition prédeutéronomiste de l'<histoire de la succession>", *RB* 89 (1982), pp. 5–47.

[8] E.g., Conroy, *Absalom Absalom!*, 1978; Gunn, *The Story of King David*, 1978; J.P. Fokkelman, *Narrative Art and Poetry in the Books of Samuel. A full interpretation based on stylistic and structural analyses* I: *King David (II Sam 9–20 & I Kings 1–2)*, Assen, 1981; K.K. Sacon, "A Study of the Literary Structure of 'The Succession Narrative'", in T. Ishida (ed.), *SPDS*, Tokyo/Winona Lake, 1982, pp. 27–54.

structure and so forth. Oddly enough, however, there is a feature that is common between these contradictory approaches: that is, a skepticism concerning the historicity of the narrative. As a result, without regard to the supposition of a contemporary or near contemporary original, the received text is regarded as having been composed either at a time "long after the United Kingdom had ceased to be" (D.M. Gunn)[9] or in the days between Hezekiah and Josiah (F. Langlamet)[10] or during the exilic (T. Veijola)[11] or the post-exilic period (J. van Seters).[12] Inasmuch as we have no effective method for controlling these anarchic postulations, historical studies of the Hebrew Bible will remain nihilistic, or at best, agnostic.

Our point of departure will be the historical fact that the Hebrew Bible is a collection of compositions from the ancient Near East that were mostly composed in the first millennium B.C. Of course, disregarding any historical consideration, we may compare 2 Samuel with other literature, for example, with the works of William Shakespeare, to gain valuable insight into human nature. This sort of comparison is valid for comparative literature, but is hardly appropriate for historical research, since the cultural milieu of each composition is entirely different from each of the others. Historians also deal with human beings and with human nature, but it is vital in their research to make clear to which definite time and what space the human beings in question were confined.

This method of historical research comes from our empirical understanding that every culture has its own sense of values. Sometimes there is a cultural phenomenon that seems so universal that it must prevail all over the world. But observation of such a phenomenon always remains superficial. In my view, knowledge about foreign cultures is highly abstract even in our present age when all corners of the world are closely connected by a dense network of modern communication. I am very doubtful of the ability of Western society to understand the sense of values of Oriental countries, and vice versa. If we feel difficulties in understanding foreign cultures in our modern

[9] Gunn, *The Story of King David*, p. 33.

[10] Langlamet, *RB* 83 (1976), p. 379.

[11] His thesis of triple redactions by DtrG, DtrP and DtrN suggests that the text in 1 Kgs 1–2 was composed in the exilic period; see Veijola, *Die ewige Dynastie*.

[12] J. van Seters, "Histories and Historians of the Ancient Near East: The Israelites", *Or* 50 (1981), p. 166; idem, *In Search of History. Historiography in the Ancient World and the Origins of Biblical History*, New Haven/London, 1983, pp. 289–291.

world, how can we correctly interpret the compositions from the ancient Near East which came to us not only from different cultures but from distant times?

It seems to me that a naive application of modern Western logic and judgement to the interpretation of ancient Near Eastern sources, including biblical literature, has led us into error. First it is necessary that we establish a set of criteria for interpretation that is free from the prejudices of our modern society. In other words, the criteria must be established on an understanding, neutral but sympathetic, of the cultures of the ancient Near East. There, various peoples lived each with their own rhetoric, customs, outlooks, senses of values and so forth, which were undoubtedly distinct from those of other cultures and, of course, from those of our own time. Naturally, we must be careful about differences among the peoples of the ancient Near East, but equally we must guard against the illusion that owing to our inheritance of the Judeo-Christian culture we can understand the ancient Israelites better than their neighbouring peoples. For instance, the concept of the ban (*ḥērem*) in a holy war in ancient Israel (e.g., Num 21:2–3; Deut 2:34; Josh 6:18; Jud 21:11; 1 Sam 15:3, etc.) is quite alien to our society, but it was familiar to the people of Mari in the 18th century B.C. as well as to the Moabites in the 9th century B.C.[13]

Unfortunately, this historical approach does not seem to be popular among biblical scholars of today. Neither those who have employed redaction-criticism nor those who have used literary-structural analysis as their method have ever made a serious comparison of the Succession Narrative with any extra-biblical sources from the ancient Near East.[14] Since their argument is essentially based on the internal analysis of the narrative without any tangible support from contemporary sources from the ancient Near East, their conclusions are often inconclusive and remain hypothetical. This is especially true of the problem of the date of the narrative. As a result, every scholar suggests any date he likes, as we have observed above.

[13] For Mari see A. Malamat, *Mari and the Early Israelite Experience* (The Schweich Lectures 1984), Oxford, 1989, pp. 70 ff. For the Moabites see "*l ʿštr . kmš . hḥrmth*" in the Moabite stone (*KAI* 181:17).

[14] Mention must be made of Whybray's study on the Succession Narrative in which he dedicated a chapter to the comparison of the narrative with Egyptian literature, *The Succession Narrative*, pp. 96–116; cf. Gunn, *The Story of King David*, pp. 29 f.

On the surface, J. van Seters' studies[15] look like an exception. On the basis of comparative studies of biblical history writings with those of Greece and the ancient Near East he maintains that the first historian of Israel was the Deuteronomist whose work resembles the Greek prose histories in terms of the scope of subject matter and the themes treated. As for the Court History (i.e., the Succession Narrative), he regards it as "an antilegitimation story" added to the Dtr history, "as the product of an antimessianic tendency in certain Jewish circles" in the post-exilic period.[16] It is strange, however, that he does not make any attempt to examine the literary character of the Court History itself in the light of Greek or ancient Near Eastern sources which he has collected, but draws his radical conclusion simply from his arbitrary judgement on the relation of the Court History and its view of David to the Deuteronomistic History. A good example of his dogmatic argument is found in his failure to produce any evidence to show that there was "an antimessianic tendency in certain Jewish circles" in the post-exilic period, which was, in his view, responsible for the composition of the Court History. All in all, so far as the study of the Succession Narrative is concerned, we can hardly regard his approach as historical.

On the other hand, P.R. Ackroyd[17] has raised a question about the relationship of the Succession Narrative to the larger context and has come to the negative conclusion that it should not be separated from the rest of Samuel-Kings, which makes part of the Deuteronomistic History. Admittedly, it is worthwhile to reconsider the problems of the place of the narrative in the Deuteronomistic History together with the extent of the Deuteronomistic editing. It was once widely accepted that the Deuteronomist's contributions to the present texts of large literary complexes like the History of David's Rise or the Succession Narrative which were supposed to be at his disposal when composing the Books of Samuel-Kings were very limited or minimal.[18] In contrast, there have been also scholars who find in the present texts a heavy Deuteronomistic revision of the older narrative sources.[19] It seems to me, however, that we still have good prospects

---

[15] J. van Seters, *Or* 50 (1981), pp. 137–185; idem, *In Search of History*.

[16] J. van Seters, *Or* 50 (1981), p. 166; idem, *In Search of History*, p. 290.

[17] P.R. Ackroyd, "The Succession Narrative (so-called)", *Int* 35 (1981), pp. 383–396.

[18] Rost, in *Das kleine Credo*, pp. 119–253; Noth, *Überlieferungsgeschichtliche Studien*, pp. 63–66.

[19] R.A. Carlson, *David, the chosen King. A Traditio-Historical Approach to the Second*

for research in proceeding with the thesis of a Succession Narrative as a working hypothesis, before marking it with a Deuteronomistic composition. Moreover, in view of mounting skepticism about the historicity of the narrative, I feel it necessary first to undertake a re-examination of the possibilities of understanding the narrative in its present historical setting, i.e., in the period of David and Solomon. In my opinion, the problem of the relationship of the narrative to the larger context of the Deuteronomistic History is to be dealt with after examining the coherence of the literary complex generally called the Succession Narrative.

2. *Royal Historical Writings of an Apologetic Nature*

When we employ historical approaches as our method, the interpretation of biblical sources has to be done after settling the question of the literary genre to which they belong. And, once again, we must look for criteria for the definition of literary genres of biblical sources by comparison with compositions from other areas in the ancient Near East. As such comparative material to the Succession Narrative, I would like to suggest a genre called "Royal historical writings of an apologetic nature in the ancient Near East"; for instance, the Telepinu Proclamation[20] and the Apology of Hattušili III[21] from the Hittite archives and the Neo-Assyrian documents of Šamši-Adad V,[22] Esarhaddon[23] and Ashurbanipal[24] which H.A. Hoffner[25] and H. Tadmor[26] classify under this category. In addition, I will suggest later that the

Book of Samuel, Stockholm/Göteborg/Uppsala, 1964; G.N. Knoppers, *Two Nations under God. The Deuteronomistic History of Solomon and the Dual Monarchies* I: *The Reign of Solomon and the Rise of Jeroboam* (HSM 52), Atlanta, 1993, pp. 57–77.

[20] I. Hoffmann, *Der Erlaß Telipinus* (TH 11), Heidelberg, 1984.

[21] A. Götze, *Ḫattušiliš. Der Bericht über seine Thronbesteigung nebst den Paralleltexten* (MVÄG 29/3, Hethitische Texte, Heft 1) Leipzig, 1924, pp. 6–41; Cf. A. Ünal, *Ḫattušili III.* I: *Ḫattušili bis zu seiner Thronbesteigung* 1: *Historischer Abriß* (TH 3), Heidelberg, 1974, pp. 29–35.

[22] A.K. Grayson, *Assyrian Rulers of the Early First Millennium BC* II (*858–745 BC*) (RIMA 3), Toronto/Buffalo/London, 1996, pp. 182 f. (A.O. 103.1, i 1–53a).

[23] R. Borger, *Die Inschriften Asarhaddons Königs von Assyrien* (AfO Beih. 9), Graz, 1956, pp. 39–45 (Nin. A I:1–II:11).

[24] M. Streck, *Assurbanipal und die letzten assyrischen Könige bis zum Untergange Niniveh's* II (VAB 7/2), Leipzig, 1916, pp. 252–271 (K3050 + K2694).

[25] H.A. Hoffner, "Propaganda and Political Justification in Hittite Historiography", in H. Goedicke and J.J.M. Roberts (eds.), *Unity and Diversity. Essays in the History, Literature, and Religion of the Ancient Near East*, Baltimore/London, 1975, pp. 49–62.

[26] H. Tadmor, "Autobiographical Apology in the Royal Assyrian Literature", in

inscription of Kilamuwa, king of Y'DY-Śam'al in the ninth century B.C., also belongs to this category.[27]

The Succession Narrative is not written in the autobiographical style of these other historical writings, but it is clearly similar to them in its essential character. Hoffner[28] finds the following outline common to the fundamental structure of the Telepinu Proclamation (T) and the Apology of Hattušili III (H):

a) Introduction: T § 1, H §§ 1–2.

b) Historical survey—noble antecedents: T §§ 1–9, H §§ 3–10.

c) Historical survey—the unworthy predecessor: T §§ 10–22a, H §§ 10–12.

d) The *coup d'état*: T § 22b, H §§ 12–13.

e) The merciful victor: T §§ 23 and 26, H §§ 12–13.

f) The edict: T §§ 27–50, H §§ 13–15.

In my opinion, the apology of Esarhaddon (Nin. A I:1–II:11),[29] the most detailed composition among the Assyrian royal apologetic historical writings, is comparable with these Hittite compositions in its general outline in many respects:

a) Introduction: I:1–7.

b) Historical survey—the divine election and appointment by his father: I:8–22.

c) Historical survey—the rival princes' acts against the divine will: I:23–40.

d) Rebellion: I:41–52.

e) Esarhaddon's counter-attack and victory: I:53–79.

f) The establishment of the kingship: I:80–II:7.

g) The punishment of the rebels: II:8–11.

With reference to these outlines of the Assyrian and Hittite historical writings together with those of the Kilamuwa inscription and the Succession Narrative we may find the following six elements as common items in all the apologetic historical writings:

a) The royal ancestry of the king designate.

b) The unworthiness of his predecessor(s) and/or rival prince(s).

c) The rivals' rebellious attempt to gain the crown.

d) The counter-attack of the king designate and his victory.

H. Tadmor and M. Weinfeld (eds.), *History, Historiography and Interpretation. Studies in Biblical and Cuneiform Literatures*, Jerusalem, 1983, pp. 36–57.

[27] See below pp. 166 ff.

[28] Hoffner, in *Unity and Diversity*, p. 51.

[29] Borger, *Die Inschriften Asarhaddons*, pp. 39–45.

e) His magnanimous pardon and/or purge of his enemies.
f) The establishment of a just kingship.

In addition, one of the most important features common to all is that the kings, who were not usurpers from outside the royal family, ascended the throne either by overruling primogeniture or by taking the place of someone who belonged to the direct royal line. Needless to say, this establishment of the king's connection with the royal family was the fundamental motivation behind the composition of these narratives.

I have no intention in the present chapter of making a detailed comparative study between the Succession Narrative and the apologetic royal histories from the ancient Near East,[30] but will limit myself to making some observations of significant points. The fundamental idea in these historiographies is nothing less than the royal ideology in the ancient Near East, according to which the legitimacy of the king was proved by his royal lineage and divine election as well as by his competence to rule.[31] It is one of the striking features of the apologetic histories that the present king's competency as a ruler is put in sharp contrast to the ineffective rule of his predecessor's or the rival prince's incompetent character as a ruler. This observation will provide us with criteria for the tendencies of the apologetic historical writings.

Scholars have disagreed on the character of the Succession Narrative as to whether it is pro-David/Solomonic or anti-David/Solomonic and some scholars have found pro- as well as anti-Solomonic polemics.[32] None of these arguments is conclusive, since they have been made mainly with the biases of the moral judgement of our modern society.

[30] For a comparative study between the Succession Narrative and Esarhaddon's apology see below pp. 175 ff.

[31] For divine election and royal lineage as the foundation of royal legitimation in the ancient Near East see T. Ishida, *The Royal Dynasties in Ancient Israel. A Study on the Formation and Development of Royal-Dynastic Ideology* (BZAW 142), Berlin/New York, 1977, pp. 6–25; cf. also Mettinger, *King and Messiah*, pp. 107–297. The competence of rule of a king can be regarded as confirmation of his divine election. A similar situation is found in charismatic leaders called *šōpᵉṭîm* in the pre-monarchical period who could establish their charismatic ordination only through victories in the field; see above pp. 50 ff.

[32] L. Delekat, "Tendenz und Theologie der David-Salomo-Ezählung", in F. Maass (ed.), *Das ferne und nahe Wort. L. Rost Festschrift* (BZAW 105), Berlin, 1967, pp. 26–36; M. Noth, *Könige* I: *I. Könige 1–16* (BKAT 9/1), Neukirchen-Vluyn, 1968, pp. 1–41; Würthwein, *Die Erzählung von der Thronfolge Davids*, 1974; Langlamet, *RB* 83 (1976), pp. 321–379, 481–528; idem, *RB* 89 (1982), pp. 5–47; cf. McCarter, *II Samuel*, pp. 13–16.

Against these arguments, I will show that the Succession Narrative was composed as a legitimation of Solomon in which David is criticized as the incompetent predecessor but, at the same time, in which the throne of David is regarded as the foundation of the legitimacy of Solomon's kingship.[33] Therefore, though anti-Davidic polemics are obvious in some sections, there is neither an anti-Solomonic element nor any criticism against David's dynasty. Neither should the report on the court intrigue nor the story of Solomon's political murder be interpreted as anti-Solomonic. In the structure of the apologetic historical writings, the court intrigue was the legitimate king's counterattack against an unlawful attempt by an incompetent rival prince to gain the crown. As in these historical writings, Solomon's purge of his enemies shows his competence as a ruler.

In the following study I will demonstrate that, in the Succession Narrative, Solomon plays the role of a legitimate successor to the throne, while David and Adonijah play the roles of an incompetent predecessor and an unworthy rival prince, respectively, in the apologetic historical writings.

3. *Solomon's Supporters*

I will begin with an analysis of the political situation in the last days of David, as described in 1 Kgs 1–2. The narrative tells us that, at that time, the leading courtiers were divided into two parties revolving about the two rival candidates for the royal throne: Adonijah the son of Haggith and Solomon the son of Bathsheba. The former was supported by Joab, commander-in-chief of the army, and Abiathar the priest, while the latter was backed by Zadok the priest, Nathan the prophet, Benaiah, the leader of the royal bodyguard called the "Cherethites and the Pelethites", and David's heroes (1:7–8, 10; cf. 1:19, 25–26, 32, 38, 44; 2:22, 28).[34]

---

[33] There are scholars who hold that the narrative was composed as a Davidic apology; see McCarter, *Int* 35 (1981), pp. 355–367; idem, *II Samuel*, pp. 9–16; Whitelam, *JSOT* 29 (1984), pp. 61–87. By this assumption it is difficult to explain the nature of the descriptions of David's shortcomings in the narrative.

[34] In addition, "Shimei and Rei" are found among Solomon's supporters (1:8). However, we do not know exactly who or what they were. Since no mention is made about them elsewhere, we cannot assume anything about their roles in the struggle for the throne of David; for various conjectural readings see Noth, *Könige* I, pp. 16 f.; J. Gray, *I & II Kings. A Commentary* (OTL), London, 1977^3, p. 79.

What was the root cause of the antagonism between the two parties? Some scholars have suggested that it was a conflict between Yahwism and the Jebusite-Canaanite religion, represented by Abiathar and Zadok respectively.[35] It is not easy to accept this view, however, since there is no clear evidence for the Jebusite origin of Solomon's supporters. As is well known, Zadok's origins have been a vexing question, but, so far as I know, arguments for his Jebusite origin rely solely on indirect or circumstantial evidence.[36] Even if he had been a Jebusite priest, it seems misleading to consider him the leader of Solomon's party. The fact that Abiathar, the rival of Zadok, was not put to death but just banished from Jerusalem after the establishment of Solomon's kingship (2:26–27) would seem to show that both the priests played rather a secondary role in the struggle for the throne of David from the political point of view. On the contrary, Nathan must be regarded as the ideologue of Solomon's party. Although no information is available at all about his provenance, there is no reason to doubt that Nathan, who spoke by Yahweh's name (2 Sam 7:3–4, 8, 11; 12:1, 7, 11) and gave the name with Yah-element "Jedidiah" to Solomon (12:25), was a prophet of Yahweh.[37] If Nathan, the father of Azariah, one of the high officials of Solomon (1 Kgs 4:5) was identical with Nathan the prophet, we have another Yah-name which he gave.

It is clear that Uriah the Hittite, Bathsheba's former husband, was a foreigner, but I am skeptical about the view that he was of Jebusite

[35] G.W. Ahlström, "Der Prophet Nathan und der Tempelbau", *VT* 11 (1961), pp. 113–127; Jones, *The Nathan Narratives*, pp. 31 ff., 119 ff.

[36] For a summary of various views of Zadok's Jebusite and other origins, see A. Cody, *A History of Old Testament Priesthood* (AnBib 35), Rome, 1969, pp. 88–93; G.W. Ramsey, "Zadok", in *ABD* VI, New York, 1992, pp. 1034–1036. The Jebusite hypothesis was defended by e.g., A. Tsukimoto, "'Der Mensch ist geworden wie unsereiner'. Untersuchungen zum zeitgeschichtlichen Hintergrund von Gen. 3,22–24 und 6,1–4", *AJBI* 5 (1979), pp. 29–31; Jones, *The Nathan Narratives*, pp. 20–25, 40–42, 131–135. According to G.W. Ahlström, David himself was a non-Israelite coming from Bethlehem, a city under Jebusite rule, *Royal Administration and National Religion in Ancient Palestine* (SHANE 1), Leiden, 1982, p. 29. However, the Jebusite hypothesis has been refuted by F.M. Cross, *Canaanite Myth and Hebrew Epic. Essays in the History of the Religion of Israel*, Cambridge, Mass./London, 1973, pp. 209 ff.

[37] Jones who argues in detail for Nathan's Jebusite origin concludes that "in view of the culmulative evidence . . . . and the analysis of the Nathan tradition, the 'Jebusite-hypothesis' does provide for Nathan a background for a comprehensive understanding of his life and contribution", *The Nathan Narratives*, p. 141. In other words, the Jebusite-hypothesis is based soley on circumstantial evidence. It seems difficult for me to accept it.

stock.[38] Some scholars assume Bathsheba's non-Israelite origin because of her foreign husband.[39] Admittedly her provenance is also not so clear, but it is most likely to regard her as the daughter of Eliam, the son of Ahithophel of Gilo (2 Sam 11:3; 23:34) in the mountains of Judah (Josh 15:51).[40] By contrast, we are well informed about the origins of Benaiah and David's heroes. Benaiah came from Kabzeel, or Jekabzeel, one of the towns of Judah in the Negev (2 Sam 23:20; cf. Josh 15:21; 1 Chr 11:22; Neh 11:25), and David's heroes were mostly from Judah and Benjamin, though some of them were from the mountains of Ephraim, on the east side of the Jordan, or some foreign countries (2 Sam 23:8–39; 1 Chr 11:10–47).[41] As these data show, Solomon's supporters were mixed in their provenance and ethnic origins, but the Judahites and Israelites clearly accounted for the great majority of them. I can hardly assume that they were adherents of the Jebusite-Canaanite religion or the representatives of the Jebusite population in Jerusalem.

It has been observed that Adonijah and his supporters were men who had held positions at the court already in the days of David's reign at Hebron, whereas the members of Solomon's party appeared for the first time after David transferred his capital from Hebron to Jerusalem.[42] It is interesting to note that members of these rival parties were opposed to each other in contesting for the same positions, i.e., Adonijah vs. Solomon for the royal throne, Haggith vs. Bathsheba as the mother of the heir apparent, Abiathar vs. Zadok as the chief priest, and Joab vs. Benaiah as the commander of the army. Judging from the fact that Solomon replaced Joab by Benaiah as the com-

[38] Against A. Malamat, "Aspects of the Foreign Policies of David and Solomon", *JNES* 22 (1963), p. 9; B. Mazar, "King David's Scribe and the High Officialdom of the United Monarchy of Israel", in *The Early Biblical Period. Historical Studies*, Jerusalem, 1986, p. 129. It is difficult to regard the Jebusites as a branch of the Hittites; see above p. 34, n. 64.

[39] Jones, *The Nathan Narratives*, pp. 43 f.

[40] It seems that the narrator restricted himself to suggest indirect evidence on Bathsheba's relationship to Ahithopel, Absalom's counseler in his rebellion against David. Cf. J.D. Levenson and B. Halpern, "The Political Import of David's Marriages", *JBL* 99 (1980), p. 514. Bailey, *David in Love and War*, pp. 87–90, argues that David's marriage to Bathsheba, the granddaughter of Ahithophel, should be viewed as one of the political marriages of David to recementing his tie to the southern tribes after the defection of Ahithophel to Absalom.

[41] For David's heroes and their origin see B. Mazar, "The Military Élite of King David" (1963), in *The Early Biblical Period*, pp. 83–103; McCarter, *II Samuel*, pp. 499–501; D.G. Schley, "David's Champions", in *ABD* II, New York, 1992, pp. 49–52.

[42] See Ishida, *The Royal Dynasties*, pp. 157 f.

mander of the army, and Abiathar by Zadok as the chief priest, after the purge of his opponents (1 Kgs 2:35), it is legitimate to assume that both Benaiah and Zadok were upstarts. The conflict seems to have been caused by the newcomers' challenge to the old authority.

An exception to the above analysis is presented by David's heroes. They were, for the most part, soldiers who had followed David since the days of his wandering in the wilderness (1 Sam 22:1–2; 1 Chr 12:8, 16), like Joab and Abiathar, or the days of his staying at Ziklag (1 Chr 12:1, 20) and came up to Hebron with David when he was made the first king of the kingdom of Judah (2 Sam 2:1–4a). Nevertheless, they did not join Adonijah's party together with Joab and Abiathar but took sides with Solomon. Although the reason for their associating themselves with Solomon's party is not stated explicitly, it is possible to assume that animosity towards Joab had been growing among them, as their importance had been diminishing with the establishment of the national army under Joab.[43]

There is reason to believe that the rivalry between Joab and Benaiah originated with the situation in which the latter was appointed to be leader of the royal bodyguard (2 Sam 23:23). Although Benaiah is mentioned as "over the Cherethites and the Pelethites" in the first list of David's high officials (8:18), I am inclined to assume that his appointment was actually made some time after Sheba's revolt. Otherwise, it is extremely difficult to explain the reason for his absence at the time of both Absalom's and Sheba's revolts, in both of which the Cherethites and the Pelethites served as foreign mercenaries loyal to David (15:18; 20:7). The leaders of David's army at the time of Absalom's rebellion were Joab, Abishai, and Ittai (18:1, 12), and those during Sheba's revolt were Joab and Abishai (20:6–7, 10b). It is clear that Joab and Abishai, the sons of Zeruiah, held the first and second places, respectively, in the hierarchy of David's army after Sheba's revolt had been suppressed. Oddly enough, however, while Joab regained the position of commander-in-chief of the army, Abishai disappeared from the scene forever. Instead, Benaiah ranked next to Joab as the leader of the Cherethites and the Pelethites (20:23b). Owing to lack of information, we do not know anything certain about Abishai's final fate. It is unlikely, however, that Abishai, the commander of David's heroes (23:18–19), was opposed to Joab,

---

[43] Cf. Mazar, in *The Early Biblical Period*, pp. 102 f.

his brother, in the struggle for the throne of David, since he had always served David as Joab's right-hand man from the days of the cave of Adullam (1 Sam 26:6, etc.) up to Sheba's revolt. Perhaps, Abishai died a natural death after Sheba's revolt, and in his place Benaiah became a military leader, sharing with Joab the exercise of power in the kingdom. It is not difficult to imagine that Joab felt uneasy about Benaiah from the beginning. Probably, Benaiah's appointment was backed by a circle which was interested in checking the growing power of Joab at the court. In other words, it was Joab against whom Solomon's supporters made common cause.

4. *The Presentation of Adonijah*

Following the episode of Abishag and the aging King David (1 Kgs 1:1–4), which provides a general background as well as a motif for the Abishag episod (2:13–25), the narrative mentions the name "Adonijah the son of Haggith" without any other introduction (1:5). Evidently, the readers are expected to know about Adonijah, originally the fourth son, but now the eldest surviving son of David (2 Sam 3:4). According to the narrative, Adonijah was recognized by the general public as the first candidate for succeeding David, probably based on the priority of the eldest living son (1 Kgs 2:15, 22). The principle of primogeniture had been accepted in the royal succession since the inception of the Hebrew monarchy. While Saul expected that Jonathan's kingdom would be established (1 Sam 20:31), David "loved Amnon because he was his firstborn" (2 Sam 13:21b LXX, 4Q Sam[a]).[44]

However, Adonijah's attempt to gain the crown is commented upon here as an act of "exalting himself" (*miṯnaśśēʾ*). Though the term *hiṯnaśśēʾ* does not always have a negative connotation, here it clearly denotes one who exaggerates his own importance.[45] Undoubtedly, this is a biased judgement on Adonijah by his enemy, i.e., Solomon. The comment is followed by a direct quotation of Adonijah's words: "I will be king" (*ʾănî ʾemlōḵ*). There is no reason to doubt that

---

[44] For the principle of primogeniture in the royal succession in the kingdoms of Israel and Judah see Ishida, *The Royal Dynasties*, p. 152.

[45] A positive use: e.g., *wᵉḵaʾarî yiṯnaśśāʾ* (Num 23:24); a negative use: e.g., *ʾim nāḇaltāh bᵉhiṯnaśśēʾ* (Prov 30:32), see *HALOT* II, p. 727.

they were his true words, but it is difficult to regard them as his manifesto of a rebellion against David. Judging from the political situation at that time, he had no reason to be in a hurry to seize the throne by force. He was expected by the people to succeed David, and David's remaining days were numbered. We may assume, therefore, that this declaration was originally made to Solomon and his supporters in order to demonstrate Adonijah's determination to be king after David. In that case, a temporal condition such as "after the demise of my father" (*ʾaḥarê môṯ ʾaḇî*) should have been included in the original (cf. 1 Kgs 1:24). We submit that the conditional phrase was omitted to give the reader the false impression that Adonijah had attempted to attain the throne without David's consent. The supposed omission is further evidence for the Solomonic character of the composition.

The effect of the distortion of Adonijah's words is intensified by the report of his preparation of a *reḵeḇ* and *pārāšîm*[46] with fifty outrunners. It immediately reminds us of a similar arrangement made by Absalom when he had schemed to rebel (2 Sam 15:1). An important difference between these almost identical reports is found in the terms used for the items which the two princes prepared. While Absalom provided himself with a *merkāḇāh* and *sûsîm*, Adonijah prepared a *reḵeḇ* and *pārāšîm*. Concerning the *merkāḇāh*, examples in the Manner of the King (1 Sam 8:11b), the Joseph story (Gen 41:43) and many other sources from the ancient Near East, show that Absalom's *merkāḇāh* was an imitation of a royal display chariot and that his *sûsîm* were horses for it;[47] thus, his *merkāḇāh* and *sûsîm* do not stand for chariotry and cavalry. In other words, they formed a ceremonial troop or procession but not a rebel army. Indeed, his preparation of a *merkāḇāh* and *sûsîm* was not regarded as a rebellious act until he raised the standard in Hebron; otherwise, David would have dealt with Absalom before the latter "stole the hearts of the men of Israel" (2 Sam 15:6b).

It seems justified to assume that Adonijah's *reḵeḇ* and *pārāšîm* were synonymous with the *merkāḇāh* and *sûsîm* of Absalom. Mention must

---

[46] Commentators suggest reading *pᵉrāšîm* for MT *pārāšîm*, a lost form of the plural of *pārāš* "horse"; see J.M. Montgomery and H.S. Gehman, *A Critical and Exegetical Commentary on the Books of Kings* (ICC), Edinburgh, 1951, p. 83; Gray, *I & II Kings*, p. 78.

[47] See Y. Ikeda, "Solomon's Trade in Horses and Chariots in Its International Setting", in T. Ishida (ed.), *SPDS*, Tokyo/Winona Lake, 1982, pp. 223–225.

be made, however, that the pair of terms *reke̲b̲* and *pārāšîm* stands, except in the Adonijah passage, for the chariotry and cavalry of Solomon's army (1 Kgs 9:19; 10:26; cf. 5:6; cf. also *KAI* 202:B 2 [Zakir]). Since the use of this set of terms rather than the other does not seem incidental, we cannot but suppose that these exaggerated terms were used here to mislead the reader with the false idea that Adonijah not only had followed in the footsteps of Absalom but also had made the decisive step toward a rebellion by gathering a military force. Undoubtedly, the distortion came from the Solomonic historiographer.

The portrayal of the character of Adonijah is completed by three explanatory notes about him (1 Kgs 1:6). The first tells about David's laxity toward Adonijah: "His father had never displeased him" (*lōʾ ʿaṣāb̲ô*). It calls to mind David's similar attitude toward Amnon (2 Sam 13:21 LXX, 4Q Sam[a]) and Absalom (18:5, 12). It is worth noting that the same verb עצב is used in the report of David's lament over Absalom's death: "He is grieving" (*neʿeṣab̲*) (19:3) and in the reconstructed text about David's indulgence towards Amnon: "He has never harmed Amnon's humor" (*wᵉlōʾ ʿāṣab̲ ʾet̲ rûaḥ ʿamnôn*) (13:21b LXX).[48] Since David had displeased (*ʿāṣab̲*) neither Amnon nor Absalom, they eventually hurt (*ʿāṣᵉb̲û*) him. Thus the implication becomes clear that it is now Adonijah's turn to hurt David as had Amnon and Absalom. At the same time, we can hardly dismiss a critical tone toward David according to which Adonijah's audacious behaviour is understood as a consequence of David's own failure in his paternal duty.

The second note on Adonijah is a comment on his handsome appearance: "He was also (*wᵉḡam-hûʾ*) a very handsome man". The word "also" indicates that he is being compared with someone else. Although we have been informed about the beautiful figure of Saul (1 Sam 9:2) as well as that of David (16:12, 18), it is most probable that Adonijah is being compared with Absalom (2 Sam 14:25), for this comment is made here not as a compliment, but as a reason why David had spoiled Adonijah.

The third note reads: "And she bore (*yālᵉd̲āh*) him after Absalom". Commentators have generally felt a difficulty with the verb *yālᵉd̲āh*, since no subject is found for it in the sentence.[49] They hold that

---

[48] Cf. the text-critical notes on the verse in Conroy, *Absalom Absalom!*, pp. 152 f.

[49] Noth, *Könige* I, pp. 1, 6, holds that an indefinite subject is to be supposed, while Gray, *I & II Kings*, p. 78, n.g, suggests that *ʾimmô* has dropped out after the verb.

Haggith in v. 5a is too remote to be taken as the subject of the verb.[50] There is an opinion that the phrase "Adonijah the son of Haggith" in v. 5a makes an inclusio with the sentence "And she bore . . .".[51] Still, this literary-structural analysis does not explain the reason for the omission of the subject of the verb. In my opinion, the name of Adonijah's mother was omitted from v. 6b intentionally. If it had been repeated here, the name of Absalom's mother would also have to be mentioned. Otherwise, Haggith would be taken for the mother of both Absalom and Adonijah. The omission of the name Haggith indicates the aim of the third note. The message of the note is not to provide the name of Adonijah's mother but the fact that he was born *after Absalom*.

Indeed, the third note is not added here to provide general information. The narrative presupposes the reader's awareness of Absalom and his frustrated rebellion. Up to this point, the historiographer has accumulated parallel action and character traits between Adonijah and Absalom without mentioning the latter's name, i.e., arrogance (*mitnaśśēʾ*), pretension to the throne (*ʾănî ʾemlōk*), preparation of a royal chariot with horses and outrunners, lack of paternal discipline and a handsome appearance. After having read these parallels, every reader must have had an impression that Adonijah was really a second Absalom. At this juncture, by finally mentioning the name Absalom, the third note confirms the reader's impression and serves as the proper conclusion of the portrayal of Adonijah.

For the above reasons, I am convinced that the portrayal of Adonijah in 1 Kgs 1:5–6 was made from the consistently inimical viewpoint of the party opposing Adonijah.

5. *The Alleged Rebellion of Adonijah*

Judging from the political situation in the narrative in 1 Kgs 1, it is fairly evident that Adonijah was not under the pressure of raising the standard of a *coup d'état* in the last days of David. As David was near death (1:1–4), and Adonijah was expected to become David's successor by everybody but Solomon's supporters (2:15, 22), he had no reason to be in a hurry to usurp the throne. Moreover, it seems

[50] See Montgomery and Gehman, *The Books of Kings*, p. 83.
[51] Fokkelman, *Narrative Art and Poetry*, p. 349.

that David himself had given Adonijah his tacit approval (cf. 1:16).[52]

Nevertheless, the narrative is strikingly ambiguous about a crucial question: What was the purpose of the feast at En Rogel to which Adonijah invited all his brothers and all the royal officials, except Solomon and his supporters? Two possible answers are: a) Adonijah, like Absalom, called a meeting to revolt against David and to perform his coronation rite; b) Adonijah held the feast only for the purpose of strengthening the unity of his party and of demonstrating his determination to gain the crown. According to my analysis, the latter was the reason.[53]

As those who supported Adonijah, the following people are mentioned: Joab the son of Zeruiah the commander of the army, Abiathar the priest, Jonathan the son of Abiathar the priest, all the sons of the king except Solomon, and all the royal officials of Judah except Solomon's supporters. They are also called "the guests of Adonijah" (1:41, 49). In addition, Adonijah regarded "all Israel", i.e., the people of the kingdom, as his supporters (2:15). In contrast to Solomon's faction, Adonijah's group of supporters certainly was the dominant party. It is entirely conceivable that they did not feel it necessary to prepare for an armed rebellion when they met at En Rogel.

We also have some support within our text for this argument: a) In her plea to David, Bathsheba says: "Otherwise it will come to pass, when my lord the king sleeps with his fathers, that I and my son Solomon will be counted offenders" (1:21; cf. 1:12). If Adonijah had already become king without David's consent, why should he wait for David's death before executing Solomon and Bathsheba? b) As soon as a report of Solomon's accession arrived, Adonijah and his supporters at En Rogel dispersed (1:49). This easy collapse of Adonijah's party shows that they had made no preparation for revolt and were taken by surprise by the court intrigue of Solomon's faction. Otherwise, they would have offered armed resistance to David and Solomon. c) If Joab and Abiathar had conspired with Adonijah against David, how could they have kept their high position at the court under the co-regency of David and Solomon (cf. 2:35)? We can see other evidence as well in the Testament of David (2:1–9), with which I will deal later.

---

[52] Cf. Gray, *I & II Kings*, p. 81.

[53] Cf. Würthwein, *Das Erste Buch der Könige*, pp. 12 f.; Whitelam, *The Just King*, pp. 150 f.

Next, how can we interpret the allegation of Nathan and Bathsheba that reports repeatedly about Adonijah's accession at En Rogel, i.e., Nathan says to Bathsheba: "Have you heard that Adonijah the son of Haggith has become king?" (1:11; cf. 1:13, 24–25), and Bathsheba to David: "And now, behold, Adonijah is king" (1:18)? It is instructive that a scrutiny of the narrative makes it clear that the credibility of the allegation is problematic: a) Although the alleged coronation of Adonijah is reported soley through the direct quotations of the words of Nathan and Bathsheba, it is also suggested that neither Nathan nor Bathsheba can stand as eyewitness for their allegation, since they were not invited to the feast (1:8, 10, 26). b) Since it was not until Nathan came to her that Bathsheba learned of Adonijah's accession (1:11), her claim obviously had no foundation. c) We cannot expect Nathan's words to be credible, either. He told her the story in the context of his counsel (*'ēṣāh*) for saving her and Solomon (1:12). The term *'ēṣāh* implies here "stratagem" or "scheme", as in the counsel of Ahithophel or that of Hushai (2 Sam 15:31; 16:20, 23; 17:7, 11, 14). Nathan's words must be interpreted in the context of his stratagem.

Now we may reconstruct Nathan's stratagem as follows: a) To alarm Bathsheba by telling her of the alleged coronation of Adonijah, based on an exaggeration of the details of the feast at En Rogel (1 Kgs 1:11). b) To make David resent Adonijah when she passed on this report to him (1:18–19). c) To take advantage of David's senility by inducing him to believe that he had once sworn to Bathsheba that Solomon would be his successor (1:13, 17, 30; cf. 1:24).[54] However, when Bathsheba says: "And now, my lord the king, the eyes of all Israel are upon you, to tell them who shall sit on the throne of my lord the king after him" (1:20), and Nathan adds: "You have not told your servants who should sit on the throne of my lord the king after him" (1:27), their words betray that David's pledge to Solomon was a fabrication. Evidently, there was neither pledge nor designation, but the indecision of a senile king who was vaguely expecting that the eldest surviving son would be designated as his successor. d) While confirming her story, Nathan asks David a leading

[54] Cf. Noth, *Könige* I, p. 20; Gray, *I & II Kings*, p. 88; Gunn, *The Story of King David*, pp. 105 f.; Whitelam, *The Just King*, pp. 150 f. Bailey, *David in Love and War*, p. 89, regards Bathsheba's words to David: "I am pregnant" (2 Sam 11:5) as a sign of an arrangement concluded between David and Bathsheba.

question in order to elicit a negative response to Adonijah's adventure (1:22–27). In short, Nathan's stratagem consisted of the use of deception, instigation, auto-suggestion and a leading question in order to extract Solomon's designation as royal successor from the senile king.

It is true, however, that the narrative gives us the impression that Adonijah did ascend the throne at En Rogel without David's consent. This false impression comes, in addition to the allegations of Nathan and Bathsheba, from suggestive references to episodes which remind us of similar incidents during Absalom's rebellion and its aftermath: a) The counseling with Joab and Abiathar (1 Kgs 1:7) and that with Ahithophel (2 Sam 15:12). b) The feast at En Rogel (1 Kgs 1:9, 19, 25) and the sacrifices at Hebron (2 Sam 15:12). c) The acclamation of royalty given to Adonijah (1 Kgs 1:25) and to Absalom (2 Sam 16:16). d) Adonijah, who expected good news, was informed of Solomon's accession (1 Kgs 1:41–48) and David, who had waited to hear of Absalom's safety, was instead told of his death (2 Sam 18:24–32).[55] e) The dispersion of Adonijah's supporters (1 Kgs 1:49) and the dispersion of Israel after Absalom's rebellion failed (2 Sam 19:9bγ). f) Solomon's pardon given to Adonijah (1 Kgs 1:50–53) and David's amnesty granted to Shimei and Mephibaal (2 Sam 19:17–31). Evidently, in these references the literary scheme is reflected for making an impression that Adonijah was a second Absalom.

Both the recounting of the alleged rebellion of Adonijah and Solomon's snatching of the designation as royal successor by maneuvering David reflect irregular situations. The best explanation seems to be that the ambiguity in the story stems from an apologetic attitude toward the court intrigue on behalf of Solomon. Since the fact that Solomon received the designation from David as his successor was of fundamental importance for the Solomonic legitimation, it was unavoidable that the historiographer should tell how it came about. Therefore, he tried to describe the court intrigue by which Solomon received the designation in a manner that would further his aim. The historiographer had Nathan and Bathsheba tell the story of Adonijah's rebellion and bolstered the allegation by implicit references to Absalom's rebellion. Still, he avoided making up an outright fabri-

[55] Rost, in *Das kleine Credo*, pp. 222–225, analyses all the messenger-reports in the Succession Narrative (2 Sam 13:30 ff.; 15:13 ff.; 17:15 ff.; 18:19 ff.; 1 Kgs 1:42 ff.) in comparison with the messenger-report in the Ark Narrative (1 Sam 4:12 ff.).

cation to keep his narrative plausible. As a result, though some ambiguous impressions remain, he succeeded in persuading the reader to believe that Solomon and his party were compelled to resort to an intrigue in order to overcome the ambitions of an unworthy contender to the throne. In other words, what the narrative tries to tell us is that if Solomon's supporters had stood idle, Adonijah would have been king. The one who changed the current was not Adonijah but Solomon by challenging the existing order supported by the regime, whose nominal ruler was doting David, and whose strongman was Joab, commander-in-chief of the army.

From the foregoing we may conclude that the feast which Adonijah gave at En Rogel was nothing but another demonstration of his intention to be king as the legitimate successor to David after the latter's demise, just as was his preparation of "chariots and horsemen, and fifty men to run before him" (1 Kgs 1:5).

6. *The Structure of the Solomonic Apology*

Royal lineage and divine election served as the fundamental principles for the legitimation of kingship in the ancient Near East, including Israel.[56] Both principles can be found also in the narrative in 1 Kgs 1–2 for legitimatizing the kingship of Solomon. It is striking, however, that the fact that Solomon sat upon the throne of David is repeatedly told by either the narrator (2:12), Solomon himself (2:24; cf. 2:33, 45) or David (1:30, 35, 48; cf. 1:13, 17; 2:4), while the divine approval of Solomon's kingship is mentioned just a few times in an indirect way, i.e., in a prayer of Benaiah (1:36–37; cf. 1:47) and confirmation by David (1:48) and Adonijah (2:15). This phenomenon has nothing to do with the so-called non-charismatic character of Solomon's kingship.[57] The narrator of the Succession Narrative has already dealt with the divine legitimation of Solomon's kingship in the narrative of Nathan's prophecy (2 Sam 7:1–17)[58] and the

[56] See Ishida, *The Royal Dynasties*, pp. 6–25.

[57] Against A. Alt, "Die Staatenbildung der Israeliten in Palästina" (1930), in *Kleine Schriften zur Geschichte des Volkes Israel* II, München, 1953, pp. 61 f.; idem, "Das Königtum in den Reichen Israel und Juda" (1951), in *Kleine Schriften zur Geschichte des Volkes Israel* II, pp. 120 f.; cf. also J. Bright, *A History of Israel* (OTL), London, 1972², p. 206.

[58] See below pp. 137 ff.

episode of Solomon's birth (12:24–25).[59] In the present narrative, the emphasis on the throne of David on which Solomon sat derived from certain problems with which our narrator was concerned.

Undoubtedly, our narrator knew that Solomon had actually usurped the throne of David by a court intrigue, though he described it with ingenious obscurity. However, I can hardly agree with the view that he composed the narrative with the intention of denouncing either Solomon or the dynasty of David, let alone monarchy as such.[60] From his point of view, in spite of the intrigue and usurpation, Solomon is the legitimate king. The court intrigue by which Solomon outmaneuvered Adonijah and seized the throne of David reminds us of the story of Jacob in Gen 27.[61] By exploiting the blindness of his old father, Jacob snatched away the blessing of Isaac, his father, from Esau, his elder brother, with a trick devised by Rebecca, his mother. Although the acts of Jacob and Rebecca were clearly immoral, the narrator, who was interested in Jacob's fate, does not mind telling the story. What he was most concerned with was not a moral judgement on Jacob's acts but the fact that the blessing of Isaac was diverted from Esau to Jacob, the ancestor of the people of Israel. The same spirit seems to be found in the narrative of the court intrigue which set Solomon on the throne. What was important for our narrator was not the process by which Solomon established his kingship but its establishment. Therefore he could insist without embarrassment that it came "from Yahweh" (1 Kgs 2:15). This does not mean that he did not care about the defence of the legitimacy of Solomon's kingship. On the contrary, he was very sensitive about it, since when Solomon's kingship was established it had neither popular support nor the consent of the majority of senior officials but only the backing of his faction which consisted of part of the courtiers and professional soldiers. The styles of royal legitimation correspond to the situations in which the kingship is established. If Solomon had been a genuine usurper from another house than the Davidides or an Absalom who had seized the throne of his father by force with popular support, our narrator could have simply underlined the divine

---

[59] See below pp. 151 ff.

[60] Against Delekat, in *Rost Festschrift*, pp. 26–36; Würthwein, *Die Erzählung von der Thronfolge Davids*, pp. 11–17, 49; Langlamet, *RB* 83 (1976), pp. 321–379, 481–528; van Seters, *In Search of History*, pp. 289–291.

[61] Cf. Mettinger, *King and Messiah*, p. 29; H. Hagan, "Deception as Motif and Theme in 2 Sam 9–20; 1 Kgs 1–2", *Bib* 60 (1979), p. 302.

election. But the situation was more complicated. Solomon gained designation as the successor from his father, but he gained it by a court intrigue. Under these circumstances, the regime of Solomon had to lay emphasis first on the continuity of the dynasty, since the throne of David was the sole foundation of his kingship when it was established. At the same time, it was necessary to legitimatize the drastic measure which Solomon's supporters took to secure the kingship for him, for Solomon became king contrary to general expectation (cf. 2:15).

In my opinion, these two elements of the Solomonic legitimation are blended in the words of congratulation offered by Benaiah (1:37) and David's servants (1:47): "May your God make the name of Solomon more famous than yours, and make his throne greater than your throne". I have tried to explain these words elsewhere as a blessing to David, symbolizing a dynastic growth.[62] This interpretation seems correct but insufficient. I am now inclined to think that these words imply not only the growth of the Davidic dynasty but also a real wish on the part of Solomon's supporters that the name and throne of Solomon should literally become superior to those of David. This wish originated in their judgement that the regime of David had long been deteriorating and had to be taken over by Solomon, even though this meant resorting to a court intrigue, in order to establish the dynasty of David in the true sense.[63]

7. *David as a Disqualified King*

It has been noted that the figure of David as described in the Succession Narrative presents a striking contrast to that in the History of David's Rise.[64] In the latter, he is described as a blessed person

[62] Ishida, *The Royal Dynasties*, pp. 105 f.

[63] If we accept B. Mazar's suggestion that Ps 72 originated in the days of co-regency of David and Solomon, "The Phoenicians in the Levant", (1965), in *The Early Biblical Period. Historical Studies*, Jerusalem, 1986, p. 228, we may find in the psalm a development of the theme of the congratulation offered to David on the occasion of Solomon's accession to the throne, especially compare v. 17: "May his name endure for ever, his fame continue as long as the sun" with 1 Kgs 1:47.

[64] For the History of David's Rise see J.H. Grønbaek, *Die Geschichte vom Aufstieg Davids (1.Sam.15–2.Sam.5). Tradition und Komposition*, Copenhagen, 1971; Ishida, *The Royal Dynasties*, pp. 55–80; Mettinger, *King and Messiah*, pp. 33–47; P.K. McCarter, *I Samuel. A New Translation with Introduction, Notes and Commentary* (AB 8), Garden City, N.Y., 1980, pp. 27–30. According to R.A. Carlson, in 2 Sam 2–7 David is described

chosen by Yahweh as king, while David in the former is an object of scandal and a man of indecision and finally a dotard. Scholars have puzzled over the intention of the narrator of the Succession Narrative who persistently discloses the weak points of David and his decadence. The answers propounded to the question differ mainly according to the way the critics define the purpose of the narrative. From the viewpoint of finding a Solomonic legitimation in it, I am convinced that the purpose of the description of David's shortcomings in the Succession Narrative can be elucidated solely from the political standpoint of those with a critical attitude towards the regime of David, who assisted Solomon in establishing his kingship.

It is important to note that the criticism is leveled against David not as a private person but as a king.[65] For instance, David is described with much sympathy when he, as a father, wept over the death of his rebellious son (2 Sam 19:1). But, what the narrator intends to show by this moving description is that David is disqualified from being king in the sense of a military leader, as Joab's remonstrance indicates (19:6–8). This is a typical example of a description of David's disqualification to be king, in which Joab's influence over the regime increases in inverse proportion to the decline of David's control over the kingship. The key to understanding the purpose of the narrator of the Succession Narrative lies in this interrelation between David and Joab.[66]

When the people of Israel demanded that Samuel installs a king over them, they expected the king to be *šōpēṭ*, i.e., the ruler and supreme judge, as well as the war-leader of the kingdom (1 Sam 8:20; cf. 8:5; 12:12; Ps 72). These two functions were regarded as the fundamental duties of a king in the ancient Near East.[67] David,

---

as a person under the blessing, while in 2 Sam 9–24 he is described as a man under the curse, see *David, the chosen King: A Traditio-Historical Approach to the Second Book of Samuel*, Stockholm/Göteborg/Uppsala, 1964.

[65] K.R.R. Gros Louis finds in the narrative many conflicts between David's personal desires and his public obligations as king, "The Difficulty of Ruling Well: King David of Israel", *Semeia* 8 (1977), pp. 15–33.

[66] H. Schulte has pointed out that Joab dominates the narrative from the beginning to the end, *Die Entstehung der Geschichtsschreibung im alten Israel* (BZAW 128), Berlin/New York, 1972, pp. 141–143.

[67] See H. Frankfort, *Kingship and the Gods. A Study of Ancient Near Eastern Religion as the Integration of Society & Nature*, Chicago, 1948, pp. 51–60; T. Jacobsen, "Early Political Development in Mesopotamia" (1957), in W.L. Moran (ed.), *Toward the Image of Tammuz and Other Essays on Mesopotamian History and Culture* (HSS 21), Cambridge, Mass., 1970, p. 154; idem, "Ancient Mesopotamian Religion: The Central Concerns" (1963), in *Toward the Image of Tammuz*, p. 43; cf. also above pp. 43 ff., 68.

while he was still competent to perform the task of being ruler and supreme judge of the kingdom, is mentioned in the first list of his high officials as follows: "So David reigned over all Israel; and David administered justice and equity to all his people" (2 Sam 8:15).[68] By contrast, he puts on a very poor performance or gets just failing marks for this duty in the Succession Narrative.

David betrayed the people's confidence in him as a just judge by his adultery with Bathsheba and his murder of Uriah the Hittite, her husband, to cover up his crime (11:2–27). It was Joab who first learned the secret from David (11:14–21). We do not know how the affair came to Nathan's knowledge. It is possible to assume that, by informing Nathan of the fact, Joab vindicated himself in the matter of Uriah's death in battle. In the disclosure of the affair through Nathan's prophetic reproach (12:7–15), David was disgraced, but Joab escaped from having his reputation ruined as the commander of the army.

No action was taken by David as a judge concerning Amnon's rape of Tamar. "When King David heard of all these things, he was very angry; but he did nothing to harm Amnon, his son, for he loved him, because he was his firstborn" (13:21 LXX). This unjust treatment of the affair caused Absalom, Tamar's brother, to kill Amnon in revenge. This time David once again did nothing but weep with his sons and all his servants (13:36). Moreover, in the stories of Amnon's rape of Tamar and Absalom's revenge on Amnon, by stupidly granting the respective requests of Amnon and Absalom without penetrating into their hearts (13:6–7, 26–27; cf. 15:7–9), David indirectly helped them realize their evil designs. These mistakes also call into question his competence as a wise ruler.

Though David wanted to pardon Absalom, he hesitated to take any initiative towards healing the breach between himself and Absalom. In the meantime, Joab took an active hand in the problem by sending a woman of Tekoa to David (14:1–3). We are not explicitly told the reason for Joab's intervention. But the conversation between David and the woman from Tekoa indicates that Joab was concerned about the problem of the royal succession (14:4–20). Since Absalom was the first candidate for the throne at that time, we can assume that Joab also expected Absalom to become king in the future. It is quite possible, therefore, that by mediating a settlement between

[68] For the list of David's high officials see below pp. 128 f.

David and Absalom, Joab wanted to place Absalom under an obligation to himself and to exert influence on him when he should become king. However, contrary to his expectation, Absalom kept aloof from Joab (cf. 1 Kgs 2:28b), and appointed Amasa commander of the army instead of Joab (2 Sam 17:25). Absalom undoubtedly felt much more at ease with Amasa than with Joab, since the former was much less brilliant than the latter (cf. 20:4–5). But, this appointment proved fatal to Absalom. He was not only defeated at the battle in the forest of Ephraim (18:6–8) but also killed by Joab (18:9–15), who was a man of vengeful character (cf. 3:27). In any case, as the woman from Tekoa told David, "in order to change the course of affairs", Joab intervened in the problem and succeeded in reconciling David with Absalom (14:33). The fact that the course of events was determined not by David but by Joab testifies to the existence of a situation in which David was not active enough to exercise the office of ruler, while Joab actually conducted the affairs of state.

According to the Succession Narrative, the direct cause of Absalom's rebellion was David's negligence in his duty as the supreme judge of the kingdom. Absalom said to any person who "had a suit to come before the king for judgement. . . . See, your claims are good and right; but there is no man deputed by the king to hear you. . . . Oh that I were judge in the land! Then every man with a suit or cause might come to me, and I would give him justice" (15:2–4). By these words, "Absalom stole the hearts of the men of Israel" (15:6), and succeeded in rising in revolt with them against the regime of David. Then, the people dethroned David and elevated Absalom to the position of king (cf. 15:10; 19:10–11). This episode is one of the clearest pieces of evidence for David's disqualification for the office of ruler.

Simply because of Absalom's death, David was restored to the throne, contrary to the people's original intention (cf. 19:23). David tried to save a difficult situation after the rebellion but eventually sowed the seeds of new trouble. Resenting David's one-sided dealing with the tribe of Judah (19:42–44), the northern tribes decided to dissolve their covenant with David, according to which he had reigned over them (5:1–3), by the instigation of Sheba, the son of Bichri (20:1–2). By calling Sheba "a worthless fellow" (20:1), the narrator shows his pro-Davidic stance, but he does not hesitate to tell about David's mismanagement of the affair. After Absalom's defeat, David appointed Amasa commander of the army in place of Joab

(19:14). Although this change was made to appease the people of Judah who had taken part in Absalom's rebellion,[69] it was clearly an unjust action, for Amasa had served as the commander of the rebel army, while Joab had rendered the most distinguished service to David in suppressing the rebellion, though he had killed Absalom in disobedience to David's order (18:10–15). To make matters worse, Amasa was an incompetent commander. He was not able to call up the people of Judah in time to quell Sheba's revolt (20:4–5). David was obliged to ask Abishai and his soldiers, among whom Joab was included, to deal with the trouble. While going on an expedition against Sheba, Joab assassinated Amasa and seized command of the expeditionary force (20:8–13). When Joab returned triumphant from the campaign, David was compelled to restore him to the command of the army (20:22–23). The unmistakable message of the story is that David was only a nominal ruler, and Joab had become the strong-man holding sway over the kingdom.

Also in the performance of his duty as the war-leader of the kingdom, David in the Succession Narrative is a thoroughly incompetent person. During the Ammonite war David committed adultery with Bathsheba. His behaviour is described in sharp contrast to that of Uriah the Hittite, who refused to go down to his house because of his strict self-control (11:11). It is clear that the story implicitly accuses David of negligence in his duty as the war-leader by his adultery with Bathsheba and murder of Uriah during the war.[70] Moreover, Joab's urging to David to capture the city of Rabbath Ammon himself, "lest I take the city, and it be called by my name" (12:28), shows that the war was virtually conducted by Joab under the nominal supervision of David.

In the battle against Absalom, David first tried to assume his responsibility as war-leader by mustering the men who were with him (18:1). But being dissuaded by the people from going out with them, he easily conceded and said to them: "Whatever seems best to you I will do" (18:4). These words are nothing but a dereliction

[69] Although there are some scholars who maintain that Judah was not involved in the rebellion, we can hardly explain the situation by that assumption, see Ishida, *The Royal Dynasties*, pp. 69 f., n. 61.

[70] It is probable that Uriah kept continence in accordance with the obligations of cleanliness which the holy war imposed on him, see R. de Vaux, *Ancient Israel. Its Life and Institutions*, London, 1961, pp. 258 f., 263; cf. also Bailey, *David in Love and War*, pp. 96–98.

of his duty as war-leader. In addition, he could not restrain himself from giving such an order, improper to troops going to the front, as to deal gently with Absalom, the leader of the enemy (18:5). Judging from the consequences, it is likely that Joab prevented David from going into battle. David's leniency towards Absalom must have been an obstacle to Joab, who had determined to eliminate Absalom, most probably since Absalom had appointed Amasa commander of the army instead of Joab. He ignored David's command and killed Absalom (18:14–15). As for the story of David as a father in a frenzy of grief at the death of his rebellious son (19:1), I have already dealt with the narrator's intention. In fact, no one can deny that the episode tells us that the real commander in the battle against Absalom was not David but Joab.

In the campaign against Sheba the son of Bichri, Joab murdered Amasa, the commander of the army appointed by David, and usurped the position of commander of the expeditionary force. So, David could not help giving his consent to Joab's self-appointment as commander of the army. As I have suggested above, if Benaiah was appointed commander of the royal bodyguard at the same time, this appointment was made, most probably, with the intention of counterbalancing Joab's growing power. Those who were loyal to the dynasty of David must have been alarmed at Joab's self-appointment as commander of the army and David's impotent rule. In any case, there is no reason to doubt that Joab was then at the zenith of his power. It cannot be an accident that David as the ruler of the land is omitted from the second list of his high officials (20:23–26), which is placed immediately after the story of Joab's victorious campaign against Sheba. There are three such lists; two of David's high officials and one of Solomon's. Except for the second list of David's, either David or Solomon is mentioned at the top of the list as the ruler reigning over all Israel (2 Sam 8:15 = 1 Chr 18:14; 1 Kgs 4:1).[71] Accordingly, we may assume that by omitting David's name from it, the second list of David's high officials tells us, though implicitly,

[71] T.N.D. Mettinger regards 2 Sam 8:15 as editorial, *Solomonic State Officials. A Study of the Civil Government Officials of the Israelite Monarchy* (CBOTS 5), Lund, 1971, p. 7, n. 4. He seems right from the stylistic point of view. However, I cannot but find in this verse an intentional addition of the author of the narrative to the original list. For various views on the two lists of David's high officials see Bailey, *David in Love and War*, pp. 149 f. n. 83.

that the *de facto* ruler was then Joab, who ranked at the top of the list (2 Sam 20:23a).

The episode concerning Abishag the Shunamite (1 Kgs 1:1–4) tells us that David had lost his physical strength, especially his virility, in his last days. This episode adds another proof of his disqualification as king. It is unlikely, however, that the narrator found in David's impotence his inability in the royal duty in fertility cults like in the neighbouring countries in the ancient Near East, since we have no evidence for such royal ceremonies in the kingdom of Judah.[72] What the narrator tells in the passage is David's impotence in the literal sense of the word. This episode implies that a king who cannot beget his successor is not a king any longer.

However, in the present context, the episode of Abishag the royal nurse rather serves as an introduction to the narrative of the court intrigue, by which Solomon gained David's designation as his successor (1:5–53), as well as a preparation for the narrative of Solomon's execution of Adonijah (2:13–25). In the narrative of the court intrigue David is portrayed as a king who became not only too senile to bring the ambitions of Joab and Adonijah under his control but also too hesitant to decide upon his successor by himself. David is described here as a completely disqualified king who can perform no royal duty any more. In portraying David in this way, the narrator skillfully provids a reason for the intrigue. According to his analysis of the situation, the *de facto* ruler of the regime was Joab; if Joab had succeeded in making Adonijah king, the latter would have been the former's puppet, just like Ishbaal, who was placed on the throne by Abner, the commander of Saul's army (2 Sam 2:8–9). In his opinion, this was a sort of usurpation to be prevented. However, David had no power to administer justice as a king. Under these circumstances, it was legitimate, so asserts the narrator, to take all possible steps to interfere with the plan of Joab and Adonijah. This was the reason for the intrigue by which Solomon's supporters secured his designation as the heir apparent by turning the tables on Adonijah's party at the last moment.

[72] See Würthwein, *Das Erste Buch der Könige*, p. 10, n. 6.

8. *The Abishag Episode*

After several years of co-regency with David, Solomon became the sole sovereign after his father's death. Judging from his passive role in the court intrigue, we may assume that Solomon was under adult age at the time of his accession.[73] Besides, in contrast to broad support from important courtiers and the general public which Adonijah enjoyed (1 Kgs 1:7, 9, 19, 25; 2:15, 22), Solomon was helped by nobody but a few newcomers who enlisted David's mercenaries as their allies (1:8, 10, 26).[74] Undoubtedly, the main purpose of the co-regency was to protect young Solomon against Adonijah and his supporters.[75] The fact that no purge was made in the days of the co-regency suggests that the foundation of Solomon's regime was shaky at the beginning, while Adonijah's party remained intact. Especially, Joab was threatening who continued to have influence with the coutiers and the people. Under these circumstances, the demise of David doubtless brought Solomon's regime to a crisis (cf. 2:22).

Against the background of this political crisis, the Abishag affair must be elucidated. The narrative begins with Adonijah visiting Bathsheba (2:13a). The names of Adonijah's mother and of Bathsheba's son are pointedly mentioned again, in order to show that this visit was made in the framework of a confrontation between the two rival parties. Indeed, Bathsheba entered into conversation with Adonijah in a tense atmosphere. She asked: "Do you come *šālôm*?" and he answered: "*šālôm*" (2:13). The identical question and answer were exchanged between the elders of Bethlehem and Samuel, when Samuel visited Bethlehem to find a future king as a substitute for Saul (1 Sam 16:4–5). The report on the elders' "trembling" (*wayyeḥerᵉḏû*) when coming to meet Samuel tells that they felt misgiving about the purpose of his visit. Similarly, Bathsheba's question signifies her grave suspicion about Adonijah's real intention.

However, before disclosing the purpose of his visit, Adonijah skillfully relaxed her tension by telling her of his resignation of political

---

[73] According to S. Yeivin's calculation, Solomon was 16 years old at his accession, "שלמה", in *Encyclopaedia Biblica* VII, Jerusalem, 1976, col. 693 (Hebrew); cf. also T. Ishida, "Solomon", in *ABD* VI, New York, 1992, p. 105.

[74] See above pp. 110 ff.

[75] For the institution of co-regency in the kingdom of Judah, see Ishida, *The Royal Dynasties*, p. 170.

ambition (1 Kgs 2:15). This was done to convince her that his request for Abishag had nothing to do with a claim upon the throne. It is a well-known fact, however, that one way royal legitimacy was acquired was by the appropriation of the previous kings' harem, both in Israel and in the rest of the ancient Near East.[76] In that case, why did Adonijah make such a request which might endanger his life? The answer is bound up with the ambiguous status of Abishag at the court.

It is by no means clear exactly what her title *sōḵeneṯ* stood for (1 Kgs 1:2, 4), since she is the only bearer of the title in the Hebrew Bible.[77] Her task was "to lie in the king's bosom to make him warm" (1:2). As such she "stood before the king" (1:2) and served him (1:4, 15). But the king "had no intercourse with her" (1:4b). Owing to the last remark it is on the one hand possible to regard her not as a concubine of David but as a mere nurse. However, on the other hand, we may contend that though no intercourse occurred between David and her because of his impotence, she was certainly included among David's concubines since her task was "to lie in the king's bosom".

Evidently, there were differences of opinion about the status of Abishag at Solomon's court and it appears that Adonijah attempted to take advantage of the ambiguity of the situation. First, he approached Bathsheba to use her as a backdoor to Solomon. He knew well that Solomon would hardly refuse her request (2:17a). After making her lower her guard by stating his resignation of the kingship (2:15), he induced her to believe that his request for Abishag was innocent. She was willing to intercede with Solomon for Adonijah (2:18, 20–21). When hearing of Adonijah's request, however, Solomon was enraged with Adonijah and ordered the latter's execution (2:22–24). According to a common interpretation, whatever motivation Adonijah might have had, whether romantic or political, Solomon seized the request as a legal pretext to execute him, and most commentators discover

[76] de Vaux, *Ancient Israel*, pp. 116 f.; M. Tsevat, "Marriage and Monarchical Legitimacy in Ugarit and Israel", *JSS* 3 (1958), pp. 237–243; Ishida, *The Royal Dynasties*, p. 74. There are several scholars who have tried to refute the thesis, e.g., Würthwein, *Die Erzähung von der Thronfolge Davids*, pp. 37–39; Gunn, *The Story of King David*, p. 137, n. 4; but their argument does not seem convincing enough.

[77] "Servitress", BDB, p. 698; "nurse, (maid-)servant", KB, p. 658; "nurse, female local government official responsible for particular duties", *HALOT* II, p. 755.

some sympathetic tones for Adonijah in the narrative.[78] I would like to suggest a different interpretation, however.

Solomon's answer to Bathsheba reveals the problem involved: "Why do you ask Abishag the Shunamite for Adonijah? Ask for him the kingdom also!" (2:22). In his view, wherein the appropriation of Abishag is regarded as the equivalent of seizing the kingship, if he had granted Adonijah's request for Abishag, Adonijah would have exploited her as a pretext for pretending again to the throne; Bathsheba had been deceived by Adonijah. Although no mention is made of Adonijah's plot, it is clear for the reader who has knowledge about Solomon's critical situation that he made the correct judgement of the problem and penetrated Adonijah's plot. Besides, the request for Abishag should remind the reader of Absalom's taking possession of David's harem (2 Sam 16:21–22). In any case, as Solomon had once warned Adonijah, when "wickedness" was found in Adonijah (1 Kgs 1:52), Solomon did not hesitate to kill him. The execution was licit.

The opinion that the narrative of the Abishag affair was composed as an anti-Solomonic propaganda since it revealed Solomon's cruel action toward his innocent brother[79] is a good example of the misunderstanding of a biblical passage based on the humanistic sentiment of our modern society. We must understand the original message of the narrative in light of the royal ideology of the ancient Near East, as praise of Solomon who was wise enough to prevent Adonijah's cunning plot.[80] In so doing, Solomon succeeded in establishing his kingship in the kingdom.

9. *The Testament of David and Solomon's Purge*

The Testament of David (1 Kgs 2:1–9)[81] provides us with additional evidence for the argument that there was no uprising against David at En Rogel. In his final words to Solomon on his death-bed, David

[78] Delekat, in *Rost Festschrift*, p. 27; Noth, *Könige* I, pp. 32–34; Würthwein, *Die Erzähung von der Thronfolge Davids*, pp. 11–17; Langlamet, *RB* 83 (1976), p. 335; Mettinger, *King and Messiah*, pp. 27–29.

[79] See above p. 105.

[80] Whitelam, *The Just King*, p. 152, argues that Solomon's execution of Adonijah was "a contrived judicial murder" by the monarchical authority.

[81] The Testament of David (1 Kgs 2:1–9) is generally regarded as a composite work consisting of an original source (vv. 5–9) and Deuteronomistic material, see Gray, *I & II Kings*, pp. 15 f., 97–104. However, W.T. Koopmans reads the peri-

charged Joab with the assassination of Abner and Amasa and accused Shimei of cursing David at the time of Absalom's rebellion. Some commentators are puzzled over the fact that there is no charge against Adonijah and Abiathar in the testament.[82] This is not surprising, however, since the crimes with which Joab and Shimei were charged have nothing to do with Adonijah's attempt to gain the crown. In other words, David did not find any offence in Adonijah and his supporters in connection with their struggle with Solomon's party over the kingship.

However, Adonijah was executed by Solomon as a rebel who had plotted against Solomon's regime. Likewise, Abiathar was condemned solely for taking sides with Adonijah. Indeed, his loyalty toward David is even mentioned as grounds for commuting a death sentence to banishment from Jerusalem to Anathoth, his home village (2:26). At the same time, this fact suggests that Abiathar did not play a significant role in the strugle for the throne from the political point of view. By contrast, Solomon had to get rid of Joab by any possible means, since it was the aim of Solomon's *coup d'état* to remove Joab's influence over the regime. Therefore, exploiting Adonijah's request for the hand of Abishag as a sign of a conspiracy, on this pretext Solomon ordered Benaiah to execute Joab together with Adonijah. Admittedly, Joab was guilty of offences against David (2:5, 31–33). However, the short explanation of the reason for his execution reads: "For Joab had supported Adonijah although he had not supported Absalom" (2:28). This comment reveals that Joab was actually executed not for his disobedience to David in the early days but for his conspiracy with Adonijah against Solomon.[83] It seems that Solomon had a need for the authority of David's testament to execute Joab who was still so influential that Solomon felt uneasy about dealing with him alone. At the same time we have to keep it in sight that the charge against Joab with his assassination of Abner and Amasa in the Testament of David (2:5–6) is placed here according to the historiographical design to legitimatize Solomon's execution of Joab.[84]

cope as a "poetic narrative" and argues for an original unity of the work, "The Testament of David in 1 Kings ii 1–10", *VT* 41 (1991), pp. 429–449. For various opinions concerning the literary-critical analysis of the passage see ibid., p. 429, n. 2.

[82] E.g., Montgomery and Gehman, *The Books of Kings*, p. 83.

[83] Cf. Gray, *I & II Kings*, p. 109.

[84] See below pp. 164 f.

The Testament of David was not a sufficient pretext for Shimei's execution, since David had sworn to him that he would not kill him (2 Sam 19:24). Therefore, Solomon entrapped him and succeeded in getting rid of him. Shimei was the archenemy of the house of David. Ever since David had taken over Saul's kingship, the house of Saul had continued to lay claim to the kingship even after David had become the king of Israel. Ziba's words about Meribaal's expectation of the restoration of Saul's kingship (16:3), Shimei's curse on David (16:5–8) and Sheba's revolt (20:1–2) show that David had not succeeded in silencing that claim by the end of his reign. By the execution of Shimei, Solomon demonstrated that this latent claim of Saul's house to the kingship was rejected for good. The execution of Shimei, together with that of Joab, must be regarded not as a token of Solomon's coldblooded character but as an episode of Solomon's wisdom (cf. 1 Kgs 2:9) as well as one of his political achievements in a matter which David had left unfinished.

As I have suggested above, the relationship between David and Solomon in the Succession Narrative basically had two aspects: continuation of David's throne on the one hand and criticism against David's regime on the other. This ambivalence toward David is the characteristic feature of the Solomonic legitimation. These double aspects are also found in the Testament of David (2:1–9) and the narrative about Solomon's purge of his enemies (2:13–46). The view for the continuity of the dynasty is expressed in the words placed before the narrative of the purge: "Solomon sat upon the throne of David his father, his kingdom was firmly established" (2:12). Solomon's purge is understood here as a confirmation of the eternal stability of the house of David and its throne (2:33, 45), but not as a prerequisite to the establishment of his kingdom.

Evidently, the dynastic continuity between David and Solomon is the prevailing aspect in the Succession Narrative. But the Solomonic historiographer could not finish without adding the other aspect. We find it in the very last words of the narrative: "So the kingdom was established *bᵉyaḏ šᵉlōmōh*" (2:46b). This Hebrew phrase is generally translated as "in the hand of Solomon". But the context requires its rendering as "by the hand of Solomon".[85] The passage implies that

[85] For the use of *bᵉyaḏ* with the meaning of "by the agency or instrumentality of", see BDB, p. 391. As intensifying expression of *bᵉ* with the meaning of "through", see *HALOT* II, p. 388.

the kingdom was established only after Solomon had solved difficult problems left unsolved by David. Solomon is contrasted here with David, whose awkward treatment of political problems had caused one rebellion and unrest after another in the kingdom.

10. *Conclusions*

I have no intention to deal in detail in the present chapter with the questions of the boundaries, date, and author of the Succession Narrative. It seems necessary, however, to make some remarks about these questions in order to complete the analysis. Since the relationship between David and Joab and the way of dealing with the claim of Saul's house to the kingship may be regarded as the main and second themes, respectively, the story of the beginning of David's kingdom of Judah, established by taking over Saul's kingship, the conflict between David and Ishbaal, culminating in Joab's assassination of Abner and David's curse on Joab, and the assassination of Ishbaal signifying the end of Saul's kingdom in 2 Sam 2–4, seems the most suitable beginning to the narrative.[86] By the same reasoning, I am inclined to find the concluding remark in the words: "So the kingdom was established by the hand of Solomon", placed after the execution of Shimei (1 Kgs 2:46b), rather than in the similar words in 2 Kgs 2:12.[87]

The date of composition could not be as late as the second half of Solomon's reign. For the regime of Solomon must have felt it necessary to make this sort of legitimation only in its early years. Besides, the narrator's candid attitude towards the disgraceful conduct of the members of David's house, such as David's adultery with Bathsheba, his murder of Uriah or Amnon's rape of Tamar, would also indicate the same early years. It appears that these scandals were still too fresh in the memory of the general public to be concealed, when it was composed.

[86] See below pp. 158 ff. Cf. also Schulte, *Die Entstehung der Geschichtsschreibung*, pp. 140 f., 165; Gunn, *The Story of King David*, pp. 65–84; Bailey, *David in Love and War*, pp. 14 f.

[87] As one of the critical views agaisnt Rost's thesis there has been a tendency to find the end of the Succession Narrative in 2 Sam 20 instead of 1 Kgs 1–2, see McCarter, *II Samuel*, pp. 12 f. For various opinions about the end of the Succession Narrative see Bailey, *David in Love and War*, pp. 15 f.

I am convinced that the author of the Succession Narrative was one of the supporters of Solomon. Judging from Nathan's role as the driving force of Solomon's party in the court intrigue, one of Nathan's followers may be a likely candidate for author. An examination of the roles which Nathan played in the Succession Narrative also confirms that he was the ideologue of the movement for establishing Solomon's regime. Apart from the episode of the court intrigue (1 Kgs 1), he appears only twice in the Succession Narrative, viz., in his prophecy about the perpetuation of David's dynasty (2 Sam 7:1–17)[88] and in his prophetic verdict on David's sins of adultery and murder (12:1–25).[89] It is important to note that both episodes are directly connected with the claim of Solomon's party that the name and throne of Solomon were superior to those of David. In the prophecy, it is expressed as a prediction about the establishment of the Davidic dynasty: "When your days are fulfilled and you lie down with your fathers, I will raise up your son after you . . . . . and I will establish his kingdom" (7:12) and the builder of the Temple: "He (i.e., your son) shall build a house for my name" (7:13a). This is nothing but a declaration that Solomon did in fact establish the dynasty and build the Temple which David had failed to build. In the verdict, Solomon loved by Yahweh and called Jedidiah (12:24–25) presents a striking contrast to David under Yahweh's curse (11:27; 12:10–11). It is conspicuous that Yahweh's curse brought on by David's adultery with Bathsheba and his murder of Uriah no longer has any unfavourable influence upon Solomon's birth to David and Bathsheba. This was a sin to be redeemed by David himself, involving the life of the first son of David and Bathsheba.

From the foregoing study I conclude that Nathan was a prophet who, being disappointed in David, placed his hopes in young Solomon to restore the rule of the dynasty of David with justice and equity over the kingdoms of Israel and Judah.[90] And someone from Nathan's circle composed the Succession Narrative in a historiographical style to defend the legitimacy of Solomon's kingship.

[88] See below pp. 137 ff.

[89] See below pp. 151 ff.

[90] It is worth comparing this attitude of Nathan towards David with that of Samuel, who regretted having made Saul king (1 Sam 15:10–35) and that of Ahijah the Shilonite, who predicted the downfall of Jeroboam whom he had helped to the throne (1 Kgs 14:6–16).

CHAPTER EIGHT

THE NARRATIVE OF NATHAN'S PROPHECY*

1. *Limitations of Analytical Studies*

The narrative of Nathan's prophecy (2 Sam 7:1–17; 1 Chr 17:1–15; cf. Ps 89), a fundamental document for the covenant of David,[1] is one of the biblical texts which have been most repeatedly studied. Numerous suggestions have been advanced to analyze its complicated structure and to give an interpretation of its ambiguous implication. However, no study has received general support among scholars.[2]

After the pioneering study of L. Rost appeared in 1926, the narrative of Nathan's prophecy was once regarded by the majority of critics as a text composed from the oldest nucleus of the prophecy and several strata from different periods of which the last one was Deuteronomistic.[3] In contrast, the fundamental unity of the text was also defended once and again.[4] Among others, the proposal of

* This essay is a revised version of the study which appeared in S. Arai et al. (eds.), *The Message of the Bible—Ways of its Communication. Essys in Honour of Professor Masao Sekine on the Occasion of His Seventy-Seventh Birthday* (Biblical Studies 23), Tokyo, 1989, pp. 147–160 (Japanese).

[1] For the Davidic covenant see above p. 86, n. 18.

[2] For a survey of previous studies see T.N.D. Mettinger, *King and Messiah. The Civil and Sacral Legitimation of the Israelite Kings* (CBOTS 8), Lund, 1976, pp. 48–63; T. Ishida, *The Royal Dynasties in Ancient Israel. A Study on the Formation and Development of Royal-Dynastic Ideology* (BZAW 142), Berlin/New York, 1977, pp. 81–117. See also E. von Nordheim, "König und Tempel. Der Hintergrund des Tempelbauverbotes in 2 Samuel vii", *VT* 27 (1977), pp. 434–453; P.K. McCarter, *II Samuel. A New Translation with Introduction, Notes and Commentary* (AB 9), Garden City, N.Y., 1984, pp. 190–231; P.J. Botha, "2 Samuel 7 against the Background of Ancient Near-Eastern Memorial Inscriptions", in W.C. van Wyk (ed.), *Studies in the Succession Narrative*, Pretoria, 1986, pp. 62–78; G.H. Jones, *The Nathan Narratives* (JSOTSup 80), Sheffield, 1990, pp. 59–92; 157–165.

[3] L. Rost, "Die Überlieferung von der Thronnachfolge Davids" (1926), in *Das kleine Credo und andere Studien zum Alten Testament*, Heidelberg, 1965, pp. 159–183. According to Rost's analysis, the prophecy consisits of vv. 11b + 16 (the nucleus) and vv. 1–4a, 4b–7 from the time of David, vv. 8–11a, 12, 14, 15, 17 from the time of Isaiah, Deuteronomistic v. 13 from the time of Josiah. Cf. M. Noth, *Überlieferungsgeschichtliche Studien. Die sammelnden und bearbeitenden Geschichtswerke im Alten Testament*, Tübingen, 1943, 1957², pp. 64 f.

[4] S. Mowinckel, "Ntansforjettelsen 2 Sam. kap. 7", *SEÅ* 12 (1947), pp. 220–229.

S. Herrmann once brought substantial support for the unity. His argument was based on a comparison of the narrative of Nathan's prophecy with the Egyptian *Königsnovelle*.[5] However, this proposal was discarded after the analogy had been proved as inappropriate.[6] According to the prevailing view, obtained by methods of redaction-criticism, the present narrative of Nathan's prophecy composed from different layers edited by the Deuteronomistic historian.[7]

Admittedly there are obvious difficulties in the narrative from the literary critical point of view. Analytical studies are effective to indicate problems deriving from the difficulties. However, scholars who employ methods of redaction-criticism are, it seems, scarecely concerned to give a satisfactory explanation for the *unity* of the present text in which difficulties remain side by side. In other words, we can find few, if any, analytical study giving a satisfactory answer to the question why such obvious difficulties remain in an important text like Nathan's prophecy, if the present text was a result of a consistent editorial work of the Deuteronomistic historian. I am of the opinion that it is worthwhile to seek after a possibility to find a design in the present narrative with the inclusion of difficulties as original elements.

---

[5] S. Herrmann, "Die Königsnovelle in Ägypten und in Israel. Ein Beitrag zur Gattungsgeschichte in den Geschichtsbüchern des Alten Testaments", *WZ Leipzig* 3 (1953/54). *Gesellschafts- und sprachwissenschaftliche Reihe* 1, pp. 51–62. Cf. M. Noth, "David und Israel in 2. Samuel 7" (1957), in *Gesammelte Studien zum Alten Testament*, München, 1960², pp. 334–345; A. Weiser, "Tempelbaukrise unter David", *ZAW* 77 (1965), pp. 153–168.

[6] E. Kutsch, "Die Dynastie von Gottes Gnaden. Probleme der Nathanweissagung in 2. Sam 7", *ZTK* 58 (1961), pp. 137–153; cf. also McCarter, *II Samuel*, pp. 212–215. As to comparative materials for Nathan's prophecy documents from Mesopotamia seem more relevant than Egyptian texts, see Ishida, *The Royal Dynasties*, pp. 83–92. A comparison with the Karatepe texts from the 8th century B.C. is suggested by Kutsch, *ZTK* 58 (1961), p. 148 and Botha, in *Studies in the Succession Narrative*, pp. 70–75.

[7] McCarter, *II Samuel*, pp. 215–220, assumes a threefold development: a) the earliest form of the oracle of the establishment of the Davidic dynasty in association with the erection of a temple in Jerusalem; b) a prophetic expansion with a negative view towards David's plan to build a royal temple and a divine promise of the Davidic dynasty; c) the Deuteronomistic redaction which softens the negativie attitude towards David's temple plan when incorporating it and the dynastic promise into the Deuteronomistic history. According to the analysis of Jones, *The Nathan Narraitives*, pp. 70–92, 2 Sam 7:1–17 consists of two oracles: the first one, on behalf of the Jebusite community, preventing David's plan to build a temple in Jerusalem (vv. 1–7) and the second one, a royal oracle on the occasion of David's enthronement or at celebrations of it (vv. 8–16); and the Deuteronmists who modified and linked both oracles are responsible for an apparent unity of the present form with Deuteronomistic theological views.

2. *David's Building Plan of a Temple in Jerusalem*

The narrative of Nathan's prophecy consists of the introductory and concluding frameworks (2 Sam 7:1–4 + 17) and the prophecy proper (vv. 5–16) composed from three sections: a) A historical recollection of Yahweh's preference for a tent to move about with the people of Israel since the Exodus to the days of David (vv. 5–7); b) Yahweh's merciful works for David and the people of Israel in past and future (vv. 8–11a); c) Yahweh's promise of founding the Davidic dynasty with a prediction about a temple built by a son of David (vv. 11b–16).

The introductory framework begins with the description of the situation (vv. 1–3) which presupposes David's building of his palace in Jerusalem, his new capital (5:6–12) and his transfer of the ark of God there (2 Sam 6; 1 Chr 13; 15–16). Taking it into consideration that the ark was the sacred symbol of the tribal confederation of Shiloh in the pre-monarchical period (1 Sam 4–6), the last operation is to be understood as David's religio-political action to establish the legitimation of Jerusalem as the new capital of his double kingdoms of Israel and Judah by connecting the city with the Shilonite tradition.[8] David had good reason to make every effort to do so, because Jerusalem had been an alien city outside the territories of the Israelite tribes before his capture (2 Sam 5:6–9). Moreover, he came from Bethlehem of Judah (1 Sam 16:1–13), one of the southern tribes, most probably, outside the confederation of Shiloh. It is conceivable, therefore, that David already had a plan to build a temple in Jerusalem for the lasting abode of the ark when its transfer to Jerusalem was decided. Moreover, it is to be remembered that the king's building or repairing of a temple was regarded in the ancient Near East as a sign of divine approval of the king's rule.[9] In every respect the building of a temple in the new capital was an indispensable project for David.

When David sought advice of Nathan the prophet for his idea of building a temple for Yahweh, the prophet extemporarily gave full

---

[8] See Ishida, *The Royal Dynasties*, pp. 140–143; H. Kruse, "David's Covenant", *VT* 35 (1985), p. 146.

[9] See H. Frankfort, *Kingship and the Gods. A Study of Ancient Near Eastern Religion as the Integration of Society & Nature*, Chicago, 1948, pp. 267–269; A.S. Kapelrud, "Temple Building: A Task for Gods and Kings", *Or* 32 (1963), pp. 56–62; V.(A.) Hurowitz, *I Have Built You an Exalted House. Temple Building in the Bible in Light of Mesopotamian and Northwest Semitic Writings* (JSOTSup 115), Sheffield, 1992.

support to it (2 Sam 7:3), but at night he imparted Yahweh's answer to David in a somewhat negative tone (vv. 4–7). Scholars have searched for the reason why the prophet changed his attitude towards David's plan overnight.[10] Regarding all the solutions proposed as unsatisfactory, I suggested in a previous study that a change of mind on the part of Nathan seems to have resulted from antagonism at the royal court at that time, especially, from his failure to make consensus of the two chief priests, Abiathar and Zadok, on the king's plan.[11] In that case, Nathan's hasty support to the king's plan should be regarded as his misjudgement on the balance of power at the court. I still hold that we could imagine this sort of political situation behind the narrative of Nathan's prophecy. However, if the narrative was composed as a historiography, the narrator's concern was not to give a report on the real situation, let alone Nathan's mistake. His seemingly inconsistent attitude towards David's plan may be correctly interpreted only when we shall find out the narrator's own rhetoric.

3. *Explanations of David's Failure*

Biblical historiographers were interested in a hitorical fact that Solomon instead of David succeeded in leaving his mark on history as the builder of the Jerusalem Temple. They felt uneasy to accept the fact without explanation. For David was not only the founder of the dynasty under Yahweh's blessing but also the prototype of the ideal king who was loyal to Yahweh (1 Kgs 15:3–5). In contrast, Solomon was remembered as a king whose apostacy tarnished his fame (11:1–13, 31–39). There are at least two different explanations for it. While the first tells that David was preoccupied with fightings with enemies by whom he was surrounded (5:17), the second relates that Yahweh forbad David to build a temple because "he was a man of wars and had shed blood" (1 Chr 22:8; 28:3). The latter explanation develops into a word-play on the name Solomon as signifying a man of peace (22:9). What both the explanations have in common is to count

[10] While Herrmann, *WZ Leipzig* 3, p. 58, finds a literary characteristic of the Egyptian *Königsnovelle*, Noth, in *Gesammelte Studien*, p. 343, regards it as a polite formality customary before the king; accordiong to McCarter, *II Samuel*, pp. 196–197, 224–229, it is a late negative addition to the positive original view toward temple building; Kruse, *VT* 35, p. 147, holds that it was Nathan's private opinion.

[11] Ishida, *The Royal Dynasties*, pp. 94 f.

David's failure in achieving political stability as the fundamental reason for the miscarriage of his plan to build a temple.

It is very likely that the narrative of Nathan's prophecy offers another explanation of the reason why David was unsuccessful in building the Jerusalem Temple. In comparison with the other two explanations, however, the political situation related in the beginning of the narrative looks quite different. It reads: "Now when the king dwelt in his house, and Yahweh had given him rest from all his enemies round about" (2 Sam 7:1). All the biblical sources except the second half of this passage (v. 1b) tell us that David did not have rest until the end. To smooth the difficulty posed by v. 1b its omission has been proposed as a Deuteronomistic addition with its rest formula or as a marginal correction based on the synoptic passage in 1 Chr 17:1.[12] However, menetion is to be made that the very assertion that David already had rest plays an important role in the narrative to introduce David's seeking counsel from Nathan. Had not judged that he already had rest, i.e., his reign became stable enough to undertake the construction of a temple, David might have not sought the divine will about his plan of temple building. In that case, we can hardly consider 2 Sam 7:1b as a late addition but, at the same time, it cannot be an objective report on the real situation. It is most probale to find in v. 1b David's own judgement on the situation, which was proved to be wrong later.

To the David's inquiry Nathan replied: "Go, do all that is in your heart; for Yahweh is with you" (v. 3). The prophet's reply clearly indicates his guarantee for Yahweh's approval of the king's plan. However, the divine words revealed to David through Nathan that night assumed another tone as follows: "Thus says Yahweh: Would you build me a house to dwell in? I have not dwelt in a house since the day I brought up the people of Israel from Egypt to this day, but I have been moving about in a tent for my dwelling. In all places where I have moved with all the people of Israel, did I speak a word with any of the judges[13] of Israel, whom I commanded to shepherd my people Israel, saying, 'Why have you not built me a house of cedar?'" (vv. 5b–7).

---

[12] The phrase "to give you rest" is counted in the Deuteronomistic phraseologies, see M. Weinfeld, *Deuteronomy and the Deuteronomic School*, Oxford, 1972, p. 343. For the omission of v. 1b from the original prophecy see Mettinger, *King and Messiah*, p. 52. For a marginal correction see McCarter, *II Samuel*, p. 191.

[13] See above p. 43, n. 36.

Critics have felt difficulties in these passages. First, they are puzzled over Nathan's overnight change of the attitude towards David's plan. We have already dealt with the problem and found in it a point of departure of the present study. Secondly, they are perplexed with the ambiguous expressions of Yahweh's answer. In a previous study, I suggested that we may find in the periphrasis Yahweh's reluctant disapproval of David's plan.[14] It seems necessary, however, to advance another interpretation to understand the narrator's rhetoric.

First of all, a more careful perusal of the text is required to decide what Yahweh's words really imply. According to the prevailing view, in these words Yahweh dismissed David's plan to build a temple for him.[15] In addition, some scholars are of the opinion that a categorical refusal of a temple for Yahweh's dwelling is expressed here.[16] It seems to me, however, that the message of Yahweh's words in vv. 5b–7 is neither the definite disapproval of David's plan to build a temple nor the refusal of the concept of a temple for his dwelling. What is underlined in these passages is that Yahweh's continuous abide with the people of Israel all through the days of the Exodus, the period of the Judges, and the present time, i.e., the time of David. The passages tell us a historical recollection that Yahweh has never asked anybody to build a permanent dwelling for him during the period when the people of Israel have been moving about. What we learn from the passages, therefore, is that Yahweh preferred a tent to a temple since the Exodus to the time of David in order to move about with the people.

The intent of the narrator who tells Yahweh's preference for a tent over a temple to move about up to the days of David becomes clear step by step in the second and the third sections. In the second section he asserts that the people of Israel were still moving about in the time of David (v. 10) in which neither the people nor

[14] Ishida, *The Royal Dynasties*, p. 95.

[15] McCarter, *II Samuel*, p. 197, holds that the positive tone of v. 3 came from the oldest stratum upon which the negativity of vv. 5–7 was imposed.

[16] Von Nordheim, *VT* 27 (1977), pp. 445 f., finds a confrontation between the royal ideology of the ancient Near East and the traditions of ancient Israel; according to McCarter, *II Samuel*, pp. 197–201, 225–228, the negative attitude towards David's plan to build a temple of vv. 5–7 came from a prophetic editor who regarded a temple as unnecessary like the institution of monarchy. Kruse, *VT* 35 (1985), pp. 142–145, maintains that the divine disapproval of David's plan to build a temple originated in the Deuteronomistic invention but a negative view against the instituiton of temple is not expressed here.

David was given rest yet (v. 11a). And in the third section he predicts as Yahweh's promise to David that a son of David will build a temple (v. 13a). In other words, the expressions of the first section are so ambiguous that we can hardly understand correctly the narrator's intent without the second and the third sections. The characteristic feature of the ambiguity of the first section becomes clearer in comparison with Deuteronomistic references to Nathan's prophecy concerning the building of the Temple. They are Solomon's correspondence to Hiram king of Tyre (1 Kgs 5:17–19) and his dedicatory speech at the Termple in Jerusalem (8:16–19).[17] While the former lays emphasis on rest given to Solomon after David's fightings with enemies were over as the precondition for the erection of the Temple, the latter accentuates the joint election of Jerusalem and David by Yahweh (8:16 LXX) to defend the legitimacy of the founder of the dynasty. Both themes originated in Nathan's prophecy, but from both the passages disappears a historical recollection of Yahweh's preference for a tent over a temple in the past. There remains no ambiguity in the Deuteronomistic explanations of the reason for David's failure to build the Temple. It is to be assumed, therefore, the ambiguous expressions of the first section reflect a delicate situation of which the narrator tried to give an explanation.

We may thus assume the rhetorical development of the first section of Nathan's prophecy with the introductory framework (2 Sam 7:1–7) as follows: First, David judged that his rule became stable enough to undertake to build a royal temple in his new capital (v. 1b). It was proved later, though obliquely, that he made a misjudgement, as wars, rebellions, and domestic troubles reported in chapters following after 2 Sam 7 show. Secondly, Nathan from whom David sought counsel gave a favourable reply to his plan (v. 3) but it became clear later that what Nathan approved was a plan to build a royal temple for Yahweh in Jerusalem in general. Thirdly, to make David postpone his plan to his son's generation Nathan gave David divine words in which Yahweh told his preference for a tent to move about with the people of Israel over a temple to dwell in since the days of the Exodus to the time of David (vv. 5b–7). The implication of the divine words is that the time is not yet ripe for building

[17] M. Noth, *Könige* I: *I. Könige 1–16* (BKAT 9/1), Neukirchen-Vluyn, 1968, pp. 88, 90, 173 f., 183; E. Würthwein, *Das Erste Buch der Könige: Kapitel 1–16* (ATD 11/1), Göttingen, 1977, pp. 52 f., 96 f.

a temple for him because both David and the people of Israel have not yet been given permanent rest.[18] We can find here a common understanding that the stability of the society was the precondition for building a royal temple.

4. *Solomon's Superiority over David*

In the second section of the prophecy (2 Sam 7:8–11a) Yahweh's merciful works in the past and the future are related: Yahweh called David to be *nāḡîḏ*, and he was with David to save him from his enemies; he will make for David a great name, will appoint a place where the people will dwell in forever without disturbance, and will give David rest.[19]

It is striking that the same topics are dealt with in biblical passages concerning Solomon in which his kingship is always described as more legitimate and much greater than David's. While Yahweh called David to be *nāḡîḏ* from the pasture, Solomon was appointed *nāḡîḏ* by David, who was the reigning king (1 Kgs 1:35).[20] Among multiple factors contributing to determining the royal succession in the ancient Near East the reigning king's designation, together with the divine election, was most important to prove the legitimacy of the successor.[21] However, David who did not come from a royal family had naturally no designation from the reigning king. He could not but resort to his divine election to legitimatize his kingship (1 Sam 16:1–13). As to the divine election, too, Solomon was at advantage over David. While David was chosen by Yahweh when he was keeping the sheep in Bethlehem (16:11–13), Solomon was loved by Yahweh immediately after he was born (2 Sam 12:24b–25).[22] This sort of

[18] According to McCarter, *II Samuel*, pp. 202–204, 225, 230 f., the interpretation that the time was not yet right for David's plan to build a temple is found in the Deuteronomistic layer in vv. 1b, 9a–11a, 13a, and 16.

[19] Opinion is divided on the interpretation of the tense of verbs in vv. 9b–11a. Some scholars regard it as a past tense, while the other critics insist that the passages refer to the future promises, for the problems and various opinions see Ishida, *The Royal Dynasties*, p. 89, n. 41; McCarter, *II Samuel*, pp. 202 f. In a previous study I found here Yahweh's guidance given to David in the past (ibid., p. 89), but I will modify my opinion since Nathan's prophcy asserts that a name, a place, and rest have not yet given to David.

[20] For *nāḡîḏ* see above pp. 57 ff.

[21] See Ishida, *The Royal Dynasties*, pp. 6–25, 151–170.

[22] See below pp. 151 ff.

extension of the validity to the past was common in the doctrine of divine election of the king in the ancient Near East. For instance, Esarhaddon: ". . . . . whom Aššur, Šamaš . . . . . have pronounced king of Assyria ever since he was a younster" (Nin. A I:5–6).[23] Nabonidus: ". . . . . whom Sin and Ningal designated to the kingship in his mother's womb" (Nr. 1, I:4–5).[24] Refer also to the call of Jeremiah the prophet: "Before I formed you in the womb . . . . . I appointed you a prophet" (Jer 1:4).[25]

As to Yahweh's abiding with David and making a great name for him, Solomon's superiority is explicitly expressed in the words of congratulation on Solomon's accession by Benaiah and David's servants: "As Yahweh has been with my lord the king, even so may he be with Solomon, and make his throne greater than the throne of my lord the king David" (1 Kgs 1:37); "Your God make the name of Solomon more famous than yours, and make his throne greater than your throne" (1:47a).[26]

As we dealt with the first section of the prophecy (2 Sam 7:5b–7), the narrator of Nathan's prophecy was of the opinion that the divine promise to provide the people of Israel with a peaceful settlement in a fixed place[27] did not become a reality in the days of David. On the contrary, the Solomon's reign is generally described as a peaceful and prosperous period. For instance, "Judah and Israel were as many as the sand by the sea; they ate and drank and were happy. Solomon ruled over all the kingdoms from the Euphrates to the land of the Philistines and to the border of Egypt; they brought tribute and served Solomon all the days of his life" (1 Kgs 4:20–5:1); "And Judah and Israel dwelt in safety, from Dan even to Beer-sheba, every man under his vine and under his fig tree, all the days of Solomon" (5:5). Mention is to be made, however, that there are also biblical sources informing us of insurrections and secessional activities under

[23] R. Borger, *Die Inschriften Asarhaddons Königs von Assyrien* (AfO Beih. 9), Graz, 1956, pp. 39 f.

[24] S. Langdon, *Die neubabylonischen Königsinschriften* (VAB 4), Leipzig, 1912, pp. 218 f.

[25] See Ishida, *The Royal Dynasties*, pp. 12 f.; cf. S.M. Paul, "Deutero-Isaiah and Cuneiform Royal Inscriptions", *JAOS* 88 (1968), pp. 180–186.

[26] See above p. 123.

[27] The term *māqôm* (v. 10) is sometimes understood in the sense of "cult place, shrine", i.e., the place that Yahweh chose to be worshiped (Deut 12:5). See A. Gelston, "A Note on II Samuel 7_{10}", *ZAW* 84 (1972), pp. 92–94; McCarter, *II Samuel*, pp. 202 f. It is difficult to accept the view because of the context, cf. also Weinfeld, *Deuteronomy and the Deuteronmic School*, p. 170, n. 1.

Solomon's rule (11:14–40). Therefore, the information that Solomon's reign was peaceful without any trouble is not to be understood as a historical report on the real situation. It is similar to the assertion that Solomon's kingship was greater than David's.

Nor is there any information that David was given rest in his lifetime. On the contrary, David was announced from Nathan the prophet that "the sword shall never depart from your house" because of his adultery with Bathsheba and his murder of Uriah, her husband (2 Sam 12:10). In fact, David in the second half of his reign is described as a king who had to deal with disturbances and unrest one after the other such as Absalom's rebellion (2 Sam 13–19), Sheba's revolt (20:1–2, 4–22), the national census and the plague (24:1–25), and a power struggle at the court (1 Kgs 1:5–53). It was Solomon who received rest which Yahweh had promised to David. This assertion is expressed in the most explicit fashion in Solomon's words to Hiram king of Tyre: "You know that David my father could not build a house for the name of Yahweh his God because of the warfare with which his enemies surrounded him, until Yahweh put them under the soles of his feet. But now Yahweh my God has given me rest on every side; there is neither adversary nor misfortune" (5:17–18). As mentioned above, these passages are evidently a Deuteronomistic expansion of Nathan's prophecy. But I find no reason to regard the assertion that the divine promise of rest to David was fulfilled in the time of Solomon as a mere Deuteronomistic invention.

5. *The Divine Promise of the Dynasty Linking with the Temple*

The third section of the prophecy (2 Sam 7:11b–16) is closely interwoven with the first section by means of the term "house" (*bayiṯ*), which signifies "temple" as well as "dynasty". The first section begins with Yahweh's question: "Would you build me a house (*bayiṯ*) to live in?" (v. 5b). Then the answer marks the beginning of the third section: "Yahweh will make you a house (*bayiṯ*)" (v. 11b). Needless to say, a "house" in the first section stands for a "temple", while a "house" in the third section signifies a "dynasty". A skilful shift of the theme from temple to dynasty takes place between the first and the third sections via the second section of which the main theme is Solomon's greater kingship than David's. At the same time, this answer plays a role of a rubric for the third section. Both the first and the second sections have a similar formulaic rubric for prophecy, respectively: "Go and tell my servant David, 'Thus says Yahweh'" (v. 5a) and "And now thus you shall say to my servant David, 'Thus says Yahweh Zebaoth'" (v. 8aα). In contrast, the rubric of the third section reads: "And Yahweh declares to you that Yahweh will make you a house" (v. 11b).[28] The last rubric stands out by including the presentation of the main theme of the section. Since the third section is the concluding part of the prophecy, it seems necessary for the narrator to have shown explicitly the aim of the composition.

In the third section, following the general promise of the establishment of a dynasty (v. 11b), Yahweh tells how to do so precisely: after David's death he will choose a son of David (v. 12a) and will make his kingship firm (v. 12b); then, the son will build a temple (v. 13a); Yahweh will make his throne stable (v. 13b); Yahweh will have a father-son relationship with him (v. 14) and will keep the divine favour on him forever (v. 15). At the end Yahweh concludes these words with the promises about the everlasting establishment of the Davidic dynasty, his kingdom, and his throne (v. 16). Evidently, it was again Solomon who enjoyed the fruits of all the divine promises to David.

In the concluding section the theme of the erection of a temple recedes from the front which is occupied by the theme of establishing the Davidic dynasty. However, it is important to note that the theme of the erection of a temple remains, though secondary, in the divine promise: "He shall build a house for my name" (v. 13a). It is clear that this promise is in response to the question: "Would you build me a house to dwell in?" (v. 5b) in the beginning of the first section. Because of the phraseology "for my name (*lišmî*)", a characteristic expression for the Deuteronomistic "name theology", v. 13a has been regarded since long as Deuteronomistic.[29] Admittedly the phrase "for my name" is Deuteronomistic. It is unlikely, however, that v. 13a as a whole stemmed from the Deuteronomistic historian

---

[28] Since Yahweh is spoken of in the third person, v. 11b is regarded as the oldest nucleus of the prophecy by Rost, in *Das kleine Credo*, pp. 169 f. On the other hand, McCarter, *II Samuel*, p. 205, finds in it a rubric introducing the dynastic promise.

[29] For the Deuteronomistic phraseologies of "the house/city which my name is called upon", "to make his name dwell there", "to put his name there", "that his name be there" and "to build a house for the name of Yahweh", see Weinfeld, *Deuteronomy and the Deuteronomic School*, pp. 193, 325.

because of the insertion of the phrase "for my name", since the theme of building a temple is indispensable for Nathan's prophecy.[30]

In addition, the divine designation Yahweh Zebaoth in the formulaic rubric in the beginning of the second section (v. 8aα) also indicates that the theme of the Jerusalem Temple is never dropped from the prophecy. As the ark of God which David tranferred to Jerusalem was called by the name of "Yahweh Zebaoth, who sits enthroned on the cherubim" (2 Sam 6:2; cf. also 1 Sam 4:4), Yahweh Zebaoth was the designation of the deity who came from Shiloh to Jerusalem with the ark. After the ark was placed in the holy of holies under the wings of the cherubim in the Temple built by Solomon (1 Kgs 8:6), the designation Yahweh Zebaoth offered the central concept of deity for the cult at the Jerusalem Temple until replaced by the Deuteronomistic name theology.[31] Therefore, the special mention of the designation Yahweh Zebaoth in the rubric of the second section suggests that the building of the Jerusalem Temple is considered in Nathan's prophecy as one of the important consequences of David's transfer of the ark to Jerusalem.

6. *Conclusions*

From the foregoing study we may come to the following conclusions:

a) David had strong motivation to build a royal temple in Jerusalem, his new capital, but wars and rebellions together with domestic troubles prevented him from translating his plan into reality. In contrast, Solomon succeeded to David's throne by a court intrigue, instituted a severe purge of his opponents who were influential people at the court of David, established the Davidic dynasty, and demonstrated the establishment of his kingship under divine grace by building the Jerusalem Temple for Yahweh, God of Israel.

[30] Cf. Mettinger, *King and Messiah*, pp. 151–184. However, he modified the opinion later, *The Dethronement of Sabaoth. Studies in the Shem and Kabod Theologies* (CBOTS 18), Lund, 1982, p. 49; see also F.K. Kumaki, "The Deuteronomistic Theology of the Temple—as Crystallized in 2 Sam 7, 1 Kgs 8—", *AJBI* 7 (1981), pp. 16–52.

[31] See T.N.D. Mettinger, "YHWH SABAOTH—The Heavenly King on the Cherubim Throne", in T. Ishida (ed.), *SPDS*, Tokyo/Winona Lake, 1982, pp. 109–138; idem, "Yahweh Zebaoth", in *DDD*, Leiden/New York/Köln, 1995, cols. 1730–1740.

b) The narrative of Nathan's prophecy is a composition to give an interpretation of the course of history concerning the establishment of Solomon's kingship linking with the building of the Jerusalem Temple from the Solomonic point of view, although, on the surface, David was the person to whom the prophecy was delivered.

c) The rhetorical development of the narrative is intricate in correspondence with the complicated course of history. The main theme is to give an explanation of the circumstances under which the Davidic dynasty was established under the divine grace linking with the builing plan of the Jerusalem Temple, by employing the double meanings of the term *bayiṯ*: "temple" and "dynasty". At the same time, the concept "rest" plays an important role as a precondition for establishing a dynasty as well as for building a royal temple.

d) In the introductory framework (2 Sam 7:1–3) the theme "to build a temple (*bayiṯ*)" is intorduced by David's apprehension that "rest" has already given and Nathan's approval of David's plan to build a royal temple. In the first section (vv. 4–7) the theme develops into the assertion that there was no "temple (*bayiṯ*)" among the people of Israel since the Exodus to the time of David when they moved about. In the second section (vv. 8–11a) Yahweh's merciful acts on David culminates in the divine promise of rest to David, although it is fulfilled in the time of a son of David. In the third section (vv. 11b–16) Yahweh gives a promise to establish a "dynasy (*bayiṯ*)" with a son of David who will build a "temple (*bayiṯ*)".

e) The intricate structure of the narrative of Nathan's prophecy originated in Solomon's ambivalent relationship with David. Although the legitimacy of Solomon's kingship was based on David's designation, Solomon established his kingship by a court intrigue and a severe purge of his opponents who were important supporters of the regime of David. Therefore, Solomon had to defend the legitimacy of his kingship against the mainstream of David's court by asserting his superiority over David. To do so, among others, Solomonic historiographer mentions David's plan to build the Jerusalem Temple. David failed but Solomon carried it into execution. It was the crown of Solomon's achievements in a matter which David had left unfinished.

f) The purpose of the narrative of Nathan's prophecy is to confirm the legitimacy of Solomon's kingship by Yahweh's promise of a dynasty to King David, his father. Therefore, the message of the narrative is to be found in the demonstration of the legitimacy of Solomon's succession to the Davidic throne by his royal lineage as well as the divine election before he was conceived in his mother's womb. A perfect legitimation.

g) The narrative of Nathan's prophecy is skillfully placed as the first preparatory reference to Solomon in the Succession Narrative. It was the moment that, according to David's judgement, after finishing all the fightings with his enemies his kingship was established firm enough to begin to build a royal temple in the new capital but, in reality, from the moment on David would have to struggle with wars, rebellions, and domestic troubles until the end of his life. At this juncture, the historiographer suggests by the narrative of Nathan's prophecy that David will be given rest and his kingship will be firmly established when one of his sons will succeed to the Davidic throne. The identity of the son of David is evident but his real name, Solomon, is concealed until his birth. By treating carefully in this way with the theme of the Solomonic legitimation the historiographer succeeded in enhancing the credibility of the Succession Narrative.

CHAPTER NINE

THE EPISODE OF SOLOMON'S BIRTH*

1. *A Terse Report*

The short episode of Solomon's birth (2 Sam 12:24–25) is in a modest way placed as the epilogue of the David-Bathsheba story which tells about David's adultery with Bathsheba (11:2–27a), Yahweh's condemnation of the affair through Nathan the prophet (11:27b–12:15a), and the death of the first child whom Bathsheba bore to David (12:15b–23), while the account of the Ammonite war (11:1; 12:26–31) serves the framework in which the David-Bathsheba story has been incorporated.[1]

The episode of Solomon's birth is so terse in contrast to the dramatic detailed narrative about the Ammonite war and the Bathsheba affair (2 Sam 11–12) that its importance may possibly escape the reader's notice. Indeed, the significance of the episode is hidden here until being revealed in the story of the court intrigue in 1 Kgs 1, in which Solomon appears as the legitimate successor to David. The implication of the episode is hardly understood properly unless we assume a literary complex which includes in it the episode of Solomon's birth as well as the story of his succession to the throne of David. Therefore, we will try to show in the present chapter the implication of the terse report on Solomon's birth by scrutinizing the role of Nathan the prophet in the episode in view of the large context of a literary complex called the Succession Narrative.

---

* This essay is a revised version of the study which appeared in *Near Eastern Studies. Dedicated to H.I.H. Prince Takahito Mikasa on the Occasion of His Seventy-Fifth Birthday* (Bulletin of the Middle Eastern Culture Center in Japan 5), Wiesbaden, 1991, pp. 133–138.

[1] The account of the Ammonite war in 2 Sam 11–12 is the continuation of the stories of the Ammonite-Aramaean wars in 8:3–8; 10:1–19. It is not the purpose of the present study to make clear the literary structure of the whole stories of the Ammonite-Aramaean wars and the David-Bathsheba story. For various opinions on the analysis of these passages see P.K. McCarter, *II Samuel. A New Translation with Introduction, Notes and Commentary* (AB 9), Garden City, N.Y., 1984, pp. 275 f., 285, 305 f.

Nathan the prophet appears exclusively in the following three sections in 2 Samuel and 1 Kgs 1–2, viz., a) the narrative of Nathan's prophecy about the establishment of the dynasty of David (2 Sam 7:1–17; cf. 1 Chr 17:1–15), b) the David-Bathsheba story (2 Sam 11:1–12:25), and c) the story of the court intrigue (1 Kgs 1). Conspicuously, references to Solomon in 2 Samuel and 1 Kgs 1–2 are also confined to the same three sections, except for his name in the list of David's sons born in Jerusalem (2 Sam 5:14). Needless to say, the reference to Solomon is implicitly made in Nathan's prophecy which was given to David before Solomon's birth, i.e., "*your son* who shall come forth from your body" (7:12); "*he* shall build a house for my name" (7:13a); or "I will establish the throne of *his* kingdom for ever" (7:13b). In addition, mention must be made that King David is another actor who appears in all the same sections. There is no section but the above three in 2 Samuel and 1 Kgs 1(–2)[2] where David, Solomon, and Nathan are together playing the leading roles. In view of this, it seems difficult to exclude anyone of them from the same literary complex. In other words, it is legitimate to assume that they are closely related to each other.

2. *A Comparison with the Narrative of Nathan's Prophecy*

To make clear their relations among each other, we will first make a comparative examination of the narrative of Nathan's prophecy and the David-Bathsheba story. Both the prophecy and the story begin with a report on David's stay in the palace in Jerusalem: "when the king dwelt (*yāšaḇ*) in his house" (2 Sam 7:1a) in the prophecy and "David remained (*yôšēḇ*) in Jerusalem" (11:1b) in the story, but the situation is different. While in the prophecy "Yahweh had given him rest round about from all his enemies" (7:1b), it is told in the story that David sent Joab with the army against the Ammonites (11:1a). The difference in the situations leads to different developments. While in the prophecy David made a plan to build a temple for Yahweh in Jerusalem (7:2), in the story he was involved in the Bathsheba affair (11:2–27a). They are evidently different episodes in

[2] Nathan does not appear in 1 Kgs 2 in which the testament of David and Solomon's purge of his enemies are told. However, this chapter is to be regarded as the direct continuation of the preceding chapter, see above pp. 132 ff.

the character. However, they are common in causing Yahweh's negative response. In the story it is frankly related: "The thing that David had done displeased Yahweh" (11:27b). In the prophecy, however, Yahweh's response to David's plan is obliquely expressed: "Would you build me a house to dwell in?" (7:5b), because of the delicate situation.[3] In any case, David had to postpone his plan to build a temple.

In both the narrative of Nathan's prophecy and the David-Bathsheba story, after Yahweh's response was revealed, the following three subjects are dealt with: a) an explanation of the reason of Yahweh's negative response, b) a recollection of Yahweh's benevolent guidance given to David, and c) a divine decision on David's future. As the first subject, while it is told in the prophecy that Yahweh has never ordered anybody to build a temple since the Exodus (7:6–7), Nathan tells a juridical parable in the story (12:1–4). The contents of the second subject is virtually identical both in the prophecy and the story. Thus it is told in the former that Yahweh chose David as *nāḡîḏ* over Israel and destroyed David's enemies (7:8b–9a). Similarly, it is related in the latter that Yahweh anointed David king over Israel and delivered him out of Saul's hand (12:7b–8a).

Undoubtedly, the third subject is most important. In the prophecy, after promising David a great name, a peaceful dwelling for Israel, and a rest from the enemies (7:9b–11a), Yahweh gives his word for the establishment of David's dynasty and his successor's building of a temple for Yahweh (7:11b–16). On the other hand, divine punishment for David's sin is announced in the story, i.e., the everlasting curse of sword, the dispossession of David's harem by his neighbour, and the death of the first child whom Bathsheba bore to David (12:10–14).

The above comparative examination has shown that the narrative of Nathan's prophecy and the David-Bathsheba story have virtually the identical structure. Then, what is the position of the episode of Solomon's birth in this structure? Whether is it a mere appendix or an important epilogue? To answer the question it is to make clear the implication of the prophecy.[4]

---

[3] For the situation see above pp. 140 ff.

[4] For the detailed analysis of Nathan's prophecy in the Succession Narrative see above pp. 137 ff.

On the surface, the narrative of Nathan's prophecy and the David-Bathsheba story seem poles apart. Indeed, the same David who is a blessed person in the former is under curse in the latter. However, the perusal of the texts will show us another picture. As mentioned above, Yahweh's main promise is twofold in the prophecy: the establishment of the dynasty of David and the building of a temple by his successor. Although David was the recipient of the promise, the dynastic establishment was naturally achieved only when Solomon succeeded to David's throne. Therefore, after Nathan told David Yahweh's promise of the dynasty in a general way: "Yahweh will make *you* a house (= dynasty)" (7:11b), Yahweh's concern is concentrated exclusively on a son of David (= Solomon): "I will establish *his* kingdom" (7:12b); "I will establish the throne of *his* kingdom for ever" (v. 13b); "I will be *his* father, and *he* shall be my son . . ." (vv. 14–15). At the end of the prophecy, as the result of the establishment of the throne of *his*, i.e., Solomon's kingdom, David is finally told that "*your* house, *your* kingdom . . . and *your* throne shall be established for ever" (v. 16). The real recipient of the dynastic promise is not David but Solomon.

As to the building of the temple, the situation is more obvious. Yahweh accepted the plan of David with a condition which David could not achieve but approved the building of the temple by Solomon without condition: "*he* shall build a house for my name" (7:13a). From the same viewpoint, the other promises given to David in the prophecy (7:9b–11a) are also Solomonic in the implication, i.e., *the great name* of David is prerequisite to Solomon's name which should become superior to that of David (1 Kgs 1:37, 47), while biblical sources tell us that it was Solomon who achieved *the peaceful dwelling for Israel* (4:20–5:5) and enjoyed *the rest from the enemies* which David did not have during his lifetime (5:17–18). It has thus become clear that it is Solomon who really received Yahweh's blessing in Nathan's prophecy.

Supposing that the David-Bathsheba story is identical with Nathan's prophecy in the structure, the former story cannot be finished with the death of the first child whom Bathsheba bore to David. We should find here a contrast between Yahweh's displeasure toward David which culminated in the death of the child and the divine blessing given to Solomon. Accordingly, the episode of Solomon's birth (2 Sam 12:24–25) is to be regarded not as a mere appendix to the David-Bathsheba story but as its climax, though it is in appearance a modest epilogue.

3. *Jedidiah a Royal Epithet*

Before dealing with the episode itself, the implication of the death of the first child is to be examined. When David confessed his guilt, Nathan told him: "Yahweh has transferred (*heʿeḇîr*)[5] your sin; you shall not die" (2 Sam 12:13b). The words imply that David's child will die as atonement for his father's sin. This interpretation perfectly agrees with the strange behaviour of David concerning the illness and death of the child. David implored Yahweh for the child by fasting and self-humiliation during the child's illness. When hearing his death, however, David stopped the imploration, worshipped Yahweh, and returned to the normal life (12:15b–20). He made fasting and self-humiliation not for mourning the dead but for imploring divine forgiveness. The death of the child was understood by David as a sign of atonement for his sin.

Accordingly, the new relation of David to Bathsheba is told in the beginning of the episode of Solomon's birth (12:24a). This passage indicates that Bathsheba had conceived Solomon by a legitimate intercourse with David, in contrast to the ill-fated child conceived by an illicit one.[6] David called the second child Solomon (v. 24b). The explanation of the name Solomon (*šᵉlōmōh*) is given in 1 Chr 22:9 that Yahweh "will give peace (*šālôm*) and quiet to Israel in his days". However, scholars explain the significance of the name as a "replacement" (from *šillem*: make compensation) for a lost sibling.[7] The name would show that David wished the newborn child to be a comfort to himself and Bathsheba in place of the first child (cf. 2 Sam 12:24a). In that case, the name Solomon suggests that David was convinced of Yahweh's forgiveness for his relation with Bathsheba. Indeed, as to Solomon whom Bathsheba bore to David after the death of their first child, the episode explicitly tells: "Yahweh loved him (= Solomon)" (12:24bβ). At this juncture, Nathan the prophet returned to the scene and gave Solomon another name called "Jedidiah (Beloved one of Yahweh) *baʿaḇûr yhwh* (by the grace of Yahweh)" (v. 25).[8] There is no doubt that Solomon was born under Yahweh's blessing.

---

[5] For the interpretation of the word see McCarter, *II Samuel*, p. 301.

[6] Cf. C. Schäfer-Lichtenberger, *Josua und Salomo. Eine Studie zu Autorität und Legitimität des Nachfolgers im Alten Testament* (VTSup 58), Leiden/New York/Köln, 1995, p. 230.

[7] See J.J. Stamm, "Der Name des Königs Salomo", *TZ* 16 (1960), pp. 285–297; G. Gerleman, "Die Wurzel *šlm*", *ZAW* 85 (1973), pp. 1–14.

[8] For the translation of *baʿaḇûr yhwh* on the basis of *bʿbwr* DN in the Karatepe

Still it is striking that Solomon's figure never comes to the fore in the David-Bathsheba story. As his birth story it seems anomalous. It is necessary to make clear the circumstances under which the story was composed. It is not difficult to imagine that there was a serious doubt about Solomon's legitimacy for the successor to the throne among the people, because of the irregular situation in which Bathsheba had become one of David's wives. Especially, Solomon must have been severely criticized as Bathsheba's child by the supporters of Adonijah, Solomon's elder brother and the contender of the throne. It is likely, therefore, that the David-Bathsheba story was composed to dispel all the doubts about the legitimacy of Solomon's birth. Evidently, no attempt was intentionally made to conceal the Bathsheba affair. Perhaps, the scandal was too well-known to be omitted. However, the detailed report on David's adultery with Bathsheba was made, in our opinion, according to the general pattern of the Solomonic legitimation, in which David is described as a disqualified king in a sharp contrast to Solomon as the legitimate successor to the Davidic throne.[9]

In the light of the above understanding of the situation, the implication of Solomon's second name Jedidiah (Beloved one of Yahweh) (2 Sam 12:25) can be elucidated. First of all, it is undeniable to feel an abrupt change in the introductory remark: "Yahweh loved him (= Solomon)" (12:24bβ). Then, we are not told exactly when Solomon received the second name. Moreover, no biblical source mentions Jedidiah as Solomon's second name except for this passage. It is very likely, therefore, the name Jedidiah originated in an attempt to show that Solomon had received the divine election for future king immediately after his birth. As a close parallel to the name Jedidiah we may refer to *migir ilāni* (Beloved one of gods), one of the royal epithets in ancient Mesopotamia.[10] If the name Jedidiah should be regarded not as a personal name but as a sort of royal epithet, we may conclude that the episode of Solomon's second name Jedidiah was produced as the indispensable epilogue of the David-Bathsheba story.

---

inscriptions (*KAI* 26: A I 8; II 6, 11–12; III 11) see J.C.L. Gibson, *Textbook of Syrian Semitic Inscriptions* III: *Phoenician Inscriptions*, Oxford, 1982, p. 57; J. Hoftijzer and K. Jongeling, *DNWSI* II, p. 823.

[9] See above pp. 121 ff. Cf. also J.A. Soggin, *A History of Israel. From the Beginnings to the Bar Kochba Revolt, A.D. 135*, London, 1984, p. 43.

[10] See M.-J. Seux, *Épithètes royales akkadiennes et sumériennes*, Paris, 1967, pp. 162–168; *CAD* M/2, pp. 48 f.

4. *Summary*

We may summarize the foregoing study as follows:

a) The David-Bathsheba story was composed to legitimatize the birth of Solomon as David's successor.

b) Because of Yahweh's wrath which David incurred by his adultery with Bathsheba and his murder of Uria the Hittite, her former husband, David was placed under the divine curse.

c) However, David's marital relation with Bathsheba was recognized as legitimate after the death of the first child which atoned for David's sin.

d) Accordingly, David's sin no longer has any unfavorable influence on Solomon's birth.

e) From his childhood Solomon was destined for the successor to the throne of David, as the name Jedidiah (Beloved one of Yahweh) indicates.

f) The David-Bathsheba story and the narrative of Nathan's prophecy served as theological preparations for the legitimation of Solomon who succeeded to the Davidic throne through the court intrigue related in 1 Kgs 1.

g) Nathan the prophet not only played the role of the leader of Solomon's supporters but also acted as the ideologue of the Solomonic legitimation.

CHAPTER TEN

THE STORY OF ABNER'S MURDER*

1. *David's Exoneration*

The narratives in 1 Sam 29–2 Sam 4 tell us how Saul, Abner, and Ishbaal were killed. They were David's antagonists, whose deaths opened the way for his rise to power in the final stage. It is understandable, therefore, that there were prevailing suspicions among the northern tribes of Israel in the days of David that he had seized the throne of Israel by maneuvering to eliminate the royal antagonists one after the other, as Shimei's curse to David: "You are a man of blood" (2 Sam 16:7–8) indicates.

Under these circumstances, we can assume that it was of fundamental importance for David's regime to exonerate him from any accusation concerning the deaths of the Saulides, the sole royal family in Israel before David's accession to the throne.[1] David's innocence in the matter was the prime condition for legitimate transfer of the kingship of Israel from the house of Saul to David (5:1–3).[2]

Apparently, we can find in the accounts concerning the deaths of Saul, Abner, and Ishbaal common efforts to exonerate David from suspicions of his complicity in the violent deaths of these Saulides. It has been suggested from this viewpoint that all the accounts should be interpreted as the same Davidic apology running through the

---

* This essay is a revised version of the study which appeared in S. Aḥituv and B.A. Levine (eds.), *Avraham Malamat Volume* (Eretz-Israel. Archaeological, Historical and Geographical Studies 24), Jerusalem, 1993, pp. 109*–113*.

[1] The story of the execution of seven Saulides by the Gibeonites (2 Sam 21:1–14) also tells how David secured his kingship of Israel at the expense of the house of Saul. However, we shall not deal with it in the present study, since this incident is different from the deaths of Saul, Abner, and Ishbaal as far as David's involvement is concerned. While David did not conceal his consent with the execution of the seven Saulides, he tried to prove his innocence in all the deaths of the last three Saulides.

[2] For the argument that the constitutional as well as the dynastic continuity can be found in the transfer of the kingship from Saul to David see T. Ishida, *The Royal Dynasties in Ancient Israel. A Study on the Formation and Development of Royal-Dynastic Ideology* (BZAW 142), Berlin/New York, 1977, pp. 74–76.

History of David's Rise.[3] However, the perusal of the texts will show that the story of Abner's murder (2:12–3:1; 3:6–39) can hardly be regarded as an apology for David as in the other two cases.

In the present study, I shall first re-examine the Davidic apology in the accounts concerning the deaths of Saul and Ishbaal. Then I shall proceed to show how the leading actors are portrayed in the story of Abner's murder. Finally, I shall make it clear what the narrator is intent on telling in the last story.

2. *The Deaths of Saul and Ishbaal*

An alibi is carefully established for David in the narratives concerning Saul's final defeat. It is told in detail how David did not join the last campaign of the Philistines against Saul (1 Sam 29). It is also told that Saul was killed in the battle on Mount Gilboa, while David was fighting against the Amalekites in the south (1 Sam 30). Moreover, David learned of Saul's death in Ziklag (2 Sam 1:1). Thus it is perfectly proved that David was not involved in the battle on Mount Gilboa where Saul was killed.

The Amalekites who made a report of the death of Saul also brought Saul's diadem and bracelet to David (1:10). These royal insignia served not only as evidence for the death of Saul, but also as the symbol of the transfer of the kingship from Saul to David. Against his expectations, however, the Amalekite was executed by David on the charge that he killed Yahweh's anointed (1:14–16).

After Ishbaal lost power as the result of the death of Abner, his protector (4:1), two Beerothites assassinated Ishbaal and brought his head to David in Hebron (4:5–8). Again against their expectations, David promptly had them executed on the charge that they had killed a "righteous man" (4:11–12aα),[4] and made their mutilated

[3] E.g., J.H. Grønbaeck, *Die Geschichte vom Aufstieg Davids (1.Sam.15–2.Sam.5). Tradition und Komposition*, Copenhagen, 1971, pp. 186–201, 234–246; T.N.D. Mettinger, *King and Messiah. The Civil and Sacral Legitimation of the Israelite Kings* (CBOTS 8), Lund, 1976, pp. 39 f.; K.W. Whitelam, *The Just King: Monarchical Judicial Authority in Ancient Israel* (JSOTSup 12), Sheffield, 1979, pp. 100–112; P.K. McCarter, *II Samuel. A New Translation with Introduction, Notes and Commentary* (AB 9), Garden City, N.Y., 1984, pp. 64 f., 120–124, 129.

[4] Unlike Saul, Ishbaal is never called "Yahweh's anointed". It reflects David's claim that the legitimate successor to Saul was not Ishbaal but David, see Ishida, *The Royal Dynasties*, pp. 75 f.

bodies hang beside the pool in Hebron (4:12bβ), obviously to demonstrate to the public his innocence in the matter.

The situation was fundamentally identical in both cases. The death of Saul, king of Israel, enabled David to ascend the throne of the newly established kingdom of Judah in Hebron (2:1–4). Similarly, the murder of Ishbaal, the successor to Saul (2:8–9), cleared the way for David to receive the kingship of Israel offered by the elders of Israel (5:1–3). Undoubtedly, David was the sole beneficiary in both cases. David's reference to the execution of the Amalekite in passing the death sentence on the Beerothites (4:10) indicates that David found himself in a similar embarrassing situation in both incidents. He dealt with both murderers by the same measure to show his legitimacy to the public.

It is worth noting, however, that there is also a delicate difference between the two cases. The execution of the Beerothites implied that Ishbaal's assassination was not committed at David's instigation. As to Saul's death, however, there was no necessity for David for setting up an alibi in addition to the one mentioned above. David tried to demonstrate in the punishment of the Amalekite that he was loyal to Saul in paying reverence for the inviolability of Yahweh's anointed. The gesture of loyalty culminated in his composition of an elegy for Saul and Jonathan (1:17–27).

The above clearly indicates that David's portrait is painted in the same bright colours in all the narratives concerning the deaths of Saul and Ishbaal. In this portrait, David is an impeccable person, who remained loyal to Saul and his son; he had nothing to do with Saul's death in battle; nor was he instrumental in Ishbaal's assassination; moreover, he put the Amalekite to death on the grounds of the latter's own confession of his sacrilegious act; similarly, he punished the assassins of Ishbaal for their crime by exercising jurisdiction; in so doing, he not only performed his royal duties as a just king, but also exercised his right of the *gōʾēl* on behalf of the house of Saul;[5] as a result, without coveting the kingship of Israel, he became king of Israel as the legitimate successor to Saul by Yahweh's election, as well as with the approval of the people of Israel.

This portrait of David agrees well with his figure in the rest of the History of David's Rise, in which David did not resist Saul despite Saul's unjust attempt to kill David (1 Sam 18:10–11, etc.);

[5] Ibid., pp. 73 f.

moreover, David spared Saul's life twice, even when the latter had fallen into his hands, because of his reverence for Saul as Yahweh's anointed (24:4–8; 26:6–12); indeed, Yahweh chose David as the future king already during Saul's reign (16:6–13). It is clear that the same Davidic apology is found in the narratives concerning the deaths of Saul and Ishbaal.[6]

3. *Abner's Murder*

After Saul's death, his kingdom was divided between David in Hebron and Ishbaal in Mahanaim (2 Sam 2:1–4, 8–9),[7] and as a result, a war between them broke out, and continued (2:12–3:1). Against this background, Abner's murder by Joab is told as the culmination of a chain of events.

The story of Abner's murder consists of two parts: the account of the battle between Abner and Joab (2:12–3:1) and the narrative of Abner's treachery, his murder, and his funeral (3:6–39). While the first part tells how a blood feud started between Abner and the sons of Zeruiah,[8] the second begins with David's successful dealings with Abner and Ishbaal by his exploitation of the conflicts between them. After recovering the familial ties to the house of Saul by making Michal return, David made a pact with Abner, which confirmed that the kingship of Israel would be peacefully transferred from the house of Saul to David (vv. 6–21a). However, David's initial success was

[6] For the judicial structure of the two narratives in 2 Sam 1:1–16 and 4:5–12 and their function in the History of David's Rise see C. Mabee, "David's Judicial Exoneration", *ZAW* 92 (1980), pp. 89–107; Whitelam, *The Just King*, pp. 100–105, 110–112.

[7] It is likely that the territories described as Ishbaal's kingdom in 2 Sam 2:9 were actually those of Saul's kingdom, see Y. Aharoni, *The Land of the Bible. A Historical Geography*, London, 1966, pp. 255–257. It is assumed that the heartland of Saul's kingdom in the hillcountry was under Philistine occupation at that time (cf. 1 Sam 31:7).

[8] According to 1 Chr 2:16 Zeruiah was David's sister, and Joab was her second son between Abishai and Asahel. Abishai was commander of the Thirty of David's army (2 Sam 23:18–19) and played an important role in David's military operations since the days of his wanderings in the wilderness (1 Sam. 26:6–10; 2 Sam 10:9–14; 18:2; 20:6–10; 21:15–17). In these pericopes, however, Joab is always mentioned either as his brother or as his senior. Disappearing from the scene after Sheba's revolt, Abishai is absent from the narratives of the court intrigue and Solomon's consolidation of the kingdom in 1 Kgs 1–2. It is clear that Joab is regarded as a representative of the "sons of Zeruiah" in these narratives.

torpedoed by Joab who, together with his brother Abishai, had been seeking revenge for the blood of their brother Asahel, killed by Abner in battle (vv. 21b–27). Learning of Abner's murder, David was upset; he promptly declared his innocence and the guiltlessness of his kingdom in Abner's blood, cursed Joab and his house, took to mourning, held a funeral, composed a dirge, and kept a fast (vv. 28–35).

In addition to the detailed description of David's reactions to Abner's murder, the narrator takes much pains to prove David's innocence in the matter. It is stated twice that Joab killed Abner to revenge the death of Asahel (vv. 27, 30). It is explicitly told three times that David sent Abner away "in peace" (vv. 21–23). Moreover, after telling about Joab's trap for Abner, a superfluous note is added: "But David did not know (about it)" (v. 26). Finally, it is told that David succeeded in convincing all the people including "all Israel" under Ishbaal's rule that Abner's murder had not been committed at David's instigation (v. 37). We can hardly find such an insistent apology for David in any other narrative in the History of David's Rise.[9] From the story we can assume that David was really embarrassed by Abner's murder caused by the personal revenge of the sons of Zeruiah. Indeed, Abner's death was a great loss to David at this stage, since he wanted to gain support from the people of Israel by means of the pact which he had made with Abner (vv. 12–13; cf. v. 21).

Accordingly, it is extremely difficult to find in the story of Abner's murder the same Davidic apology running through the History of David's Rise, which gives explanations for David's royal legitimacy against Saul and his sons. To begin with, however, Abner ben Ner was not in the line to succession to Saul's throne, though he was Saul's cousin (1 Sam 14:50; cf. 1 Chr 9:36).[10] There is no evidence that David regarded Abner as a contender for the throne of Israel. David had no reason to defend his legitimacy against Abner.

It is very doubtful whether David is portrayed in this story as a just king. He did not kill Abner, but neither could he prevent Joab's revenge. Moreover, David could not bring Joab, the murderer, to

[9] Cf. McCarter, *II Samuel*, p. 121.

[10] According to 1 Chr 8:33 and 9:39, Ner was Saul's grandfather. Consequently, Abner was Saul's uncle (cf. 1 Sam 14:50bβ). However, Saul's grandfather was called Abiel in 1 Sam 9:1. The tradition that identifies Ner as Saul's grandfather seems confused. Cf. P.K. McCarter, *I Samuel. A New Translation with Introduction, Notes and Commentary* (AB 8), Garden City, N.Y., 1980, p. 256.

justice as in the cases of the Amalekite, who allegedly killed Saul, and the assassins of Ishbaal. In other words, David failed to carry out his judicial responsibilities in the crime. Instead, he just complained: "I am this day weak, though anointed king, and these men, the sons of Zeruiah, are harder than I am" (2 Sam 3:39). Can we regard these words as a positive assessment of David? On the contrary, they are nothing but an acknowledgement of his inability to rule as king. This sort of negative remark concerning David cannot be found in any narrative in the History of David's Rise.[11]

It is also remarkable that Joab is described as the leading villain in the story, while David plays a passive role. In the first part (2:12–3:1), Joab at the head of the servants of David was fighting against the men of "Israel" (vv. 17, 28), while David kept in the background. The situation reminds us of Absalom's rebellion, in which Joab, who was in command of David's servants, defeated Israel, while David stayed behind (18:1–17). In both battlefields, the one who ruthlessly beat Israel was Joab, while David did not fight against Israel directly. It is suggested that the real enemy of Israel was not David but Joab.[12]

From the episode in which Abner was reluctant to kill Asahel in battle (2:18–23), we can learn that Asahel was killed by his own fault. In addition, it is clear that the right of blood-vengeance should not be extended to killing in battle.[13] Therefore, the episode tells that Joab's revenge for Asahel's blood was carried out from unjustified resentment.

It should be mentioned that the story of Abner's murder is very similar in many respects to the account of Amasa's assassination (20:8–13). Both killings were committed by Joab with premeditation. From the circumstances it is assumed that the second murder had its source in Joab's resentment, after David had given his position as commander of the army to Amasa (19:14). Although it is explicitly told that the first murder was caused by blood-vengeance, it is likely that the real cause was also Joab's misgivings about David's promise to grant the position of commander of the army to Abner.

[11] For the History of David's Rise and its positive attitude towards David see the studies mentioned above in n. 3.

[12] The Davidic apology originated in efforts to convince the northern tribes of Israel that the house of David legitimately succeeded to the kingship of Saul over Israel, see Ishida, *The Royal Dynasties*, p. 108.

[13] David accuses Joab of "avenging in time of peace blood which had been shed in war" (1 Kgs 2:5), cf. Whitelam, *The Just King*, p. 108.

In any case, the narrative records that Joab outrageously killed Amasa, while David was completely innocent of the crime.

It is strange, however, that no report is given about a punishment for Joab's crime. Like in the case of Abner's murder, David here again gave up the royal responsibilities of exercising jurisdiction. Surprisingly, Joab is reappointed to the position of commander of the army at the top in the second list of David's high officials (20:23), following the account of Sheba's revolt during which Joab killed Amasa.[14] It is clear that in both accounts of the killings of Abner and Amasa the narrator is intent on recording David's inability in the face of Joab's unlawful actions.

From the foregoing discussion it has become clear that in the story of Abner's murder David's portrait is sketched as an incompetent king who could neither control Joab's vendetta nor exercise his royal authority to bring the latter to justice. At the same time, Joab is described as a violent soldier who had his own way in every decision, in defiance of the king's will. Then, what is the narrator intent on telling in this story? This can be elucidated only from the later development in the relations between David and Joab.

4. *The Beginning of the Succession Narrative*

Both the murders of Abner and Amasa are referred to in the Testament of David (1 Kgs 2:5)[15] and Solomon's injunction upon Benaiah to execute Joab (2:31–33). In these references Joab was not only accused of his unjustified murders but also cursed by words which remind us of David's utterance against Joab about Abner's murder (2 Sam 3:28–29).[16] In addition to these direct references, the story

---

[14] It is worth noting that David is placed before the first list of his high officials as king who "reigned over all Israel and administered justice and equity to all his people" (2 Sam 8:15). In contrast, no mention is made of David in connection with the second list (20:23–26). David's absence suggests that the *de facto* ruler was then Joab, who ranked at the top of the list, see above pp. 128 f.

[15] For The Testament of David in 1 Kgs 2:1–9 see above p. 132, n. 81.

[16] 2 Sam 3:28–29 and 1 Kgs 2:31–33 are sometimes regarded as Deuteronomistic insertions to link these two parts of the larger history, e.g., T. Veijola, *Die ewige Dynastie. David und die Entstehung seiner Dynastie nach der deuteronomistischen Darstellung*, Helsinki, 1975, pp. 30 f.; McCarter, *II Samuel*, pp. 117 f. In my opinion, however, these pericopes accord well with the Solomonic apology.

of Abner's murder has a point of view common to the Succession Narrative.

As I have suggested in a previous chapter, we can find in the Succession Narrative a charge against Joab, who conducted himself violently by exploiting David's incompetence as king.[17] It follows logically from this charge that Joab should be eliminated in order to establish a just rule of the house of David in the kingdom. This is an argument of the Solomonic apology for justifying the execution of Joab who took sides with Adonijah, Solomon's contender for the Davidic throne.[18]

We can conclude that the story of Abner's murder, in which Joab appears for the first time on the scene, is composed as the beginning of the Succession Narrative,[19] the aim of which is to defend the legitimacy of Solomon against the old regime whose nominal ruler was the aging David and whose strongman was Joab. Accordingly, it is one of the important themes of the Succession Narrative to justify Joab's execution as the victorious climax in Solomon's struggle for the Davidic throne. From this point of view, an *inclusio* for the Succession Narrative is recognized between the story of Abner's murder by Joab at the beginning, and the episode of Joab's execution by Solomon at the end. Thus we find in David's concluding words in the story of Abner's murder: "I am this day weak, though anointed king, and these men, the sons of Zeruiah, are harder than I am" (2 Sam 3:39), a problem posed by the Solomonic apologist asserting that the problem which David had left without taking any action, Solomon finally solved by Joab's execution.

---

[17] See above pp. 124 ff., 132 ff.

[18] According to L.M. Muntingh, "The Role of Joab in the Succession Narrative", in W.C. van Wyk (ed.), *Studies in the Succession Narrative*, Pretoria, 1986, p. 213, Joab was made the sacrifice of David's indecision who had become old and senile. On the other hand, J.W. Wesselius, "Joab's Death and the Central Theme of the Succession Narrative (2 Samuel ix 1–1 Kings ii)", *VT* 40 (1990), pp. 344–346, contends that the real reason for Joab's execution was Bathsheba's revenge on the murderer of her first husband. It seems that neither Muntingh nor Wesselius succeed in explaining the nature of the criticism against David running through the Succession Narrative.

[19] D.M. Gunn, *The Story of King David. Genre and Interpretation* (JSOTSup 6), Sheffield, 1978, pp. 65–84, has suggested that the beginning of the story in 2 Sam 9–20 + 1 Kgs 1–2 is found in 2 Sam 2–4 (2:8 or 2:12 to 4:12, or more likely 5:3) on grounds of plot and style.

CHAPTER ELEVEN

SOLOMON'S SUCCESSION IN THE LIGHT OF THE INSCRIPTION OF KILAMUWA, KING OF Y'DY-ŚAM'AL*

1. *The Solomonic Legitimation*

In the foregoing chapters I have suggested that the Succession Narrative (2 Sam 2–20 + 1 Kgs 1–2) was composed as a historiography aiming at the defence of Solomon against the old regime of David.[1] From this point of view, the Succession Narrative can be summarized in the following fashion: a) Solomon, one of the younger sons of David, gained his designation as David's successor by a court intrigue; b) the legitimacy of Solomon's accession is defended by a claim that the irregular procedure involved was unavoidable under abnormal circumstances; c) the regime which Solomon challenged was supported by the administration whose nominal ruler was the aging David and whose strong-man was the commander-in-chief Joab; d) the description of David's shortcomings in the narrative reflects the political standpoint of Solomon's historiographer; e) Solomon's purge of his opponents is regarded by his historiographer as an initial achievement of his monarch in a matter left unfinished by David.

On the basis of these observations, I shall try to show in the present chapter that the concluding section of the Succession Narrative, i.e., 1 Kgs 1–2, is an apologetic composition from the early days of Solomon, aiming at legitimatizing not only his irregular succession but also his execution of his brother, high officials of the old regime and a leader of the Saulides. I shall attempt to explain the substance of the Solomonic legitimation by analysing the pertinent biblical texts and by referring to relevant extra-biblical material. The latter may provide us with a much needed analogy for the narrative of Solomon's succession and the events it relates.

---

* This essay is a revised version of the study which appeared in J.A. Emerton (ed.), *Congress Volume*, Salamanca 1983 (VTSup 36), Leiden, 1985, pp. 145–153.

[1] See above pp. 102 ff.

I believe that the Solomonic legitimation consists of two conflicting elements: an apology for his legitimacy and a defence for his deeds. Both elements are skillfully blended in the congratulation offered to David by Benaiah (1 Kgs 1:37) and by similar words of David's servants (1:47) on the occasion of Solomon's accession: "May your God make the name of Solomon more famous than yours, and make his throne greater than your throne".[2] The implication of the words is twofold: on the one hand, an explicit congratulation to David on having a successor, on the other, an implicit wish that the reign of his successor may surpass that of David.[3] This congratulation must have originated in the Solomonic scribal circle, since the canonical view in the biblical traditions regards Solomon as inferior to David in every respect.[4]

2. *A Comparison between the Early Monarchies of Śam'al and Israel*

We come now to the extra-biblical parallel to the Solomonic succession, which augments the biblical narrative by providing a point of departure for historiographical and historical analysis. The comparative analogue we are looking for comes from the inscription of Kilamuwa, king of *y'dy*-Śam'al, an Aramaean king in North Syria in the latter half of the ninth century B.C.[5] Both archaeological and epigraphical evidence shows that Kilamuwa reigned about a century

---

[2] Cf. T. Ishida, *The Royal Dynasties in Ancient Israel. A Study on the Formation and Development of Royal-Dynastic Ideology* (BZAW 142), Berlin/New York, 1977, pp. 105 f.; see above pp. 123, 154.

[3] For the second implication, compare the following text of Esarhaddon, king of Assyria: "*ēnu* ^{d}*Aššur . . . eli šarrāni . . . šarrūtī ušarriḫma ušarbâ zikri šumija.* When Aššur made my royal power more famous and my fame greater than (that of all) kings", R. Borger, *Die Inschriften Asarhaddons Königs von Assyrien* (AfO Beih. 9), Graz, 1956, p. 98, line 32; cf. *CAD* Z, p. 116a.

[4] E.g. "And his heart was not wholly true to Yahweh his God, as was the heart of David his father" (1 Kgs 11:4); "So solomon did what was evil in the sight of Yahweh , and did not wholly follow Yahweh, as David his father had done" (11:6). For the biblical traditions about David's loyalty to Yahweh in contrast to Solomon's apostasy see G.N. Knoppers, *Two Nations under God. The Deuteronomistic History of Solomon and the Dual Monarchies* I: *The Reign of Solomon and the Rise of Jeroboam* (HSM 52), Atlanta, 1993, pp. 135 ff.; C. Schäfer-Lichtenberger, *Josua und Salomo. Eine Sudie zu Autorität und Legitimität des Nachfolgers im Alten Testament* (VTSup 58), Leiden/New York/Köln, 1995, pp. 341 ff.,

[5] *KAI* 24; F. Rosenthal, "Canaanite and Aramaic Inscriptions", in *ANET*, Princeton, 1969^{3}, pp. 654 f.; J.C.L. Gibson, *Textbook of Syrian Semitic Inscriptions* III: *Phoenician Inscriptions*, Oxford, 1982, no. 13.

after the inception of the Aramaean monarchy in Śam'al.[6] Accordingly, we may suppose that with Kilamuwa, as with Solomon, we have the last generation of the early monarchy in his kingdom.

The introduction of the Kilamuwa inscription reads: "I am Kilamuwa, the son of Hayya. Gabbar became king over *y'dy*, but he did nothing. There was[7] *bmh*, but he did nothing. And there was my father Hayya, but he did nothing. And there was my[8] brother *š'l*, but he did nothing. But I am Kilamuwa, the son of *tm-*.[9] What I have done my predecessors[10] did not do" (lines 1–5).

We have here the names of five successive rulers of Śam'al in the ninth century B.C. The series of names gives us an impression that all the five kings belonged to the same dynasty founded by Gabbar. And indeed, Hayya is called "Haianu/ni, the son of Gabbari" in a ninth-century Assyrian source.[11] Yet, since the Assyrians used to call the land after the name of king who reigned there when they first became acquainted with it, it does not necessarily imply that Hayya

---

[6] F. von Luschan et al., *Ausgrabungen in Sendschirli* I–IV (Königliche Museen zu Berlin: Mitteilungen aus den orientalischen Sammlungen XI–XIV), Berlin, 1893–1911; B. Landsberger, *Sam'al. Studien zur Entdeckung der Ruinenstätte Karatepe*, Ankara, 1948, p. 37; D. Ussishkin, "'Der alte Bau' in Zincirli", *BASOR* 189 (1968), pp. 50–53; N. Na'aman, "שמאל", in *Encyclopaedia Biblica* VIII, Jerusalem, 1982, cols. 308–316 (Hebrew).

[7] The implication of the verb *kn* here is obviously *mlk*, "he became king" or "he ruled". M. O'Connor suggests that the term *kn* here functions as a marker of a verb phrases deletion transformation, "The rhetoric of the Kilamuwa inscription", *BASOR* 226 (1977), p. 20; cf. also C.-F. Jean and J. Hoftijzer, *DISO*, p. 117; J. Hoftijzer and K. Jongeling, *DNWSI* II, pp. 493 f.

[8] There is no possibility of rendering *'ḥ* here by "his brother", making *š'l* Kilamuwa's uncle, from the orthographical as well as morphological point of view, against W. Röllig, *KAI* II, p. 32; T. Collins, "The Kilamuwa Inscription—A Phoenician Poem", *WO* 6 (1970/71), p. 184. It must be read as *'ḥi*, "my brother", see F.M. Cross and D.N. Freedman, *Early Hebrew Orthography. A Study of the Epigraphic Evidence* (AOS 36), New Haven, 1952, p. 16; O'Connor, *BASOR* 226 (1977), p. 20; Gibson, *Textbook* III, p. 36; cf. *DNWSI* I, p. 28.

[9] A letter is missing after *tm*. I am skeptical about the reading *tm*, "perfection", against Collins, *WO* 6 (1970/71), pp. 184 f.; Landsberger, *Sam'al*, p. 45, n. 112; p. 56, n. 139, has suggested a possibility that "Bar-tumm" may be regarded as the Aramaic translation of the Anatolian name Kilamuwa; cf. *DNWSI* I, p. 1219. For my interpretation see below p. 170.

[10] There is a difficulty with the second *h* of *hlpnyhm*. Still, the rendering "my predecessors" is most suitable for the context, see Cross and Freedman, *Early Hebrew Orthography*, pp. 16 f.; O'Connor, *BASOR* 226 (1977), pp. 20 f. The rendering "their predecessors", making the reference to the kings preceding to Gabbar, is untenable, against Gibson, *Textbook* III, p. 36; cf. *DNWSI* I, p. 580.

[11] ᵐ*ḫa-ia-(a)-nu/ni* DUMU *ga(b)-ba-ri*, (Shalmaneser III), A.K. Grayson, *Assyrian Rulers of the Early First Millennium BC* II *(858–745 BC)* (RIMA 3), Toronto/Buffalo/London, 1996, p. 18 (A.O.102.2, ii 24), p. 23 (ii 83); cf. p. 9 (A.O.102.1, i 53'–54').

was actually Gabbar's son. Nor is it absolutely clear that Hayya was a member of Gabbar's house. We should rather look for a clue to the relations among these kings in the curse formula in the end of the inscription (lines 15–16). Kilamuwa invokes here three deities with their titles one after the other: "Baal-Ṣemed who belongs to Gabbar", "Baal-Ḥammon who belongs to *bmh*", and "Rakkabel, lord of the dynasty (*bʿl bt*)". If these three divine names stand for the three tutelary deities of Gabbar, of *bmh*, and of the other three kings, respectively, we may assume that there were dynastic changes from Gabbar to *bmh*, and from *bmh* to Hayya, the latter being the founder of the ruling dynasty to which Kilamuwa belonged.[12]

If this reconstruction, suggested first by B. Landsberger, is tenable, we can find here a remarkable parallel to the pattern of the royal succession in early Israel. Both Gabbar of Śam'al and Saul of Israel were the first kings who introduced the monarchical regime into their countries, but each failed to found a lasting dynasty. As for the second set of kings, there is some difference. While *bmh* of Śam'al was a usurper, Ishbaal of Israel was a legitimate successor to the throne. Yet, despite this difference, they played the similar role of representing a transitional stage between the establishment of the monarchy and its consolidation by another dynasty. The third set of kings, Hayya and David, succeeded at last in founding the stable dynasties. They bequeathed the throne to their sons, but the succession in both kingdoms was not achieved without trouble. The position of *šʾl*, the fourth king of Śam'al, corresponds to that of Adonijah in Israel, though again there is a difference between them, i.e., while the former became king, the latter failed to seize the throne. But both had a common fate as losers, defeated by their half-brothers in the struggle for the kingship.[13] Finally, the kingship was firmly established by Kilamuwa and Solomon, respectively, the fifth candidate for the throne in both kingdoms.

---

[12] Landsberger, *Sam'al*, pp. 46 f. He has also pointed out that there is no filiation between Gabbar, *bmh* and Hayya (p. 47, n. 118); cf. also W. Röllig, *KAI* II, p. 34. The dynastic groupings are perceived also from the rhetorical structure of the inscription, in which the introductory section and the curse formula "are linked together by their references to the rulers of Ya'diya", O'Connor, *BASOR* 226 (1977), p. 24. For the tutelary deities of dynasties see Ishida, *The Royal Dynasties*, pp. 113 f.

[13] It is unlikely that Kilamuwa succeeded *šʾl* by a normal procedure. He maintains, "I sat upon my father's throne" (line 9), but not "brother's throne"; cf. Landsberger, *Sam'al*, pp. 51, 56 f. In the monarchies of Israel and Judah, the succession from brother to brother took place only in irregular situations, see Ishida, *The Royal Dynasties*, pp. 151 f.

In this context, it seems possible to expect the name of Kilamuwa's mother in *tm-*, a defective word after *klmw. br* in line 4. The queen-mother's involvement in the problems of royal succession was a phenomenon common to the "Western courts".[14] We may suggest that Kilamuwa's mother's intervention in the struggle for the kingship, like that of Bathsheba, may have been the reason for the special mention of her name in the inscription.

The characterization of the five kings in both kingdoms is summarized as follows:

	Śam'al	Israel
1. Founder of monarchy	Gabbar	Saul
2. Transitional king	*bmh*	Ishbaal
3. Founder of dynasty	Hayya	David
4. Loser in the struggle for the kingship	*š'l*	Adonijah
5. King who established his kingship	Kilamuwa	Solomon

3. *Priority on the Predecessors*

One of the most striking features of the Kilamuwa inscription is a bold statement accompanying each of his four predecessors in the introduction: "but he did nothing (*wbl. pʿl*)" (lines 2–4). This negative evaluation of the former kings is put in a sharp contrast to Kilamuwa's own achievements: "What I have done my predecessors did not do" (lines 4–5). The same is emphasized in conjunction with his social reform, contrasted with the days of the former kings (lines 9–10). The theme of the inscription is what we may call Kilamuwa's propaganda which claims that he is the sole, just king after a series of the ineffective rulers who preceded him.

The Kilamuwa inscription has been subjected to a critical analysis by F.M. Fales, who pointed out the propagandistic and literary typological features of the text.[15] Of the special significance is the literary motif called "heroic priority" or "priority on the predecessors"

[14] See ibid., pp. 155–157; H. Tadmor, "Autobiographical Apology in the Royal Assyrian Literature", in H. Tadmor and M. Weinfeld (eds.), *History, Historiography and Interpretation. Studies in Biblical and Cuneiform Literatures*, Jerusalem, 1983, pp. 54, 57; cf. also N.-E.A. Andreasen, "The Role of the Queen Mother in Israelite Society", *CBQ* 45 (1983), pp. 179–194; cf. above p. 84.

[15] F.M. Fales, "Kilamuwa and the Foreign Kings: Propaganda vs. Power", *WO* 10 (1979), pp. 6–22.

expressed there. This is one of the recurrent motifs in the historiographical literature of Mesopotamian kings, i.e., a reigning monarch claims that he is the first to perform successfully a task or tasks which none of his predecessors has done.[16] A typical eclectic text would read: "(I accomplished) what no one among the kings who preceded me had done (*ša ina šarrāni ālikūt maḫrīya mamman lā ēpušū*)".[17] In this pattern the events are presented as moving from "negative past" to "positive present", i.e., against the shortcomings of the predecessors, the present king is not only a more successful ruler but also the just king and the "restorer of order".[18]

It is to be stressed, however, that there is also a significant difference between Kilamuwa's assertion and the stereotyped statement of the "priority on the predecessors". While former kings in the latter texts are always generalized and their names are no longer important, the four predecessors of Kilamuwa are mentioned by their names and their ineffective rule is clearly remembered in his time.[19]

So far the introduction of the Kilamuwa inscription. The major part of the inscription is devoted to his own personal achievements (in contrast to the lack of achievement on the part of his predecessors). First, he tells how he liberated Śamʾal from the oppression of the Danunian king (lines 5–8). Then, he relates his achievement in the sphere of domestic administration, i.e., how he made the *mškbm* happy and prosperous (lines 9–13). It is generally held that the word

---

[16] See M. Liverani, "The Ideology of the Assyrian Empire", in M.T. Larsen (ed.), *Power and Propaganda—A Symposium on Ancient Empires*, Copenhagen, 1979, pp. 308 f. A dissertation on this theme: R. Gelio, *Ša ina šarrāni abbēya mamman lā ēpušu . . . Il motivo della priorità eroica nelle iscrizioni reali assire*, Università di Roma, 1977, was not available to me. This is a frequent theme particularly in the commemorative inscriptions, see A.K. Grayson, "Histories and Historians of the Ancient Near East: Assyria and Babylonia", *Or* 49 (1980), p. 191; cf. also H. Tadmor, "History and Ideology in the Assyrian Royal Inscriptions", in F.M. Fales (ed.), *Assyrian Royal Inscriptions: New Horizons in Literary, Ideological, and Historical Analysis* (Orientis Antiqvi Collectio 17), Roma, 1981, pp. 13–25.

[17] Liverani, in *Power and Propaganda*, p. 309; cf. *CAD* M/1, p. 200.

[18] For the pattern of the "restorer of order" see M. Liverani, "Memorandum on the Approach to Historiographic Texts", *Or* 42 (1973), pp. 186–188. For the ideological explanation of the motif of the "priority on the predecessors" by the pattern of the "restorer of order" see Fales, *WO* 10 (1979), pp. 7–9.

[19] Fales has also noted that in the Kilamuwa inscription "this opposition between the age before the king and the age of the king is charged with more definite connotations", *WO* 10 (1979), p. 7. Because of the lack of the real names of the predecessors, neither the inscriptions of Kapara, ruler of Guzana (AfO Beih. 1 [1933], pp. 71–79), nor that of Azitiwadda from Karatepe (*KAI* 26: A I 18–19) can be regarded as compositions belonging to the same category with the Kilamuwa inscription.

mškbm (lines 10, 14, 15) refers to the conquered Anatolian population, whereas the word *bʿrrm* (line 14) stands for the Aramaean ruling class.[20] Evidently, there had been conflicts between these two elements with the *bʿrrm* ultimately prevailing over the *mškbm*. Then, it was Kilamuwa who put an end to the futile struggle between them and restored the social justice in Śam'al.[21]

It is clear that this is the central motif of the text. Kilamuwa appears to be the just king, provider for the poor, and restorer of the good order who brings peace and security to his realm. The parallel to Solomon immediately comes to mind. Under his just rule (cf. 1 Kgs 3:4–28) the people of Israel enjoyed peace and prosperity (5:5). We shall return to this motif somewhat later.

The analogy to Solomon is more explicit in the relationship between Kilamuwa and his two immediate predecessors, his father Hayya and his brother *šʾl*. Kilamuwa clearly maintains that not only is he the son of Hayya (lines 1, 9; cf. *KAI* 25, line 3) but also he succeeded to his father's kingship (line 9). Needless to say, the throne of Hayya is mentioned here as the foundation of Kilamuwa's legitimacy. When he won the royal throne in struggle with his brother, he could not but legitimatize his kingship by his royal descent.[22] Yet, at the same time, he did not hesitate to announce that he would not continue the policies of his father and brother. This seems to be the implication of the negative evaluation attached to Hayya and *šʾl*.

Before making a comparison between Kilamuwa's propaganda and the Solomonic legitimation, we cannot fail to observe that there are also some differences between them. An important difference is found in the situations in which they inaugurated the kingship. While

---

[20] See M. Lidzbarski, *Ephemeris für semitische Epigraphik* III, Giessen, 1915, pp. 233–236; Rosenthal, in *ANET*, p. 654; Röllig, *KAI* II, pp. 33 f.; Jean and Hoftijzer, *DISO*, pp. 40, 170; Gibson, *Textbook* III, pp. 37 f.; Hoftijzer and Jongeling, *DNWSI* I, p. 185; II, p. 701. But Landsberger, *Sam'al*, p. 56, n. 140, has held that the *mškbm* and the *bʿrrm* were two classes of "Ministerialen".

[21] It has been suggested that Kilamuwa was the new Anatolian name which he took upon his accession for appeasing his Anatolian subjects; see Gibson, *Textbook* III, pp. 31, 35; Na'aman, in *Encyclopaedia Biblica* VIII, col. 309 (Hebrew).

[22] Strikingly, reference to Kilamuwa's divine election is entirely lacking from the text. According to the royal ideology in the ancient Near East, the royal authority was normally legitimatized by royal lineage and divine election. Since Kilamuwa was doubtless a worshipper of Rakkabel (*KAI* 24:16; 25:4–6), his silence about his divine election must be regarded as intentional. It could be assumed, therefore, that he avoided mentioning any deity belonging to any class or national element as a god who chose him, in order to establish his kingship as the neutral authority over the mixed population.

Kilamuwa, as it seems, dethroned his brother and established his kingship for himself, Solomon was designated co-regent by David and reigned with him, though he resorted to a court intrigue. Evidently, the formal designation and co-regency prevented Solomon from expressing a negative criticism of David as explicitly as Kilamuwa criticized his predecessors. There was also no need for Solomon's historiographer to deal with Adonijah as if he were equal in rank to Solomon. Adonijah was stigmatized as a second Absalom, a rebel.[23]

These differences aside, the Kilamuwa inscription offers close parallel to the Solomonic legitimation, especially in the following three items: a) the emphasis on the father's throne as the foundation of the legitimate kingship;[24] b) the negative evaluation to his father: Solomon's historiographer made it in the description of David's shortcomings[25] as well as in the wish of David's servants that Solomon's kingship may be superior to that of David;[26] c) the establishment of the kingship based on the restoration of social justice or order. As for this last point, we should note that Solomon's purge of his adversaries was different in nature from Kilamuwa's appeasement policy. But both the political actions brought about a common effect: the restoration of social order. As a result, "the kingdom was established by the hand of Solomon" (1 Kgs 2:46b).[27]

4. *Royal Historiographies of Apologetic Nature*

Before closing the present inquiry, I should like to suggest in brief my view of the historical circumstances under which Kilamuwa's propaganda and the Solomonic legitimation were composed. H.A. Hoffner for the Hittite texts[28] and H. Tadmor for the Neo-Assyrian sources[29] have assumed that royal historiographies of an apologetic

---

[23] See above pp. 114 ff., 117 ff.

[24] For Kilamuwa see above p. 172; for Solomon see above pp. 121 ff.

[25] See above pp. 123 ff.

[26] See above pp. 123, 154.

[27] See above p. 134.

[28] H.A. Hoffner, "Propaganda and Political Justification in Hittite Historiography", in H. Goedicke and J.J.M. Roberts (eds.), *Unity and Diversity. Essays in the History, Literature, and Religion of the Ancient Near East*, Baltimore/London, 1975, pp. 49–62; idem, "Histories and Historians of the Ancient Near East: The Hittites", *Or* 49 (1980), pp. 325–327.

[29] Tadmor, in *History, Historiography and Interpretation*, pp. 36–57.

nature in the ancient Near East were composed with specific aims in the present and future. Accordingly, we may suppose that one of the strongest motivations for writing this sort of royal historiography arose from the necessity of general support for the new enterprise undertaken by the king who had just overcome a crisis. For Kilamuwa, it is likely that the crisis was the struggle against the domination of the *bʿrrm* supported by the followers of *šʾl*, his brother; and the new enterprise was the building of his palace.[30] For Solomon, the crisis was the struggle with the leading members of the regime of David when he became the sole sovereign after his father's demise;[31] and the new enterprise was the building of his palace and the Temple in Jerusalem (cf. a prediction about the builder of the Temple in Nathan's prophecy [2 Sam 7:13a]).[32]

Admittedly, the details of the historical reconstruction of the early monarchies in Śamʾal remain hypothetical. Still, it is the best means conceivable to regard both the texts of 1 Kgs 1–2 and the Kilamuwa inscription as compositions belonging to the category of royal historiographies of apologetic nature. And the pattern of transfer of the royal throne in Israel and Śamʾal indicates that there were common features in the political development in the early—inexperienced—monarchies in the national kingdoms of Syro-Palestine at the beginning of the first millennium B.C.

---

[30] Although there is no reference to building operations in the text, it is likely that the inscription was composed on the occasion of the dedication of the palace, since it was found on an orthostat at the entrance to a vestibule leading into the palace, see von Luschan et al., *Ausgrabungen in Sendschirli* IV, p. 374 and Taf. IL; cf. Rosenthal, in *ANET*, p. 654; Gibson, *Textbook* III, p. 30.

[31] E. Ball has laid emphasis on the fact that Solomon became "co-regent with his father David in the full sense", "The Co-Regency of David and Solomon (1 Kings i)", *VT* 27 (1977), p. 270. He seems to overlook, however, the fact that Solomon did not, or perhaps could not, purge any adversary in David's lifetime. In the period of his co-regency with David, Solomon was actually a young boy under the protection of David and Bathsheba. The purpose of Solomon's co-regency was to confirm David's designation of him and its announcement, see Ishida, *The Royal Dynasties*, p. 170; cf. also K.W. Whitelam, *The Just King: Monarchical Judicial Authority in Ancient Israel* (JSOTSup 12), Sheffield, 1979, pp. 149–155.

[32] See above pp. 136, 146 ff.; cf. also Ishida, *The Royal Dynasties*, p. 97.

CHAPTER TWELVE

THE SUCCESSION NARRATIVE AND ESARHADDON'S APOLOGY*

1. *Royal Apology*

In one of his studies Hayim Tadmor shed light on circumstances under which apologetic autobiographies were composed by royal authors in Neo-Assyria.[1] After submitting his thesis, he devoted half the study to an analysis of Esarhaddon's apology, the introductory section to the Prism Nin. A,[2] as the most important source material for the study. Then, he dealt with the apologies of Ashurbanipal and Šamši-Adad V. In the final section, he testified to the wide-spread diffusion of the genre of royal apology from the second millennium B.C. Hittite Anatolia and North Syria to the first millennium Israel, Babylon, and Persia. In this connection, he suggested that, though not a case of autobiography, the Davidic and Solomonic succession stories in the Hebrew Bible are also to be regarded as compositions belonging to this genre.[3] It is the purpose of the present study to examine this suggestion by comparing Esarhaddon's apology in Nin. A I:1–II:11 with the Succession Narrative in the Books of 2 Samuel and 1 Kings 1–2.

---

* This essay is a revised version of the study which appeared in M. Cogan and I. Ephʿal (eds.), *Ah, Assyria . . . Studies in Assyrian History and Ancient Near Eastern Historiography. Presented to Hayim Tadmor* (Scripta Hierosolymitana 33), Jerusalem, 1991, pp. 166–173.

[1] H. Tadmor, "Autobiographical Apology in the Royal Assyrian Literature", in H. Tadmor and M. Weinfeld (eds.), *History, Historiography and Interpretation. Studies in Biblical and Cuneiform Literatures*, Jerusalem, 1983, pp. 36–57.

[2] R. Borger, *Die Inschriften Asarhaddons Königs von Assyrien* (AfO Beih. 9), Graz, 1956, pp. 39–45; A.L. Oppenheim, "Babylonian and Assyrian Historical Texts", in *ANET*, Princeton, 1969[3], pp. 289 f.

[3] Tadmor, in *History, Historiography and Interpretation*, p. 56.

2. *Esarhaddon's Apology Compared with Hittite Apologies*

To begin with, the structure of Esarhaddon's apology will be examined to show the nature of its genre. At this juncture, it is worth referring to the general structure of Hittite apologies of which the two main works are the Telepinu Proclamation[4] and the Apology of Hattušili III.[5] According to H.A. Hoffner, though differing in detail, the following outline is discernible in both the compositions:[6]

1. Introduction (T § 1, H §§ 1–2).
2. Historical survey: noble antecedents (T §§ 1–9, H §§ 3–10).
3. Historical survey: the unworthy predecessor (T §§ 10–22a, H §§ 10–12).
4. The *coup d'état* (T § 22b, H §§ 12–13).
5. The merciful victor (T §§ 23 and 26, H §§ 12–13).
6. The edict (T §§ 27–50, H §§ 13–15).

Referring to the above outline, we may suggest that Esarhaddon's apology consists of the following seven sections:

1. Introduction (I:1–7).
2. Preliminary remark: the reigning king's designation of a legitimate successor (I:8–22).
3. Preliminary remark: rival princes' evil acts (I:23–40).
4. Rebellion (I:41–52).
5. The legitimate successor's counter-attack and victory (I:53–79).
6. The establishment of the kingship (I:80–II:7).
7. The punishment of the rebels (II:8–11).

Owing to the different situation, at first sight, the contents of each section in Esarhaddon's apology is quite different from those in the Hittite works. While the Hittite monarchs justify their usurpation of the throne from the reigning kings, Esarhaddon defends his assumption of the kingship by overruling primogeniture. Nevertheless, a

[4] E.H. Sturtevant and G. Bechtel, *A Hittite Chrestomathy*, Philadelphia, 1935, pp. 175–200; I. Hoffmann, *Der Erlaß Telipinus* (TH 11), Heidelberg, 1984, pp. 12–55.

[5] A. Götze, *Hattušiliš. Der Bericht über seine Thronbesteigung nebst den Parallleltexten* (MVÄG 29/3, Hethitische Texte, Heft 1), Leipzig, 1924, pp. 6–41; cf. A. Ünal, *Hattušili III.* I. *Hattušili bis zu seiner Thronbesteigung* 1: *Historischer Abriß* (TH 3), Heidelberg, 1974, pp. 29–35.

[6] H.A. Hoffner, "Propaganda and Political Justification in Hittite Historiography", in H. Goedicke and J.J.M. Roberts (eds.), *Unity and Diversity. Essays in the History, Literature, and Religion of the Ancient Near East*, Baltimore/London, 1975, p. 51.

comparative examination of each section in the Hittite works and Esarhaddon's apology will show that both the compositions share a general pattern in essence.

In the introduction, while a royal genealogy is given by Hattušili, Telepinu is silent about it on the basis of different circumstances.[7] Esarhaddon does not mention his royal lineage in the introduction (Nin. A I:1–7) either, although it is given in II:14–15: "the son of Sennacherib, king of the world, king of Assyria, the son of Sargon, king of the world, king of Assyria". In the apology, instead of a stereotyped royal lineage, Esarhaddon especially mentions his divine election from his youth (I:5–7). These observations show that the subject of the introduction is not necessarily of royal lineage but is chosen according to circumstances under which defenders had to cope with their succession problems. The subject common to the introduction of all the apologies is a self-introduction by the defenders as a legitimate king.

There is a contrast between a just past in section 2 and the subsequent deterioration in section 3. The Hittite monarchs tell about the glorious reigns of their ancestors in section 2 and the shameful days of the recent predecessors in section 3.[8] On the other hand, after emphatically referring to his father's designation of him as successor in section 2 (I:9–12; cf. I:13–19), Esarhaddon tells how his brothers caused a disturbance by violating this solemn decision in section 3 (I:23–29).

Section 4 of the Hittite works corresponds to sections 4 and 5 of Esarhaddon's apology. Since the Hittite defenders actually usurped the throne from the reigning kings, there was no merit for them in giving a full report of the *coup d'état* executed by themselves. An element which they did not forget to mention in the terse account of their *coup d'état* is their unworthy predecessors' attempt to kill them.[9] This murder attempt corresponds to the rebellion of Esarhaddon's brothers and the *coup d'état* itself in the Hittite works to the legitimate successor's counter-attack and victory in Esarhaddon's apology.

Sections 5 and 6 in the Hittite works correspond to sections 6 and 7 in Esarhaddon's apology. In order to control a delicate situation after having seized the throne, both the Hittite monarchs were

[7] See Hoffner, ibid., pp. 51, 53.
[8] See Hoffner, ibid., pp. 52 f.
[9] See Hoffner, ibid., p. 53.

magnanimous and dealt leniently with their evil predecessors.[10] In contrast, Esarhaddon punished the rebels severely (II:8–11). Though differing in their attitude towards their enemies, however, there was no difference between them in aiming for the firm establishment of their kingship. The proclamation of the edict by the Hittite monarchs in the final section is also to be regarded as their effort to establish a just kingship.

From the above, it is clear that we may classify Esarhaddon's apology under the same genre as the Hittite apologetic works.

3. *A Comparison between Esarhaddon's Apology and Solomon's Defence*

As to the date, purpose, genre, boundary, and other problems of the Succession Narrative in the Books of 2 Samuel and 1 Kings 1–2, I have suggested in the foregoing chapters the early reign of Solomon as the date, the Solomonic legitimation as the purpose, historical writings of an apologetic nature as the genre, and 2 Sam 2–20, 1 Kgs 1–2 as the boundary.[11] Without repeating my arguments for these theses, I will proceed with the present study.

Esarhaddon's apology serves as good comparative material for the Succession Narrative, since both Solomon and Esarhaddon assumed their offices under similar circumstances and their common problem was obtaining an appointment as royal successor by overruling primogeniture. It is not surprising, therefore, that both monarchs are eager to speak in defence of their inferior position in the order of succession. With regard to this problem, first of all, they defend the legitimacy of their kingship by referring to divine election which they received in their youth as well as their father's designation of them as royal successors.

Thus, in the introduction, Esarhaddon tells: *rēʾûm kēnu migir ilāni rabûti ša ultu ṣeḫerišu* ^{d}*Aššur* ^{d}*Šamaš* ^{d}*Bēl u* ^{d}*Nabû* ^{d}*Ištar ša Ninua* ^{d}*Ištar ša Arbaʾili ana šarrūti māt Aššur ibbû zikiršu*, "The true shepherd, favorite of the great gods, whom Ashur, Shamash, Bel and Nabu, Ishtar of Nineveh (and) Ishtar of Arbela have pronounced king of Assyria (ever) since he was a youngster" (Nin. A I:4–7). In the Succession Narrative, a short account on Solomon's birth reads: *wattēleḏ bēn*

[10] See Hoffner, ibid., pp. 54 f.
[11] See above pp. 102 ff., 137 ff., 151 ff., 158 ff.

wayyiqrāʾ eṯ-šᵉmô šᵉlōmōh waYHWH ʾᵃhēḇô. wayyišlaḥ bᵉyaḏ nāṯān hannaḇîʾ wayyiqrāʾ eṯ-šᵉmô yᵉḏîḏyāh baʿᵃḇûr YHWH, "And she bore a son, and he called his name Solomon. And Yahweh loved him; and he sent by the hand of Nathan the prophet, and he called his name Jedidiah, for Yahweh's sake" (2 Sam 12:24b–25). No mention is made here explicitly about Solomon's kingship, but it is clear that the name Jedidiah "Yahweh's favorite" implies, as one of Esarhaddon's epithets: *migir ilāni rabûti*, "favorite of the great gods" shows, Solomon's divine election for future king.[12]

Esarhaddon's divine election is confirmed by an oracle which was given to his father: *ᵈŠamaš u ᵈAdad ina bīri išālma annu kēnu īpulušuma umma šū tēnûka*, "He asked Shamash and Adad by means of an oracle and they gave him a reliable answer and saying: He is your successor" (I:13–14). Though differing a little in situation, Solomon also receives confirmation of divine election from David: *bārûḵ YHWH ʾᵉlōhê yiśrāʾēl ʾᵃšer nāṯan hayyôm yōšēḇ ʿal-kisʾî wᵉʿênay rōʾôṯ*, "Blessed be Yahweh, the God of Israel, who has granted one to sit on my throne this day, my eyes even seeing it" (1 Kgs 1:48b).

Both Esarhaddon and Solomon lay great emphasis upon their fathers' designation of them as royal successors. By doing so, they mention explicitly their inferior position in the order of succession, both of them make clear their fathers' decision on the succession problem. In this connection, Esarhaddon tells: *ša aḫḫēja rabûti aḫušunu ṣeḫru anāku . . . abu bānua ina puḫur aḫḫēja rēšēja kēniš ullīma umma annû māru ridûtija*, "I was (indeed) the youngest brother among my elder brothers, (but) my own father . . . has chosen me in due form and in the assembly of all my brothers—saying: This is the son to (be elevated to) the position of a successor of mine" (I:8, 10–12). Moreover, Esarhaddon maintains that his father never changed his mind about this decision even when he became estranged from Esarhaddon because of his brothers' slander and false accusation: *pašru libbi abija ša la ilāni uzennû ittija šaplānu libbašu rēmu rašîšuma ana epēš šarrūtija šitkuna ēnāšu*, "They alienated from me—against the will of the gods—the heart of my father which was (formerly) friendly, (though) in the bottom of his heart there was (always) love (for me) and his intentions were (always) that I should become king" (I:29–31).

In the Succession Narrative, after an oath sworn by David to

---

[12] See above p. 156.

Bathsheba that Solomon would be his successor is repeated three times (!) (1 Kgs 1:13, 17, 30),[13] David gives orders to make Solomon king (1:33–35a) and declares: *wᵉʾōṯô ṣiwwîṯî lihyôṯ nāḡîḏ ʿal-yiśrāʾēl wᵉʿal-yᵉhûḏāh*, "And I have appointed him to be *nāḡîḏ* over Israel and over Judah" (1:35b). Solomon's inferior position in the order of succession is expressed in his conversation with Bathsheba concerning Adonijah's request for an ex-nurse (*sōḵeneṯ*) of David: . . . *wᵉlāmāh ʾat šōʾeleṯ ʾeṯ-ʾᵃbîšaḡ haššunammîṯ laʾᵃḏōnîyāhû wᵉšaʾᵃlî-lô ʾeṯ-hammᵉlûḵāh kî hûʾ ʾāḥî haggāḏôl mimmennî*, ". . . And why do you ask Abishag the Shunammite for Adonijah? Ask for him the kingdom also; for he is my elder brother" (1 Kgs 2:22a). It is clear that the Abishag episode is closely bound up with the struggle for the throne of David between Solomon and Adonijah.[14]

It is also worth noting that Solomon and Esarhaddon assumed a similar office immediately after their appointment to royal successor had been declared. While Esarhaddon entered the *bīt ridûti* to become the crown prince (I:21–22), Solomon sat on *kissēʾ hammᵉlûḵāh*, "the throne of the kingdom" (1 Kgs 1:46; cf. 1:13, 17, 20, 24, 27, 30, 35, 37, 47, 48) to become *nāḡîḏ*.[15] Some circumstantial evidence suggests that he began to rule as co-regent with David until the latter's death. The institution of co-regency as well as crown-princeship was a device to ease the dynastic succession during the interregnum.[16] In other words, this was another form of confirmation of the royal designation. As such, report is given of Esarhaddon's entering the *bīt ridûti* or Solomon's sitting on *kissēʾ hammᵉlûḵāh*.

As mentioned above, there is a contrast between the just past in section 2 and the subsequent deterioration in section 3 in Esarhaddon's

---

[13] I agree that Nathan and Bathsheba took advantage of David's senility, inducing him to believe that he had once sworn to Bathsheba that Solomon would be his successor, see M. Noth, *Könige* I. *I.Könige 1–16* (BKAT 9/1), Neukirchen-Vluyn, 1968, p. 20; J. Gray, *I & II Kings. A Commentary* (OTL), London, 1977³, p. 88; D.M. Gunn, *The Story of King David. Genre and Interpretation* (JSOTSup 6), Sheffield, 1978, pp. 105 f. However, the question here is not whether David's oath is historical or not, but that the Succession Narrative as a Solomonic apology lays emphasis on David's designation of Solomon; cf. above p. 119.

[14] See above pp. 130 ff.

[15] For *nāḡîḏ* see above pp. 57 ff.; cf. also G.F. Hasel, "נגיד", in *TWAT* V, Stuttgart, 1984–86, col. 216.

[16] For co-regency, see E. Ball, "The Co-Regency of David and Solomon (1 Kings i)", *VT* 27 (1977), pp. 268–279; T. Ishida, *The Royal Dynasties in Ancient Israel. A Study on the Formation and Development of Royal-Dynastic Ideology* (BZAW 142), Berlin/New York, 1977, p. 170.

apology. The Succession Narrative also has a similar contrast but not between the royal designation and its violation like in the case of Esarhaddon's apology. The nature of contrast in the Succession Narrative is rather similar to that in the Hittite apologetic works, i.e., a contrast between noble antecedents and the unworthy predecessor. According to the unique development in the Davidic kingdom, the noble antecedent in the Succession Narrative is King David who rules as a just king under Yahweh's blessing: *wayyimlōḵ dāwīḏ ʿal-kol-yiśrāʾēl wayhî dāwīḏ ʿōśeh mišpāṭ ûṣᵉḏāqāh lᵉḵol-ʿammô*, "And David reigned over all Israel. And David executed justice and righteousness to all his people" (2 Sam 8:15). However, in the second half of his reign David is described as a king under a curse in 2 Sam 9–20 and 1 Kgs 1–2 and he is included in the unworthy predecessors together with his three sons, i.e., Amnon, Absalom and Adonijah. Indeed, as I have suggested in the foregoing chapters, the ambivalence towards David is the characteristic feature of the Succession Narrative as a Solomonic legitimation.[17] It is also possible to find this sort of ambivalent relationship between a royal father and his true son as his successor elsewhere in the ancient Near East.[18] For example, it is interesting to note that the sentence: *pašru libbi abija ša la ilāni uzennû ittija*, "They (i.e., my brothers) have alienated from me, against the will of the gods, the heart of my father" in Esarhaddon's apology (I:29) suggests that Esarhaddon was also by no means on good terms with Sennacherib in the latter's last days. This does not mean, however, that Esarhaddon conspired against Sennacherib, who never changed his mind about the designation of Esarhaddon as his successor (I:31). We may assume that there was an ambivalent relationship between them.[19]

As to his brothers' behaviour in struggle for the kingship, Esarhaddon condemns it as immoral by enumerating the course of their shameful conduct: *riddu kēnu eli aḫḫēja ittabikma . . . ana epšetišunu šurruḫāti ittaklūma ikappudū lemuttu lišan lemuttim karṣī tašqirti . . . elija ušabšūma surrāti*

[17] See above pp. 123 ff., 144 ff.

[18] See above pp. 166 ff.

[19] S. Parpola, "The Murderer of Sennacherib", in B. Alster (ed.), *Death in Mesopotamia. XXVIᵉ RAI* (Mesopotamia 8), Copenhagen, 1980, pp. 171–182, has clearly shown that the assassin of Sennacherib was not Esarhaddon, as once suspected, but Arad-Mulišši, biblical Adrammelech, Esarhaddon's elder brother. According to Parpola, Sennacherib, who foresaw trouble, sent Esarhaddon away from Nineveh to the western provinces (p. 175).

la šalmāti arkija iddanabubū zērāti, "The proper behaviour as reversed for[20] my brothers . . . they put their trust in bold actions, planning an evil plot. They originated against me slander, false accusation . . . and constantly were spreading evil, incorrect and hostile (rumors) behind me" (I:23–28). At the same time, he asserts that these evildoings came about because of their separation from the gods: *ša ilāni umašširūma*, "They abandoned the gods" (I:24). As a result, these actions of his brothers are against the divine will: *kī la libbi ilāni* (I:26, 46), *ša la ilāni* (I:29, 34), or *balu ilāni* (I:43). Moreover, according to Esarhaddon's criticism, since "they became insane", *immaḫûma* (I:41) and "did everything that is wicked in (the eyes of) the gods and mankind", *mimma ša eli ilāni u amēlūti la ṭāba ēpušūma* (I:41–42), they incurred the displeasure of the gods: ᵈ*Aššur* ᵈ*Sin* ᵈ*Šamaš* ᵈ*Bēl* ᵈ*Nabû* ᵈ*Ištar ša Ninua* ᵈ*Ištar ša Arbaʾili epšēt ḫammāʾē . . . lemniš ittaṭlūma*, "Ashur, Sin, Shamash, Bel, Nabu, Ishtar of Nineveh (and) Ishtar of Arbela looked with displeasure upon these doings of the usurpers" (I:45–47).

In the Succession Narrative, too, a course of bad conduct by the unworthy predecessor and rival princes of Solomon is described in great detail, i.e., David's committing adultery with Bathsheba and murdering Uriah, her husband (2 Sam 11:2–25); Amnon's committing rape upon Tamar and Absalom's murder of Amnon (13:1–29); Absalom's rebellion (15:1–18:15); Adonijah's attempt to usurp the throne (1 Kgs 1:5–27).[21] Then, these evildoings are condemned as sin against God or conduct against the divine will: *wayyēraʿ haddāḇār ʾašer-ʿāśāh dāwīḏ bᵉʿênê YHWH*, "But the thing that David had done displeased Yahweh" (2 Sam 11:27b); *kōh-ʾāmar YHWH ʾᵉlōhê yiśrāʾēl . . . maddûʿa bāzîṯā ʾeṯ-dᵉḇar YHWH laʿᵃśôṯ hāraʿ bᵉʿênaw . . . wᵉʿattāh lōʾ-tāsûr ḥereḇ mibbêṯᵉḵā ʿaḏ-ʿôlām ʿēqeḇ kî bᵉzîṯānî wattiqqaḥ ʾeṯ-ʾēšeṯ ʾûrîyāh haḥittî lihyôṯ lᵉḵā lᵉʾiššāh*, "Thus says Yahweh, the God of Israel: . . . why have you despised the word of Yahweh, to do what is evil in his sight? . . . Now, therefore, the sword shall never depart from your house, because you have despised me, and have taken the wife of

---

[20] For *ittabik* see *CAD* A/1, p. 9, but see also *AHw*, pp. 981, 1296 and Borger, *Die Inschriften Asarhaddons*, p. 41.

[21] It is very likely that the alleged rebellion of Adonijah was actually Nathan's fabrication, see above pp. 117 ff. However, it is not the point here whether Adonijah really held a coronation without David's consent or not. As in the case dealt with in n.13 above, it is important for the narrator of the Succession Narrative to give an impression that Adonijah was a second Absalom, see above pp. 114 ff.

Uriah the Hittite to be your wife" (12:7, 9, 10); *waYHWH ṣiwwāh lᵉhāpēr ʾeṯ-ʿᵃṣaṯ ʾᵃḥîṯōpel haṭṭôḇāh lᵉḇaʿᵃḇûr hāḇîʾ YHWH ʾel-ʾaḇšālôm ʾeṯ-hārāʿāh*, "For Yahweh had ordained to defeat the good counsel of Ahithophel, so that Yahweh might bring evil upon Absalom" (17:14); *wattissōḇ hammᵉlûḵāh wattᵉhî lᵉʾāḥî kî mēYHWH hāyᵉṯāh lô*, "However the kingdom has turned about and become my brother's, for it was his from Yahweh" (1 Kgs 2:15b).

While Esarhaddon counter-attacked his rebellious brothers with a military confrontation against them (I:63–76), Solomon resorted to a court intrigue to turn the tide (1:11–31). Though the measures which they took are completely different one from the other, there is a common factor in both the reports of Solomon and Esarhaddon on the circumstances under which they had to fight with their rival princes. It is an assertion that they could not but fight for the legitimate kingship which was in danger of being usurped. Thus, when *epšētišunu lemnēti . . . ašmêma*, ". . . I heard of these sorry happenings" (I:55), Esarhaddon decided to go on an expedition; and the court intrigue of Solomon began when Bathsheba heard about Adonijah's coronation from Nathan the prophet: *hᵃlôʾ šāmaʿat kî mālaḵ ʾᵃḏōnîyāhû ben-haggîṯ waʾᵃḏōnênû dāwīḏ lōʾ yāḏāʿ*, "Have you not heard that Adonijah the son of Haggith has become king and David our lord does not know it?" (1:11).

It is told in both the compositions that after gaining a decisive victory, the legitimate successor received the people's support: *nišē māt Aššur ša adê niš ilāni rabûti ina muḫḫija izkurū adi maḫrija illikūnimma unaššiqū šēpēja*, "The people of Assyria who had sworn an oath by the life of the great gods on my behalf, came to meet me and kissed my feet" (I:80–81; cf. I:50–52); *wayyiṯqᵉʿû baššôpār wayyōʾmᵉrû kol-hāʿām yᵉḥî hammeleḵ šᵉlōmōh. wayyaʿᵃlû kol-hāʿām ʾaḥᵃrāw wᵉhāʿām mᵉḥallᵉlîm baḥᵃlīlîm ûśᵉmēḥîm śimḥāh gᵉḏōlāh wattibbāqaʿ hāʾāreṣ bᵉqôlām*, "And they blew the ram's horn; and all the people said: Long live king Solomon. And all the people came up after him, playing on pipes, and rejoicing with great joy, so that the earth was split by their noise" (1:39b–40). Then, the rebellion was finished in dispersion of the rebels: *u šunu ḫammāʾē ēpiš sīḫi u barti ša alāk girrija išmûma ṣābē tuklātešunu ezibūma ana māt la idû innabtū*, "But they, the usurpers, who had started the rebellion, deserted their trustworthy troops, when they heard the approach of my expeditionary corps and fled to an unknown country" (I:82–84); *wayyeḥerᵉḏû wayyāqumû kol-haqqᵉruʾîm ʾᵃšer laʾᵃḏōnîyāhû wayyēlᵉḵû*

ʾîš leḏarkô, "And all the guests of Adonijah were afraid, and rose up, and each went his own way" (1:49). Now, the legitimate successor ascended the throne: *ina qereb Ninua āl bēlūtija ḫadîš ērumma ina kussî abija ṭābiš ūšib*, "I entered joyfully into Nineveh, the town in which I exercise my lordship and sat down happily upon the throne of my father" (II:1–2); *weḡam yāšaḇ šelōmōh ʿal kissēʾ hammelûḵāh*, "And also Solomon sat on the throne of the kingdom" (1:46).

After ascending the throne, Esarhaddon severely punished those who had joined his rebellious brothers: *ṣābē bēl ḫiṭṭi ša ana ēpeš šarrūti māt Aššur ana aḫḫēja ušakpidū lemuttu puḫuršunu kīma ištēn aḫīṭma annu kabtu emissunūtima uḫalliqa zēršun*, "The culpable military which had schemed to secure the sovereignty of Assyria for my brothers, I considered guilty as one and meted out a grievous punishment to them; I exterminated their male descendants" (II:8–11). In contrast, Solomon dealt leniently with Adonijah and his supporters at the beginning (1:50–53). As in the case of Telepinu and Hattušili, Solomon had reason to be a merciful monarch when he ascended the throne. Some evidence shows that, at that time, he had not reached adult age and was without broad support of the people. However, he did not hesitate to purge all his rivals when he became strong enough to consolidate the foundation of his regime (2:13–46a). *wehammamlāḵāh nāḵônāh beyaḏ-šelōmōh*, "And the kingdom was established by the hand of Solomon" (2:46b).[22]

4. *Conclusions*

The foregoing comparison has shown that the Succession Narrative and Esarhaddon's apology share not only basic elements but also a general structure. We find the following seven basic elements common to both compositions:

1. The legitimate successor's divine election as future king in his youth.
2. The father's designation of the legitimate successor despite of his inferior position in the order of succession.
3. A comparison between the just past and the subsequent deterioration.

[22] Cf. above pp. 134 f.

a) The noble antecedent or the solemn decision.
b) Evil acts of an unworthy predecessor and/or rival princes.

4. Rival princes' attempt to usurp the throne against the divine will.
5. The legitimate successor's counter-attack and his victory.
6. The purge of his enemies.
7. The establishment of a just kingship.

Since the structure of the Succession Narrative is more complicated than that of Esarhaddon's apology, scholars are sometimes misguided about the nature of this composition. However, if we recognize the above seven elements as the frame timbers of the structure of the composition, it becomes clear that the Succession Narrative belongs to a genre called "Royal Historical Writings of an Apologetic Nature" under which Esarhaddon's apology is also classified.

Before closing the present study, mention must be made of the fact that there are also many differences between the Succession Narrative and Esarhaddon's apology. The most important differences are perhaps found in the style and the beginning of the composition. As to the style, the latter is autobiographical while the former is a work composed by a third party with much literary augmentation. And while the latter begins with an ordinal introduction to royal historical writings, the former's beginning seems to be buried in the concluding part of the History of David's Rise. I have a feeling that there is a clue here to an explanation of the life setting of the Succession Narrative in inquiring into the differences between these two royal apologies.

BIBLIOGRAPHY

1. *Texts and Dictionaries*

Aistleitner, J. (ed. by O. Eissfeldt), *Wörterbuch der ugaritischen Sprache*, Berlin, 1963.

Albright, W.F., "Palestinian Inscriptions", in *ANET*, Princeton, 1969³, pp. 320–322.

The Assyrian Dictionary of the Oriental Institute of the University of Chicago, Chicago, 1956– [= *CAD*].

Borger, R., *Die Inschriften Asarhaddons Königs von Assyrien* (AfO Beih. 9), Graz, 1956.

Bottéro, J. and Finet, A., *Répertoire analytique des Tomes I à V des Archives Royales de Mari* (ARM XV), Paris, 1954.

Brown, F., Driver, S.R., and Briggs, C.A., *A Hebrew and English Lexicon of the Old Testament*, Oxford, 1906 [= BDB].

Donner, H. and Röllig, W., *Kanaanäische und aramäische Inschriften* I: *Texte*, 1971³; II: *Kommentar*, 1973³; III: *Glossare, Indizes, Tafeln*, Wiesbaden, 1969² [= *KAI*].

Elliger, K. and Rudolph, W. (eds.), *Biblia Hebraica Stuttgartensia*, Stuttgart, 1967–77 [= *BHS*].

Gibson, J.C.L., *Textbook of Syrian Semitic Inscriptions* II: *Aramaic Inscriptions*, 1975; III: *Phoenician Inscriptions*, Oxford, 1982.

Götze, A., *Ḫattušiliš. Der Bericht über seine Thronbesteigung nebst den Paralleltexten* (MVÄG 29/3, Hethitische Texte, Heft 1), Leipzig, 1924.

Gordon, C.H., *Ugaritic Textbook* (AnOr 38), Roma, 1965 [= *UT*].

Grayson, A.K., *Assyrian Rulers of the Early First Millennium BC* II (*858–745 BC*) (RIMA 3), Toronto/Buffalo/London, 1996.

Hoffmann, I., *Der Erlaß, Telipinus* (TH 11), Heidelberg, 1984.

Hoftijzer, J. and Jongeling, K., *Dictionary of the North-West Semitic Inscriptions* I–II (HdO I/21), Leiden/New York/Köln, 1995 [= *DNWSI*].

Jean, C.-F. and Hoftijzer J., *Dictionnaire des Inscriptions Sémitiques de l'Ouest*, Leiden, 1960–65 [= *DISO*].

Kittel, R. (ed.), *Biblia Hebraica* (3. ed.), Stuttgart, 1937, 1961¹² [= *BHK*].

Koehler, L. and Baumgartner, W., *Lexicon in Veteris Testamenti libros*, Leiden, 1953 [= KB].

Koehler, L., Baumgartner, W. and Stamm, J.J., (tr. and ed. by M.E.J. Richardson), *The Hebrew and Aramaic Lexicon of the Old Testament* I, 1994; II, 1995; III, 1996; IV, Leiden/New York/Köln, 1999 [= *HALOT*].

Langdon, S., *Die neubabylonischen Königsinschriften* (VAB 4), Leipzig, 1912.

Lidzbarski, M., *Ephemeris für semitische Epigraphik* I–III, Giessen, 1902–15.

Meissner, B., "Die Keilschrifttexte auf den steinernen Orthostaten und Statuen aus dem Tell Ḥalâf", in *Aus fünf Jahrtausenden morgenländischer Kultur. Festschrift Max Freiherrn von Oppenheim* (AfO Beih. 1), Graz, 1933, pp. 71–79.

Oppenheim, A.L., "Babylonian and Assyrian Historical Texts", in *ANET*, Princeton, 1969³, pp. 265–317.

Parpola, S., *Neo-Assyrian Toponyms* (AOAT 6), Neukirchen-Vluyn, 1970.

Pritchard, J.B. (ed.), *Ancient Near Eastern Texts Relating to the Old Testament*, Princeton, 1969³ [= *ANET*].

Reiner, E. and Civil, M., *Materialien zum sumerischen Lexikon* XI, Rome, 1974.

Rosenthal, F., "Canaanite and Aramaic Inscriptions", in *ANET*, Princeton, 1969³, pp. 653–662.

Rost, P., *Die Keilschrifttexte Tiglat-Pilesers III. nach den Papierabklatschen und Originalen des*

Britischen Museums I: *Einleitung, Trascription und Uebersetzung, Wörterverzeichnis mit Commentar*, Leipzig, 1893.
Seux, M.-J., *Épithètes royales akkadiennes et sumériennes*, Paris, 1967.
von Soden, W. (ed.), *Akkadisches Handwörterbuch* I–III, Wiesbaden, 1965–81 [= *AHw*].
Streck, M., *Assurbanipal und die letzten assyrischen Könige bis zum Untergange Niniveh's* II (VAB 7/2), Leipzig, 1916.
Sturtevant, E.H. and Bechtel, G., *A Hittite Chrestomathy*, Philadelphia, 1935.
Tadmor, H., *The Inscriptions of Tiglath-Pileser III King of Assyria. Critical Edition, with Introductions, Translations and Commentary*, Jerusalem, 1994.
Ünal, A., *Ḫattušili III*. I. *Ḫattušili bis zu seiner Thronbesteigung* 1: *Historischer Abriß*; 2: *Quellen und Indices* (TH 3–4), Heidelberg, 1974.
Weissbach, F.H., *Die Keilinschriften der Achämeniden* (VAB 3), Leipzig, 1911.

2. *Monographs and Articles*

Ackroyd, P.R., "The Succession Narrative (so-called)", *Int* 35 (1981), pp. 383–396.
Aharoni, Y., *The Land of the Bible. A Historical Geography*, London, 1966.
Ahlström, G.W., "Der Prophet Nathan und der Tempelbau", *VT* 11 (1961), pp. 113–127.
——, *Royal Administration and National Religion in Ancient Palestine* (SHANE 1), Leiden, 1982.
Albright, W.F., *Samuel and the Beginnings of the Prophetic Movement*, Cincinnati, 1961.
——, "The Role of the Canaanites in the History of Civilization", in G.E. Wright (ed.), *The Bible and the Ancient Near East. Essays in Honor of William Foxwell Albright*, London, 1961, pp. 328–362.
Alt, A., "Israels Gaue unter Salomo" (1913), in *Kleine Schriften zur Geschichte des Volkes Israel* II, München, 1953, pp. 76–89.
——, "Die Staatenbildung der Israeliten in Palästina" (1930), in *Kleine Schriften zur Geschichte des Volkes Israel* II, München, 1953, pp. 1–65.
——, "Die Ursprünge des israelitischen Rechts" (1934), in *Kleine Schriften zur Geschichte des Volkes Israel* I, München, 1953, pp. 278–332.
——, "Das Königtum in den Reichen Israel und Juda" (1951), in *Kleine Schriften zur Geschichte des Volkes Israel* II, München, 1953, pp. 116–134.
Althann, R., "Shallum", in *ABD* V, New York, 1992, p. 1154.
Anbar, M., "Genesis 15: A Conflation of Two Deuteronomic Narratives", *JBL* 101 (1982), pp. 39–55.
Andreasen, N.-E.A., "The Role of the Queen Mother in Israelite Society", *CBQ* 45 (1983), pp. 179–194.
Astour, M.C., "841 B.C.: The First Assyrian Invasion of Israel", *JAOS* 91 (1971), pp. 383–389.
Auerbach, E., *Wüste und gelobtes Land* II, Berlin, 1936.
Bailey, R.C., *David in Love and War. The Pursuit of Power in 2 Samuel 10–12* (JSOTSup 75), Sheffield, 1990.
Ball, E., "The Co-Regency of David and Solomon (1 Kings i)", *VT* 27 (1977), pp. 268–279.
——, "Introduction", in L. Rost, *The Succession to the Throne of David*, Sheffield, 1982, pp. xv–l.
Baltzer, K., *The Covenant Formulary in Old Testament, Jewish, and Early Christian Writings*, Oxford, 1971. = *Das Bundesformular* (WMANT 4), Neukirchen-Vluyn, 1964².
Bartlett, J.R., "Sihon and Og, Kings of the Amorites", *VT* 20 (1970), pp. 257–277.
Begrich, J., "Atalja, die Tochter Omris", *ZAW* 53 (1935), pp. 78–79.
Beuken, W.A.M., "*Mišpāṭ*: The First Servant Song and its Context", *VT* 22 (1972), pp. 1–30.

Beyerlin, W., "Das Königscharisma bei Saul", *ZAW* 73 (1961), pp. 186–201.
——, "Gattung und Herkunft des Rahmens im Richterbuch", in *Tradition und Situation. A. Weiser Festschrift*, Göttingen, 1963, pp. 1–29.
——, "Geschichte und heilsgeschichtliche Traditionsbildung im Alten Testament. Ein Beitrag zur Traditionsgeschichte von Richter vi–viii", *VT* 13 (1963), pp. 1–25.
Blenkinsopp, J., *Gibeon and Israel. The Role of Gibeon and the Gibeonites in the Political and Religious History of Early Israel* (The Society for Old Testament Study Monograph Series 2), Cambridge, 1972.
Boecker, H.J., *Die Beurteilung der Anfänge des Königtums in den deuteronomistischen Abschnitten des 1. Samuelbuches. Ein Beitrag zum Problem des "deuteronomistischen Geschichtswerks"* (WMANT 31), Neukirchen-Vluyn, 1969.
Böhl, F.M.T. de Liagre, *Kanaanäer und Hebräer. Untersuchungen zur Vorgeschichte des Volkstums und der Religion Israels auf dem Boden Kanaans* (Beiträge zur Wissenschaft vom Alten Testament 9), Leipzig, 1911.
Boling, R.G., *Judges. Introduction, Translation, and Commentary* (AB 6A), Garden City, N.Y., 1975.
——, "Shamgar", in *ABD* V, New York, 1992, pp. 1155 f.
Borger, R. and Tadmor, H., "Zwei Beiträge zur alttestamentlichen Wissenschaft aufgrund der Inschriften Tiglatpilesers III", *ZAW* 94 (1982), pp. 244–251.
Botha, P.J., "2 Samuel 7 against the Background of Ancient Near-Eastern Memorial Inscriptions", in W.C. van Wyk (ed.), *Studies in the Succession Narrative*, Pretoria, 1986, pp. 62–78.
Bright, J., *A History of Israel* (OTL), London, 1960, 1972^2.
Brueggemann, W., "From Dust to Kingship", *ZAW* 84 (1972), pp. 1–18.
Buccellati, G., *Cities and Nations of Ancient Syria. An Essay on Political Institutions with Speicial Reference to the Israelite Kingdoms* (Studi Semitici 26), Roma, 1967.
du Buit, M., "Populations de l'ancienne Palestine", in *DBSup* VIII, Paris, 1972, cols. 111–126.
Burney, C.F., *The Book of Judges with Introduction and Notes*, London, 1918.
Caloz, M., "Exode, XIII, 3–16 et son rapport au Deutéronome", *RB* 75 (1968), pp. 5–62.
Carlson, R.A., *David the chosen King. A Traditio-Historical Approach to the Second Book of Samuel*, Stockholm/Göteborg/Uppsala, 1964.
Cassuto, U., "Jerusalem in the Pentateuch" (1951), in *Biblical and Oriental Studies* I: *Bible*, Jerusalem, 1973, pp. 71–78.
Cazelles, H., "Institutions et terminologie en Deutéronome i 6–17", in *Congress Volume*, Genève 1965 (VTSup 15), Leiden, 1966, pp. 97–112.
Clements, R., *Abraham and David. Genesis 15 and its Meaning for Israelite Tradition* (SBTS 5), London, 1967.
Cody, A., *A History of Old Testament Priesthood* (AnBib 35), Rome, 1969.
Cogan, M. and Tadmor, H., *II Kings. A New Translation with Introduction and Commentary* (AB 11), New York, 1988.
Cohen, M.A., "The Role of the Shilonite Priesthood in the United Monarchy of Ancient Israel", *HUCA* 36 (1965), pp. 59–98.
Collins, T., "The Kilamuwa Inscription—A Phoenician Poem", *WO* 6 (1970/71), pp. 183–188.
Conroy, C., *Absalom Absalom! Narrative and Language in 2 Sam 13–20* (AnBib 81), Rome, 1978.
Cross, F.M., "The Stele Dedicated to Melcarth by Ben-Hadad of Damascus", *BASOR* 205 (1972), pp. 36–42.
——, *Canaanite Myth and Hebrew Epic. Essays in the History of the Religion of Israel*, Cambridge, Mass./London, 1973.
Cross, F.M. and Freedman, D.N., *Early Hebrew Orthography. A Study of the Epigraphic Evidence* (AOS 36), New Haven, 1952.

——, "Josiah's Revolt against Assyria", *JNES* 12 (1953), pp. 56–58.

Crüsemann, F., *Der Widerstand gegen das Königtum. Die antiköniglichen Texte des Alten Testamentes und der Kampf um den frühen israelitischen Staat* (WMANT 49), Neukirchen-Vluyn, 1978.

Davies, G.H., "Nethinim", in *IDB* III, Nashville/New York, 1962, p. 541.

Delaporte, L., "Les Hittites sont-ils nommés dans la Bible?", *RHA* 4 (1938), pp. 289–296.

——, "Hittites", in *DBSup* IV, Paris, 1949, cols. 32–110.

Delekat, L., "Tendenz und Theologie der David-Salomo-Erzählung", in F. Maass (ed.), *Das ferne und nahe Wort. L. Rost Festschrift* (BZAW 105), Berlin, 1967, pp. 26–36.

Dever, W.G., "Prolegomenon to a reconsideration of archaeology and patriarchal backgrounds", in J.H. Hayes and J.M. Miller (eds.), *Israelite and Judaean History* (OTL), London, 1977, pp. 102–117.

Donner, H., "Art und Herkunft des Amtes der Königinmutter im Alten Testament", in *J. Friedrich Festschrift*, Heidelberg, 1959, pp. 105–145.

Dossin, G., "Une mention de Canaanéens dans une lettre de Mari", *Syria* 50 (1973), pp. 277–282.

Driver, S.R., *A Critical and Exegetical Commentary on Deuteronomy* (ICC), Edinburgh, 1902^{3}.

Dus, J., "Die 'Sufeten Israels'", *ArOr* 31 (1963), pp. 444–469.

Eising, H., "חיל", in *TWAT* II, Stuttgart, 1974–77, cols. 902–911.

Eissfeldt, O., *The Old Testament. An Introduction*, Oxford, 1965. = *Einleitung in das Alte Testament*, Tübingen, 1964^{3}.

——, "The Hebrew Kingdom", in *CAH* II, ch. XXXIV, Cambridge, 1965.

Ephʿal, I., *The Ancient Arabs. Nomads on the Borders of the Fertile Crescent 9th–5th Centuries B.C.*, Jerusalem/Leiden, 1982.

Fales, F.M., "Kilamuwa and the Foreign Kings: Propaganda vs. Power", *WO* 10 (1979), pp. 6–22.

Falk, Z.W., "Two Symbols of Justice", *VT* 10 (1960), pp. 72–74.

——, "Šōpēṭ wᵉšēḇeṭ", *Lešonénu* 30 (1966), pp. 243–247 (Hebrew).

Fensham, F.C., "The Judges and Ancient Israelite Jurisprudence", *OTWSA* 2 (1959), pp. 15–22.

Fohrer, G., "Der Vertrag zwischen König und Volk in Israel" (1959), in *Studien zur alttestamentlichen Theologie und Geschichte (1949–1966)* (BZAW 115), Berlin, 1969, pp. 330–351.

——, *Geschichte der israelitischen Religion*, Berlin, 1969.

——, *Introduction to the Old Testament*, London, 1970. = Sellin, E. – Fohrer, G., *Einleitung in das Alte Testament*, Heidelberg, 1965^{10}.

Fokkelman, J.P., *Narrative Art and Poetry in the Books of Samuel. A full interpretation based on stylistic and structural analyses* I: *King David (II Sam. 9–20 & I Kings 1–2)*, Assen, 1981.

Forrer, E.O., "The Hittites in Palestine", *PEQ* 68 (1936), pp. 190–203; 69 (1937), pp. 100–115.

Forshey, H.O., "Court Narrative (2 Samuel 9–1 Kings 2)", in *ABD* I, New York, 1992, pp. 1172–1179.

Frankfort, H., *Kingship and the Gods. A Study of Ancient Near Eastern Religion as the Integration of Society & Nature*, Chicago, 1948.

Frumstein (Tadmor), H., "הבעיות הכרונולוגיות" in "אמציהו, אמציה", in *Encyclopaedia Biblica* I, Jerusalem, 1950, col. 439 (Hebrew).

Galling, K., *Die israelitische Staatsverfassung in ihrer vorderorientalischen Umwelt* (AO XXVIII 3/4), Leipzig, 1929.

Gamble, H.Y., "New Testament" in "Canon" in *ABD* I, New York, 1992, pp. 852–861.

Gelb, I.J., "Hittites", in *IDB* II, Nashville/New York, 1962, pp. 612–615.
Gelio, R., *Ša ina šarrāni abbēya mamman lā ēpušu ... Il motivo della priorità eroica nelle iscrizioni reali assire* (Diss.), Università di Roma, 1977.
Gelston, A., "A Note on II Samuel 7_{10}", *ZAW* 84 (1972), pp. 92–94.
Gerleman, G., "Die Wurzel *šlm*", *ZAW* 85 (1973), pp. 1–14.
Gese, H., "Der Davidsbund und die Zionserwählung", *ZTK* 61 (1964), pp. 10–26.
Gibson, J.C.L., "Observations on Some Important Ethnic Terms in the Pentateuch", *JNES* 20 (1961), pp. 217–238.
Ginsberg, H.L., "The Rebellion and Death of Baʿlu", *Or* 5 (1936), pp. 161–198.
——, "The Omrid-Davidid Alliance and its Consequences", in *Fourth World Congress of Jewish Studies* (1965) I, Jerusalem, 1967, pp. 91–93.
Glück, J.J., "Nagid-Shepherd", *VT* 13 (1963), pp. 144–150.
Good, R.M., *The Sheep of His Pasture. A Study of the Hebrew Noun ʿAm(m) and Its Semitic Cognates* (HSM 29), Chico, 1983.
Gordis, R., "Sectional Rivalry in the Kingdom of Judah", *JQR* 25 (1934/35), pp. 237–259.
Gordon, C.H., "Abraham and the Merchants of Ura", *JNES* 17 (1958), pp. 28–31.
Gottwald, N.K., *The Tribes of Yahweh. A Sociology of the Religion of Liberated Israel, 1250–1050 B.C.E.*, Maryknoll, N.Y., 1979.
Gray, G.B., *A Critical and Exegetical Commentary on Numbers* (ICC), Edinburgh, 1903.
Gray, J., *Joshua, Judges and Ruth* (NCB), London, 1967.
——, *I & II Kings. A Commentary* (OTL), London, 1977[3].
Grayson, A.K., "Histories and Historians of the Ancient Near East: Assyria and Babylonia", *Or* 49 (1980), pp. 140–194.
Grether, O., "Die Bezeichnung 'Richter' für die charismatischen Helden der vorstaatlichen Zeit", *ZAW* 57 (1939), pp. 110–121.
Grønbaek, J.H., *Die Geschichte vom Aufstieg Davids (1.Sam.15–2.Sam.5). Tradition und Komposition*, Copenhagen, 1971.
Gros Louis, K.R.R., "The Difficulty of Ruling Well: King David of Israel", *Semeia* 8 (1977), pp. 15–33.
Güterbock, H.G., "Hethiter, Hethitisch", in *RLA* IV, Berlin/New York, 1972–75, pp. 372–375.
Guinan, M.D., "Davidic Covenant", in *ABD* II, New York, 1992, pp. 69–72.
Gunn, D.M., *The Story of King David. Genre and Interpretation* (JSOTSup 6), Sheffield, 1978.
Gurney, O.R., *The Hittites*, Harmondsworth, 1961[2].
Hagan, H., "Deception as Motif and Theme in 2 Sam 9–20; 1 Kgs 1–2", *Bib* 60 (1979), pp. 301–326.
Haldar, A., *Who were the Amorites?*, Leiden, 1971.
Halpern, B., *The Constitution of the Monarchy in Israel* (HSM 25), Chico, 1981.
——, *The Emergence of Israel in Canaan* (SBLM 29), Chico, 1983.
——, *The First Historians. The Hebrew Bible and History*, San Francisco, 1988.
Haran, M., *Temples and Temple-Service in Ancient Israel. An Inquiry into Biblical Cult Phenomena and the Historical Setting of the Priestly School*, Winona Lake, 1985.
Hasel, G.F., "נגיד", in *TWAT* V, Stuttgart, 1984–86, cols. 203–219.
Hawkins, J.D., "Hamath", in *RLA* IV, Berlin/New York, 1972–75, pp. 67–70.
——, "Ḫatti: the I[st] millennium B.C.", in *RLA* IV, Berlin/New York, 1972–75, pp. 152–159.
Healey, J.P., "Am Ha'arez", in *ABD* I, New York, 1992, pp. 168–169.
Helck, W., *Die Beziehungen Ägyptens zu Vorderasien im 3. und 2. Jahrtausend v. Chr.* (Ägyptologische Abhandlungen 5), Wiesbaden, 1962.
Herrmann, S., "Die Königsnovelle in Ägypten und in Israel. Ein Beitrag zur Gattungsgeschichte in den Geschichtsbüchern des Alten Testaments", *WZ Leipzig* 3 (1953/54*). Gesellschafts- und sprachwissenschaftliche Reihe* 1, pp. 51–62.

Hertzberg, H.W., "Die Entwicklung des Begriffes משפט im AT", *ZAW* 40 (1922), pp. 256–287; 41 (1923). pp. 16–76.
——, "Die kleinen Richter", *TLZ* 79 (1954), cols. 285–290.
——, *Die Bücher Josua, Richter, Ruth* (ATD 9), Göttingen, 1959².
——, *I & II Samuel. A Commentary* (OTL), London, 1964. = *Die Samuelbücher* (ATD 10), Götingen, 1960².
Hoffner, H.A., "Some Contributions of Hittitology to Old Testament Study", *Tyndale Bulletin* 20 (1969), pp. 27–55.
——, "The Hittites and Hurrians", in D.J. Wiseman (ed.), *POTT*, Oxford, 1973, pp. 197–228.
——, "Propaganda and Political Justification in Hittite Historiography", in H. Goedicke and J.J.M. Roberts (eds.), *Unity and Diversity. Essays in the History, Literature, and Religion of the Ancient Near East*, Baltimore/London, 1975, pp. 49–62.
——, "Histories and Historians of the Ancient Near East: The Hittites", *Or* 49 (1980), pp. 283–332.
Hurowitz, V.(A.), *I Have Built You an Exalted House. Temple Building in the Bible in Light of Mesopotamian and Northwest Semitic Writings* (JSOTSup 115), Sheffield, 1992.
Ikeda, Y., "Solomon's Trade in Horses and Chariots in Its International Setting", in T. Ishida (ed.), *SPDS*, Tokyo/Winona Lake, 1982, pp. 215–238.
Ishida, T., *The Royal Dynasties in Ancient Israel. A Study on the Formation and Development of Royal-Dynastic Ideology* (BZAW 142), Berlin/New York, 1977.
——, "Solomon", in *ABD* VI, New York, 1992, pp. 105–113.
Jacobsen, T., "Early Political Development in Mesopotamia" (1957), in W.L. Moran, (ed.), *Toward the Image of Tammuz and Other Essays on Mesopotamian History and Culture* (HSS 21), Cambridge, Mass., 1970, pp. 132–156.
——, "Ancient Mesopotamian Religion: The Central Concerns" (1963), in *Toward the Image of Tammuz and Other Essays on Mesopotamian History and Culture* (HSS 21), Cambridge, Mass., 1970, pp. 39–47.
Jeremias, J., "*Mišpāṭ* im ersten Gottesknechtslied (Jes. XLII 1–4)", *VT* 22 (1972), pp. 31–42.
Jirku, A., "Eine hethitische Ansiedlung in Jerusalem zur Zeit von El-Amarna", *ZDPV* 43 (1920), pp. 58–61.
Jones, G.H., *The Nathan Narratives* (JSOTSup 80), Sheffiled, 1990.
Junge, E., *Der Wiederaufbau des Heerwesens des Reiches Juda unter Josia* (BWANT 75), Stuttgart, 1937.
Kallai, Z., "Tribes, Territories of", in *IDBSup*, Nashville, 1976, pp. 920–923.
——, "The Patriarchal Boundaries, Canaan and the Land of Israel: Patterns and Application in Biblical Historiography", *IEJ* 47 (1997), pp. 69–82.
Kammenhuber, A., "Hethitisch, Palaisch, Luwisch und Hieroglyphenluwisch", in *Altkleinasiatische Sprachen* (HdO I/II 1–2/2), Leiden/Köln, 1969, pp. 119–357.
Kapelrud, A.S., "Temple Building: A Task for Gods and Kings" *Or* 32 (1963), pp. 56–62.
Katzenstein, H.J., "Who Were the Parents of Athaliah?", *IEJ* 5 (1955), 194–197.
Kaufmann, Y., *The Book of Judges*, Jerusalem, 1962 (Hebrew).
——, *The Religion of Israel from its Beginnings to the Babylonian Exile* (tr. and abr. by M. Greenberg), New York, 1972.
Kenyon, K.M., *Amorites and Canaanites*, London, 1966.
Kienitz, F.K., *Die politische Geschichte Ägyptens vom 7. bis zum 4. Jahrhundert vor der Zeitwende*, Berlin, 1953.
——, "Die Saïtische Renaissance", in *Fischer Weltgeshichte* IV. *Die Altorientalischen Reiche* III. *Die erste Hälfte des 1. Jahrtausends*, Frankfurt a/M., 1967, pp. 256–282.
Kitchen, K.A., *Ancient Orient and Old Testament*, Chicago, 1966.
——, "The Philistines", in D.J. Wiseman (ed.), *POTT*, Oxford, 1973, pp. 53–78.
——, *The Third Intermediate Period in Egypt (1100–650 B.C.)*, Warminster, 1973.

Kittel, R., *Geschichte des Volkes Israel* II, Stuttgart, 1925[7].

Klengel, E. and H., *Die Hethiter. Geschichte und Umwelt*, Wien/München, 1970.

Klengel, H., *Geschichte Syriens im 2. Jahrtausend vor unserer Zeitrechnung* II: *Mittel- und Südsyrien*, Berlin, 1969.

Klostermann, A., *Der Pentateuch*, Leipzig, 1907[2].

Knoppers, G.N., *Two Nations under God. The Deuteronomistic History of Solomon and the Dual Monarchies* I: *The Reign of Solomon and the Rise of Jeroboam* (HSM 52), Atlanta, 1993.

Koehler, L., "Die hebräische Rechtsgemeinde" (1931), in *Der hebräische Mensch*, Tübingen, 1953, pp. 143–171.

Koopmans, W.T., "The Testament of David in 1 Kings ii 1–10", *VT* 41 (1991), pp. 429–449.

Kraus, H.-J., *Die prophetische Verkündigung des Rechts in Israel* (TS 51), Zürich, 1957.

Kruse, H., "David's Covenant", *VT* 35 (1985), pp. 139–164.

Kumaki, F.K., "The Deuteronomistic Theology of the Temple—as Crystallized in 2 Sam 7, 1 Kgs 8—", *AJBI* 7 (1981), pp. 16–52.

Kutsch, E., "Die Dynastie von Gottes Gnaden. Probleme der Nathanweissagung in 2. Sam 7", *ZTK* 58 (1961), pp. 137–153.

Kutscher, E.Y., "A Marginal Note to S.E. Loewenstamm's Article", *Lešonénu* 32 (1967/68), p. 274 (Hebrew).

Landsberger, B., *Sam'al. Studien zur Entdeckung der Ruinenstätte Karatepe*, Ankara, 1948.

Langlamet, F., "Israël et 'l'habitant du pays', vocabulaire et formules d'Ex., XXXIV, 11–16", *RB* 76 (1969), pp. 321–350, 481–507.

——, *Gilgal et les récits de la traversée du Jourdain* (Jos iii–iv) (CRB 11), Paris, 1969.

——, "Les récits de l'institution de la royauté (I Sam., VII–XII). De Wellhausen aux travaux récents", *RB* 77 (1970), pp. 161–200.

——, "Pour ou contre Salomon? La rédaction prosalomonienne de I Rois, I–II", *RB* 83 (1976), pp. 321–379, 481–528.

——, "Absalom et les concubines de son père. Recherches sur II Sam., XVI, 21–22", *RB* 84 (1977), pp. 161–209.

——, "Ahitofel et Houshaï. Rédaction prosalomonienne en 2 Sam 15–17?", in Y. Avishur and J. Blau (eds.), *Studies in Bible and the Ancient Near East. Presented to S.E. Loewenstamm on His Seventieth Birthday*, Jerusalem, 1978, pp. 57–90.

——, "David et la maison de Saül", *RB* 86 (1979), pp. 194–213, 385–436, 481–513; *RB* 87 (1980), pp. 161–210; *RB* 88 (1981), pp. 321–332.

——, "Affinités sacerdotales, deutéronomiques, élohistes dans l'Histoire de la succession (2 S 9–20; 1 R 1–2)", in A. Caquot and M. Delcor (eds.), *Mélanges bibliques et orientaux en l'honneur de M. Henri Cazelles* (AOAT 212), Neukirchen-Vluyn, 1981, pp. 233–246.

——, "David, fils de Jessé. Une édition prédeutéronomiste de l'<histoire de la succession>", *RB* 89 (1982), pp. 5–47.

Lemche, N.P., *Early Israel. Anthropological and Historical Studies on the Israelite Society Before the Monarchy* (VTSup 37), Leiden, 1985.

Levenson, J.D., "The Hebrew Bible, the Old Testament, and Historical Criticism", in R.E. Friedman and H.G.M. Williamson (eds.), *The Future of Biblical Studies. The Hebrew Scriptures*, Atlanta, 1987, pp. 19–60.

Levenson, J.D. and Halpern, B., "The Political Import of David's Marriages", *JBL* 99 (1980), pp. 507–518.

Levin, C., *Der Sturz der Königin Atalja. Ein Kapitel zur Geschichte Judas im 9. Jahrhundert v. Chr.* (SBS 105), Stuttgart, 1982.

Lewy, J., *Die Chronologie der Könige von Israel und Juda*, Giessen, 1927.

Lindars, B., "Gideon and Kingship", *JTS* 16 (1965), pp. 315–326.

Lipiński, E., "*Nāgîd*, der Kronprinz", *VT* 24 (1974), pp. 497–499.

——, "עם", in *TWAT* VI, Stuttgart, 1987–89, cols. 177–194.

Liver, J., "מנשה", in *Encyclopaedia Biblica* V, Jerusalem, 1968, cols. 41–45 (Hebrew).
——, "נגיד", in *Encyclopaedia Biblica* V, Jerusalem, 1968, cols. 753–755 (Hebrew).
Liverani, M., "The Amorites", in D.J. Wiseman (ed.), *POTT*, Oxford, 1973, pp. 100–133.
——, "Memorandum on the Approach to Historiographic Texts", *Or* 42 (1973), pp. 178–194.
——, "L'histoire de Joas", *VT* 24 (1974), pp. 438–453.
——, "The Ideology of the Assyrian Empire", in M.T. Larsen (ed.), *Power and Propaganda—A Symposium on Ancient Empires*, Copenhagen, 1979, pp. 297–317.
Loewenstamm, S.E., "חוי", in *Encyclopaedia Biblica* III, Jerusalem, 1958, cols. 45–47 (Hebrew).
——, "Ruler and Judge. Reconsidered", *Lešonénu* 32 (1967/68), pp. 272–274 (Hebrew).
Lohfink, N., *Das Hauptgebot. Eine Untersuchung literarischer Einleitungsfragen zu Dtn 5–11* (AnBib 20), Roma, 1963.
——, *Die Landverheissung als Eid. Eine Studie zu Gn 15* (SBS 28), Stuttgart, 1967.
von Luschan, F. et al., *Ausgrabungen in Sendschirli* I–IV (Königliche Museen zu Berlin: Mitteilungen aus den orientalischen Sammlungen XI–XIV), Berlin, 1893–1911.
Lust, J., "The Immanuel Figure: A Charismatic Judge-Leader", *ETL* 47 (1971), pp. 464–470.
Mabee, C., "David's Judicial Exoneration", *ZAW* 92 (1980), pp. 89–107.
McCarter, P.K., *I Samuel. A New Translation with Introduction, Notes and Commentary* (AB 8), Garden City, N.Y., 1980.
——, "'Plots, True or False.' The Succession Narrative as Court Apologetic", *Int* 35 (1981), pp. 355–367.
——, *II Samuel. A New Translation with Introduction, Notes and Commentary* (AB 9), Garden City, N.Y., 1984.
McCarthy, D.J., *Old Testament Covenant. A Survey of Current Opinions*, Oxford, 1972.
——, *Treaty and Covenat. A Study in Form in the Ancient Oriental Documents and in the Old Testament* (AnBib 21A), Rome, 1978².
Macholz, G.C., "NAGID—der Statthalter, 'praefectus'", in *Sefer Rendtorff. R. Rendtorff Festschrift* (Dielheimer Blätter zum Alten Testament 1), Dielheim, 1975, pp. 59–72.
McKenzie, D.A., "The Judges of Israel", *VT* 17 (1967), pp. 118–121.
McKenzie, J.L., "The 'People of the Land' in the Old Testament", in *Akten des vierundzwanzigsten Internationalen Orientalisten-Kongresses Münchens 28. Aug. bis 4. Sept. 1957*, Wiesbaden, 1959, pp. 206–208.
MacLaurin, E.C.B., "ANAK/'ANAΘ", *VT* 15 (1965), pp. 468–474.
McMahon, G., "Hitties in the OT", in *ABD* III, New York, 1992, pp. 231–233.
Maisler (Mazar), B., *Untersuchungen zur alten Geschichte und Ethnographie Syriens und Palästinas* I, Gießen, 1930.
——, "Shamgar ben Anat", in *Palestine Exploration Fund Quartely Statement*, London, 1934, pp. 192–194.
——, "Canaan and Canaanites", *BASOR* 102 (1946), pp. 7–12.
Malamat, A., "The Last Wars of the Kingdom of Judah", *JNES* 9 (1950), pp. 218–227.
——, "The Historical Background of the Assassination of Amon, King of Judah", *IEJ* 3 (1953), pp. 26–29.
——, "Cushan Rishathaim and the Decline of the Near East around 1200 B.C.", *JNES* 13 (1954), pp. 231–242.
——, "מארי", in *Encyclopaedia Biblica* IV, Jerusalem, 1962, cols. 559–579 (Hebrew).
——, "Aspects of the Foreign Policies of David and Solomon", *JNES* 22 (1963), pp. 1–17.
——, "Organs of Statecraft in the Israelite Monarchy" (1965), in *The Biblical Archaeologist Reader* III, New York, 1970, pp. 163–198.
——, "The Ban in Mari and in the Bible", in *Biblical Essays* (OTWSA 9), Potchefstroom, 1967, pp. 40–49.

——, "The Last Kings of Judah and the Fall of Jerusalem", *IEJ* 18 (1968), pp. 137–156.
——, "Mari", *BA* 34 (1971), pp. 1–22.
——, "The Period of the Judges", in B. Mazar (ed.), *WHJP* I/III: *Judges*, Tel-Aviv, 1971, pp. 129–163, 314–323.
——, "Josiah's Bid for Armageddon. The Background of the Judean-Egyptian Encounter in 609 B.C.", in *The Gaster Festschrift*, *JANES* 5 (1973), pp. 267–279.
——, *Mari and the Early Israelite Experience* (The Schweich Lectures 1984), Oxford, 1989.
Marzal, A., "The Provincial Governor at Mari: His Title and Appointment", *JNES* 30 (1971), pp. 186–217.
Mayes, A.D.H., "Amphictyony", in *ABD* I, New York, 1992, pp. 212–216.
Mazar, B., "King David's Scribe and the High Officialdom of the United Monarchy of Israel", in *The Early Biblical Period. Historical Studies*, Jerusalem, 1986, pp. 126–138. = "סופר המלך דויד ובעיית הפקידות הנבוהה במלכות ישראל" (1946/47), in *Canaan and Israel. Historical Essays*, Jerusalem, 1974, pp. 208–221 (Hebrew).
——, "החתים במקרא", *Encyclopaedia Biblica* III, Jerusalem, 1958, cols. 355–357 (Hebrew).
——, "The Military Élite of King David" (1963), in *The Early Biblical Period. Historical Studies*, Jerusalem, 1986, pp. 83–103.
——, "The Phoenicians in the Levant", in *The Early Biblical Period. Historical Studies*, Jerusalem, 1986, pp. 213–230. = "הפיניקים בחופו המזרחי של הים-התיכון" (1965), in *Cities and Districts in Eretz-Israel*, Jerusalem, 1975, pp. 244–263 (Hebrew).
——, "The Historical Background of the Book of Genesis" (1969), in *The Early Biblical Period. Historical Studies*, Jerusalem, 1986, pp. 49–62.
——, "The Philistines and their Wars with Israel", in B. Mazar (ed.), *WHJP* I/III: *Judges*, Tel-Aviv, 1971, pp. 164–179, 324–325.
——, "המלוכה בישראל", in *Types of Leadership in the Biblical Period*, Jerusalem, 1973, pp. 27–35 (Hebrew).
Mendelsohn, I., "State Slavery in Ancient Palestine", *BASOR* 85 (1942), pp. 14–17 = in *Slavery in the Ancient Near East*, New York, 1949, pp. 92–106.
Mendenhall, G.E., *The Tenth Generation. The Origins of the Biblical Tradition*, Baltimore/London, 1973.
——, "Amorites", in *ABD* I, New York, 1992, pp. 199–202.
Mendenhall, G.E. and Herion, G.A., "Covenant", in *ABD* I, New York, 1992, pp. 1179–1202.
Mettinger, T.N.D., *Solomonic State Officials. A Study of the Civil Government Officials of the Israelite Monarchy* (CBOTS 5), Lund, 1971.
——, *King and Messiah. The Civil and Sacral Legitimation of the Israelite Kings* (CBOTS 8), Lund, 1976.
——, "YHWH SABAOTH—The Heavenly King on the Cherubim Throne", in T. Ishida (ed.), *SPDS*, Tokyo/Winona Lake, 1982, pp. 109–138.
——, *The Dethronement of Sabaoth. Studies in the Shem and Kabod Theologies* (CBOTS 18), Lund, 1982.
——, "Yahweh Zebaoth", in *DDD*, Leiden/New York/Köln, 1995, cols. 1730–1740.
Meyer, E., *Die Israeliten und ihre Nachbarstämme. Alttestamentliche Untersuchungen*, Halle an der Saale, 1906.
Millard, A.R., "The Canaanites", in D.J. Wiseman (ed.), *POTT*, Oxford, 1973, pp. 29–52.
——, "Story, History, and Theology", in A.R. Millard, J.K. Hoffmeier, and D.W. Baker, (eds.), *Faith, Tradition, and History. Old Testament Historiography in Its Near Eastern Context*, Winona Lake, 1994, pp. 37–64.
Miller, J.M., "The Fall of the House of Ahab", *VT* 17 (1967), pp. 307–324.
Möhlenbrink, K., "Sauls Ammoniterfeldzug und Samuels Beitrag zum Königtum des Saul", *ZAW* 58 (1940/41), pp. 57–70.

Molin, G., "Die Stellung der Gebira im Staate Juda", *TZ* 10 (1954), pp. 161–175.
Montgomery, J.A. and Gehman, H.S., *A Critical and Exegetical Commentary on the Books of Kings* (ICC), Edinburgh, 1951.
Moore, G.F., *A Critical and Exegetical Commentary on Judges* (ICC), Edinburgh, 1898².
Mowinckel, S., "Natansforjettelsen 2 Sam. kap. 7", *SEÅ* 12 (1947), pp. 220–229.
——, "'Rahelstämme' und 'Leastämme'", in *Von Ugarit nach Qumran. O. Eissfeldt Festschrift* (BZAW 77), Berlin, 1958, pp. 129–150.
Muntingh, L.M., "The Kerethites and the Pelethites. A Historical and Sociological Discussion", in A.H. van Zyl (ed.), *Studies on the Books of Samuel*, Pretoria, 1960, pp. 43–53.
——, "The Role of Joab in the Succession Narrative", in W.C. van Wyk (ed.), *Studies in the Succession Narrative*, Pretoria, 1986, pp. 202–217.
Myers, J.M., *II Chronicles. Introduction, Translation, and Notes* (AB 13), Garden City, N.Y., 1965.
Na'aman, N., "שמאל", in *Encyclopaedia Biblica* VIII, Jerusalem, 1982, cols. 308–316 (Hebrew).
——, *Borders and Districts in Biblical Historiography. Seven Studies in Biblical Geographical Lists* (JBS 4), Jerusalem, 1986.
——, "Historical and Chronological Notes on the Kingdoms of Israel and Judah in the Eighth Century B.C.", *VT* 36 (1986), pp. 71–92.
——, "Canaanites and Perizzites", *BN* 45 (1988), pp. 42–47.
——, "The 'Conquest of Canaan' in the Book of Joshua and in History"' in I. Finkelstein and N. Na'aman (eds.), *From Nomadism to Monarchy. Archaeological and Historical Aspects of Early Israel*, Jerusalem, 1994, pp. 218–281.
Newman, M., "The Prophetic Call of Samuel", in *Israel's Prophetic Heritage. Essays in Honor of James Muilenburg*, London, 1962, pp. 86–97.
Nicholson, E.W., "The Meaning of the Expression עם הארץ in the Old Testament", *JSS* 10 (1965), pp. 59–66.
Nicolsky, N.M., "Pascha im Kulte des jerusalemischen Tempels", *ZAW* 45 (1927), pp. 171–190, 241–253.
Niehr, H., "שפט", in *TWAT* VIII, Stuttgart, 1994–95, cols. 408–428.
von Nordheim, E., "König und Tempel. Der Hintergrund des Tempelbauverbotes in 2 Samuel vii", *VT* 27 (1977), pp. 434–453.
North, R., "The Hivites", *Bib* 54 (1973), pp. 43–46.
Noth, M., *Das System der zwölf Stämme Israels* (BWANT 4/1), Stuttgart, 1930.
——, "Beiträge zur Geschichte des Ostjordanlandes I. Das Land Gilead als Siedlungsgebiet israelitischer Sippen" (1941), in *Aufsätze zur biblischen Landes- und Altertumskunde* I, Neukirchen-Vluyn, 1971, pp. 94–101.
——, *Überlieferungsgeschichtliche Studien. Die sammelnden und bearbeitenden Geschichtswerke im Alten Testament*, Tübingen, 1943, 1957².
——, *Überlieferungsgeschichte des Pentateuch*, Stuttgart, 1948.
——, "Das Amt des 'Richters Israels'" (1950), in *Gesammelte Studien zum Alten Testament* II, München, 1969, pp. 71–85.
——, *Das Buch Josua* (HAT 7), Tübingen, 1953².
——, "Das alttestamentliche Bundschließen im Lichte eines Mari-Textes" (1955), in *Gesammelte Studien zum Alten Testament*, München, 1957, pp. 142–154.
——, "David und Israel in 2. Samuel 7" (1957), in *Gesammelte Studien zum Alten Testament* , München, 1960², pp. 334–345.
——, *The History of Israel*, London, 1960². = *Geschichte Israels*, Göttingen, 1954².
——, "Samuel und Silo", *VT* 13 (1963), pp. 390–400.
——, *The Old Testament World*, London, 1966. = *Die Welt des Alten Testaments: Einführung in die Grenzgebiete der alttestamentlichen Wissinschaft*, Berlin, 1962⁴.
——, *Numbers* (OTL), London, 1968. = *Das vierte Buch Mose. Numeri* (ATD 7), Göttingen, 1966.

——, *Könige* I: *I. Könige 1–16* (BKAT 9/1), Neukirchen-Vluyn, 1968.
Nübel, H.-U., *Davids Aufstieg in der frühe israelitischer Geschichtsschreibung* (Diss.), Bonn, 1959.
O'Connor, M., "The rhetoric of the Kilamuwa inscription", *BASOR* 226 (1977), pp. 15–30.
Oppenheim, A.L., *Ancient Mesopotamia. Portrait of a Dead Civilization*, Chicago, 1964.
Orlinsky, H.M., "The Seer-Priest", in B. Mazar (ed.), *WHJP* I/III: *Judges*, Tel-Aviv, 1971, pp. 268–279, 338–344.
Ottosson, M., *Gilead. Tradition and History* (CBOTS 3), Lund, 1969.
Ottosson, M. with Bergman, J., "ארץ", in *TWAT* I, Stuttgart, 1970–73, cols. 418–436.
Parpola, S., "The Murderer of Sennacherib", in B. Alster (ed.), *Death in Mesopotamia. XXVI[e] RAI* (Mesopotamia 8), Copenhagen, 1980, pp. 171–182.
Paul, S.M., "Deutero-Isaiah and Cuneiform Royal Inscriptions", *JAOS* 88 (1968), pp. 180–186.
Pedersen, J., *Israel. Its Life and Culture* I–II, London/Copenhagen, 1926.
Pettinato, G., "The Royal Archives of Tell Mardikh-Ebla", *BA* 39 (1976), pp. 44–52.
Pitard, W.T., *Ancient Damascus. A Historical Study of the Syrian City-State from Earliest Times until its Fall to the Assyrians in 732 B.C.E.*, Winona Lake, 1987.
van der Ploeg, J., "ŠĀPAṬ et MIŠPĀṬ", *OTS* 2 (1943), pp. 144–155.
Plöger, J.G., *Literarkritische, formgeschichtliche und stilkritische Untersuchungen zum Deuteronomium* (BBB 26), Bonn, 1967.
Poulssen, N., *König und Tempel im Glaubenszeugnis des Alten Testamentes* (SBM 3), Stuttgart, 1967.
von Rad, G., "Der Anfang der Geschichtsschreibung im alten Israel" (1944), in *Gesammelte Studien zum Alten Testament*, München, 1958, pp. 148–188.
——, *Studies in Deuteronomy* (SBT 9), London, 1953. = *Deuteronomium-Studien*, Göttingen, 1948[2].
Rainey, A.F., "Compulsory Labour Gangs in Ancient Israel", *IEJ* 20 (1970), pp. 191–202.
Ramsey, G.W., "Zadok", in *ABD* VI, New York, 1992, pp. 1034–1036.
Reed, S.A., "Jebus", in *ABD* III, New York, 1992, pp. 652–653.
——, "Perizzite", in *ABD* V, New York, 1992, p. 231.
Reid, P.V., "*šbṭy* in 2 Samuel 7:7", *CBQ* 37 (1975), pp. 17–20.
Reventlow, H.G., "Das Amt des Mazkir", *TZ* 15 (1959), pp. 161–175.
Reviv, H., "The Government of Shechem in the El-Amarna Period and in the Days of Abimelech", *IEJ* 16 (1966), pp. 252–257.
——, "על ימי עתליה ויואש", *Beth Mikra* 16 (1970/71), pp. 541–548 (Hebrew).
Richter, W., *Die Bearbeitungen des "Retterbuches" in der deuteronomischen Epoche* (BBB 21), Bonn, 1964.
——, "Zu den 'Richtern Israels'", *ZAW* 77 (1965), pp. 40–72.
——, "Die *nāgīd*-Formel. Ein Beitrag zur Erhellung des *nāgīd*-Problems", *BZ* 9 (1965), pp. 71–84.
de Robert, P., "Juges ou tribus en 2 Samuel vii 7?", *VT* 21 (1971), pp. 116–118.
Rost, L., "Die Überlieferung von der Thronnachfolge Davids" (1926), in *Das kleine Credo und andere Studien zum Alten Testament*, Heidelberg, 1965, pp. 119–253 = *The Succession to the Throne of David*, Sheffield, 1982.
——, "Die Bezeichnungen für Land und Volk im Alten Testament" (1934), in *Das kleine Credo und andere Studien zum Alten Testament*, Heidelberg, 1965, pp. 76–101.
Rozenberg, M.S., *The Stem špṭ. An Investigation of Biblical and Extra-Biblical Sources* (Diss.), Pennsylvania, 1963.
——, "The *Šōf[e]ṭīm* in the Bible", in B. Mazar (ed.), *Nelson Glueck Memorial Volume* (Eretz-Israel 12), Jerusalem, 1975, pp. 77*–86*.
Rudolph, W., "Die Einheitlichkeit der Erzählung vom Sturz der Atalja (2 Kön. 11)", in *A. Bertholet Festschrift*, Tübingen, 1950, pp. 473–478.

——, "Zum Text der Königsbücher", *ZAW* 63 (1951), pp. 201–215.
——, *Chronikbücher* (HAT 21), Tübingen, 1955.
Sacon, K.K., "A Study of the Literary Structure of 'The Succession Narrative'", in T. Ishida (ed.), *SPDS*, Tokyo/Winona Lake, 1982, pp. 27–54.
Šanda, A., *Die Bücher der Könige* I–II (EHAT 9/1–2) , Münster i. Westf., 1911–12.
Sanders, J.A., "Hebrew Bible" in "Canon", in *ABD* I, New York, 1992, pp. 837–852.
Schäfer-Lichtenberger, C., *Stadt und Eidgenossenschaft im Alten Testament. Eine Auseinandersetzung mit Max Webers Studie <Das antike Judentum>* (BZAW 156), Berlin/New York, 1983.
——, *Josua und Salomo. Eine Studie zu Autorität und Legitimität des Nachfolgers im Alten Testament* (VTSup 58), Leiden/New York/Köln, 1995.
Schearing, L.S., "Queen", in *ABD* V, New York, 1992, pp. 583–586.
Schley, D.G., "David's Champions", in *ABD* II, New York, 1992, pp. 49–52.
Schmidt, L., *Menschlicher Erfolg und Jahwes Initiative. Studien zu Tradition, Interpretation und Historie in Überlieferungen von Gideon, Saul, und David* (WMANT 38), Neukirchen-Vluyn, 1970.
Schmidt, W.H., *Königtum Gottes in Ugarit und Israel zur Herkunft der Königsprädikation Jahwes* (BZAW 80), Berlin, 1966^2.
Schmitz, P.C., "Canaan (Place)", in *ABD* I, New York, 1992, pp. 828–831.
Schnell, R.F., "Perizzite", in *IDB* III, Nashville/New York, 1962, p. 735.
Schreiner, J., *Septuaginta-Massora des Buches der Richter* (AnBib 7), Roma, 1957.
——, "תולדות", in *TWAT* VIII, Stuttgart, 1994–95, cols. 571–577.
Schulte, H., *Die Entstehung der Geschichtsschreibung im alten Israel* (BZAW 128), Berlin/New York, 1972.
Schunck, K.-D., *Benjamin. Untersuchungen zur Entstehung und Geschichte eines israelitischen Stammes* (BZAW 86), Berlin, 1963.
——, "Die Richter Israels und ihr Amt", in *Congress Volume*, Genève 1965 (VTSup 15), Leiden, 1966, pp. 252–262.
Seebass, H., "Traditionsgeschichte von I Sam 8, $10_{17\,\text{ff.}}$ und 12", *ZAW* 77 (1965), pp. 286–296.
——, "Die Vorgeschichte der Königserhebung Sauls", *ZAW* 79 (1967), pp. 155–171.
Seeligmann, I.L., "Zur Terminologie für das Gerichtsverfahren im Wortschatz des biblischen Hebräisch", in *Hebräische Wortforschung. W. Baumgartner Festschrift* (VTSup 16), Leiden, 1967, pp. 251–278.
Sekine, M., "Beobachtungen zu der Josianischen Reform", *VT* 22 (1972), pp. 361–368.
Sellin, E., *Geschichte des israelitisch-jüdischen Volkes* I, Leipzig, 1924, 1935^2.
van Selms, A., "The Canaanites in the Book of Genesis", *OTS* 12 (1958), pp. 182–213.
——, "The Title 'Judge'", *OTWSA* 2 (1959), pp. 41–50.
——, "Judge Shamgar", *VT* 14 (1964), pp. 294–309.
van Seters, J., "The Terms 'Amorite' and 'Hittite' in the Old Testament", *VT* 22 (1972), pp. 64–81.
——, *Abraham in History and Tradition*, New Haven/London, 1975.
——, "Histories and Historians of the Ancient Near East: The Israelites", *Or* 50 (1981), pp. 137–185.
——, *In Search of History. Historiography in the Ancient World and the Origins of Biblical History*, New Haven/London, 1983.
Seybold, K., "משח", in *TWAT* V, Stuttgart, 1984–86, cols. 46–59.
Simons, J., "The 'Table of Nations' (Gen. X): Its General Structure and Meaning", *OTS* 10 (1954), pp. 155–184.
Skinner, J., *A Critical and Exegetical Commentary on Genesis* (ICC), Edinburgh, 1930^2.
Sloush, N., "Representative Government among the Hebrews and Phoenicians", *JQR* 4 (1913/14), pp. 303–310.

Smend, R., *Jahwekrieg und Stämmebund. Erwägungen zur ältesten Geschichte Israels* (FRLANT 84), Göttingen, 1963.
Soggin, J.A., "Der judäische *'am ha'areṣ* und das Königtum in Juda", *VT* 13 (1963), pp. 187–195.
——, *Das Königtum in Israel. Ursprünge, Spannungen, Entwicklung* (BZAW 104), Berlin, 1967.
——, *Joshua. A Commentary* (OTL), London, 1972.
——, "Tibnî, King of Israel in the First Half of the 9th Century B.C." (1972), in *Old Testament and Oriental Studies* (BibOr 29), Rome, 1975, pp. 50–55.
——, "The Davidic-Solomonic Kingdom", in J.H. Hayes and J.M. Miller (eds.), *Israelite and Judaean History* (OTL), London, 1977, pp. 332–380.
——, *Introduction to the Old Testament. From its origins to the closing of the Alexandrian canon*, London, 1980².
——, *Judges. A Commentary* (OTL), London, 1981.
——, "Compulsory Labor under David and Solomon", in T. Ishida (ed.), *SPDS*, Tokyo/Winona Lake, 1982, pp. 259–267.
——, *A History of Israel. From the Beginnings to the Bar Kochba Revolt, AD 135*, London, 1984.
Speiser, E.A., "Ethnic Movements in the Near East in the Second Millennium B.C.: the Hurrians and their Connection with the Ḫabiru and Hyksos", *AASOR* 13 (1933), pp. 13–34.
——, "Hivite", in *IDB* II, Nashville/New York, 1962, p. 615.
——, "Man, Ethnic Divisions of", in *IDB* III, Nashville/New York, 1962, pp. 235–242.
——, "Background and Function of the Biblical Nāśī'", *CBQ* 25 (1963), pp. 111–117.
——, "Amorites and Canaanites", in E.A. Speiser (ed.), *WHJP* I/I: *At the Dawn of Civilization—A Background of Biblical History*, Tel-Aviv, 1964, pp. 162–169, 364–365.
——, "The Manner of the King", in B. Mazar (ed.), *WHJP* I/III: *Judges*, Tel-Aviv, 1971, pp. 280–287, 345.
Stade, B., "Anmerkungen zu 2 Kö. 10–14", *ZAW* 5 (1885), pp. 275–297.
Stade, B. and Schwally, F., *The Book of Kings*, Leipzig, 1904.
Stamm, J.J., "Der Name des Königs Salomo", *TZ* 16 (1960), pp. 285–297. = in *Beiträge zur hebräischen und altorientalischen Namenskunde*, Freiburg i. Schweiz, 1980, pp. 45–47
Sulzberger, M., *Am ha-aretz: the Ancient Hebrew Parliament*, Philadelphia, 1910².
——, "The Polity of the Ancient Hebrews", *JQR* 3 (1912/13), pp. 1–81.
Tadmor, H., "יורם, יהורם", in *Encyclopaedia Biblica* III, Jerusalem, 1958, cols. 539–541 (Hebrew).
——, "Azriyau of Yaudi", in C. Rabin (ed.), *Studies in the Bible* (Scripta Hierosolymitana 8), Jerusalem, 1961, pp. 232–271.
——, "כרונולוגיה", in *Encyclopaedia Biblica* IV, Jerusalem, 1962, cols. 245–310 (Hebrew).
——, "'The People' and the Kingship in Ancient Israel: The Role of Political Institutions in the Biblical Period", *JWH* 11 (1968), pp. 46–68.
——, "History and Ideology in the Assyrian Royal Inscriptions", in F.M. Fales (ed.), *Assyrian Royal Inscriptions: New Horizons in Literary, Ideological, and Historical Analysis* (Orientis Antiqvi Collectio 17), Roma, 1981, pp. 13–33.
——, "Traditional Institutions and the Monarchy: Social and Political Tensions in the Time of David and Solomon", in T. Ishida (ed.), *SPDS*, Tokyo/Winona Lake, 1982, pp. 239–257.
——, "Autobiographical Apology in the Royal Assyrian Literature", in H. Tadmor and M. Weinfeld (eds.), *History, Historiography and Interpretation. Studies in Biblical and Cuneiform Literatures*, Jerusalem, 1983, pp. 36–57.
Talmon, S., "The Judaean *'Am Ha'areṣ* in Historical Perspective", in *Fourth World Congress of Jewish Studies* (1965) I, Jerusalem, 1967, pp. 71–76.
——, "עם הארץ", in *Encyclopaedia Biblica* VI, Jerusalem, 1971, cols. 239–242 (Hebrew).
Täubler, E. (ed. by H.-J. Zobel), *Biblische Studien* I. *Die Epoche der Richter*, Tübingen, 1958.

Thiel, W., "Athaliah", in *ABD* I, New York, 1992, pp. 511–512.
Thiele, E.R., *The Mysterious Numbers of the Hebrew Kings*, Grand Rapids, 1983[3].
Thompson, T.L., *Early History of the Israelite People. From the Written and Archaeological Sources* (SHANE 4), Leiden, 1994.
Thomson, H.C., "SHOPHEṬ and MISHPAṬ in the Book of Judges", *TGUOS* 19 (1961–62), pp. 74–85.
Thornton, T.C.G., "Charismatic Kingship in Israel and Judah", *JTS* 14 (1963), pp. 1–11.
Timm, S., *Die Dynastie Omri. Quellen und Untersuchungen zur Geschichte Israels im 9. Jahrhundert vor Christus* (FRLANT 124), Göttingen, 1982.
Tsevat, M., "Marriage and Monarchical Legitimacy in Ugarit and Israel", *JSS* 3 (1958), pp. 237–243.
——, "Studies in the Book of Samuel III. The Steadfast House: What was David promised in II Sam. VII 11b–16?", *HUCA* 34 (1963), pp. 71–82.
Tsukimoto, A., "'Der Mensch ist geworden wie unsereiner'. Untersuchungen zum zeitgeschichitlichen Hintergrund von Gen. 3,22–24 und 6,1–4", *AJBI* 5 (1979), pp. 3–44.
Ussishkin, D., "'Der alte Bau' in Zincirli", *BASOR* 189 (1968), pp. 50–53.
Vancil, J.W., "Sheep, Shepherd", in *ABD* V, New York, 1992, pp. 1187–1190.
de Vaux, R., *Ancient Israel. Its Life and Institutions*, London, 1961. = *Les Institutions de l'Ancient Testament* I–II, Paris, 1958–60.
——, "Le sens de l'expression 'peuple du pays' dans l'Ancien Testament et le rôle politique du peuple en Israël", *RA* 58 (1964), pp. 167–172.
——, "Les Hurrites de l'histoire et les Horites de la Bible", *RB* 74 (1967), pp. 481–503.
——, "Le pays de Canaan", *JAOS* 88 (1968), pp. 23–30.
——, *Histoire ancienne d'Israël. Des origines à l'installation en Canaan*, Paris, 1971.
——, *Histoire ancienne d'Israël* II. *La période des Juges*, Paris, 1973.
Veijola, T., *Die ewige Dynastie. David und die Entstehung seiner Dynastie nach der deuteronomistischen Darstellung*, Helsinki, 1975.
Wallis, G., "Die Anfänge des Königtums in Israel", *WZ Halle* 12 (1963), pp. 239–247.
Weinfeld, M., "ברית", in *TWAT* I, Stuttgart, 1970–73, cols. 781–808.
——, *Deuteronomy and the Deuteronomic School*, Oxford, 1972.
——, "Covenant, Davidic", in *IDBSup*, Nashville, 1976, pp. 188–192.
Weippert, M., "Menahem von Israel und seine Zeitgenossen in einer Steleninschrift des assyrischen Königs Tiglathpileser III. aus dem Iran", *ZDPV* 89 (1973), pp. 26–53.
Weiser, A., *Samuel: seine geschichtliche Aufgabe und religiöse Bedeutung. Traditionsgeschichtliche Untersuchungen zu 1. Samuel 7–12* (FRLANT 81), Göttingen, 1962.
——, "Das Deboralied: eine gattungs- und traditionsgeschichtliche Studie", *ZAW* 71 (1959), pp. 67–97.
——, "Die Tempelbaukrise unter David", *ZAW* 77 (1965), pp. 153–168.
Wellhausen, J., *Die Composition des Hexateuchs und der historischen Bücher des Alten Testaments*, Berlin, 1899[3], 1963[4].
Wesselius, J.W., "Joab's Death and the Central Theme of the Succession Narrative (2 Samuel ix 1–1 Kings ii)", *VT* 40 (1990), pp. 336–351.
Westermann, C., *Genesis* I. *Kapitel 1–11* (BKAT 1/1), Neukirchen-Vluyn, 1976[2].
Whitelam, K.W., *The Just King: Monarchical Judicial Authority in Ancient Israel* (JSOTSup 12), Sheffield, 1979.
——, "The Defence of David", *JSOT* 29 (1984), pp. 61–87.
Whitley, C.F., "The Sources of the Gideon Stories", *VT* 7 (1957), pp. 157–164.
Whybray, R.N., *The Succession Narrative. A Study of II Samuel 9–20; I Kings 1 and 2* (SBTS 9), London, 1968.
Willis, J.T., "An Anti-Elide Narrative Tradition from a Prophetic Circle at the Ramah Sanctuary", *JBL* 90 (1971), pp. 288–308.
Wilson, J.A., *The Culture of Ancient Egypt*, Chicago, 1951.

Wiseman, D.J., "Introduction: Peoples and Nations", in D.J. Wiseman (ed.), *POTT*, Oxford, 1973, pp. xv–xxi.
Würthwein, E., *Der ʿamm haʾarez im Alten Testament* (BWANT 66), Stuttgart, 1936.
——, *Die Erzählung von der Thronfolge Davids—theologische oder politische Geschichtsschreibung?* (TS 115), Zürich, 1974.
——, *Das Erste Buch der Könige: Kapitel 1–16* (ATD 11/1), Göttingen, 1977.
——, *Die Bücher der Könige: 1.Kön.17–2.Kön.25* (ATD 11/2), Göttingen, 1984.
Yamada, S., "The Editorial History of the Assyrian King List", *ZA* 84 (1994), pp. 11–37.
Yamauchi, E., "The Current State of Old Testament Historiography", in A.R. Millard, J.K. Hoffmeier, and D.W. Baker (eds.), *Faith, Tradition, and History. Old Testament Historiography in Its Near Eastern Context*, Winona Lake, 1994, pp. 1–36.
Yeivin, S., "שלמה", in *Encyclopaedia Biblica* VII, Jerusalem, 1976, cols. 693–699 (Hebrew).
Zakovitch, Y., "*bdn = ypth*", *VT* 22 (1972), pp. 123–125.
Zalewski, S., *Solomon's Ascension to the Throne. Studies in the Books of Kings and Chronicles*, Jerusalem, 1981 (Hebrew).
Zimmerli, W., *Ezekiel* I (BKAT 13/1), Neukirchen-Vluyn, 1958.

INDICES

I. Texts

1. *The Hebrew Bible*

II. Authors

III. General Index

STUDIES IN THE HISTORY AND CULTURE OF THE ANCIENT NEAR EAST

EDITED BY

B. HALPERN AND M.H.E. WEIPPERT

ISSN 0169-9024

1. Ahlström, G.W. *Royal Administration and National Religion in Ancient Palestine.* 1982. ISBN 90 04 6562 8
2. Becking, B. *The Fall of Samaria.* An Historical and Archaeological Study. 1992. ISBN 90 04 09633 7
3. Vogelsang, W.J. *The Rise and Organisation of the Achaemenid Empire.* The Eastern Iranian Evidence. 1992. ISBN 90 04 09682 5
4. Thompson, T.L. *Early History of the Israelite People.* From the Written and Archaeological Sources. 1992. ISBN 90 04 09483 0
5. el-Faïz, M. *L'agronomie de la Mésopotamie antique.* Analyse du «Livre de l'agriculture nabatéenne» de Qûṯâmä. 1995. ISBN 90 04 10199 3
6. Hallo, W.W. *Origins.* The Ancient Near Eastern Background of Some Modern Western Institutions. 1996. ISBN 90 04 10328 7
7. Toorn, K. van der. *Family Religion in Babylonia, Syria and Israel.* Continuity and Change in the Forms of Religious Life. 1996. ISBN 90 0410410 0
8. Jeffers, A. *Magic and Divination in Ancient Palestine and Syria.* 1996. ISBN 90 04 10513 1
9. Galil, G. *The Chronology of the Kings of Israel and Judah.* 1996. ISBN 90 04 10611 1
10. Ehrlich, C.S. *The Philistines in Transition.* A History from ca. 1000-730 B.C.E. 1996. ISBN 90 04 10426 7
11. Handy, L.K. (ed.). *The Age of Solomon.* Scholarship at the Turn of the Millennium. 1997. ISBN 90 04 10476 3
12. Malamat, A. *Mari and the Bible.* 1998. ISBN 90 04 10863 7
13. Krings, V. *Carthage et les Grecs c. 580-480 av. J.-C.* Textes et histoire. 1998. ISBN 90 04 10881 5
14. Stol, M. and S.P. Vleeming, *The Care of the Elderly in the Ancient Near East.* 1999. ISBN 90 04 10896 3
15. Musche, B. *Die Liebe in der altorientalischen Dichtung.* 1999. ISBN 90 04 11213 8
16. Ishida, T. *History and Historical Writing in Ancient Israel.* Studies in Biblical Historiography. 1999. ISBN 90 04 11444 0